Cortney Burns is a chef, an author, and a tastemaker who's always been in the vanguard of the food world. In this book, which combines recipes and mysticism in a way that's never been seen before, she shares guidance and wisdom about how making changes in your life will change the food you eat.

Organized into chapters by element—water, fire, earth, air, aether—here are 125 recipes, ranging from salads and mains to desserts and drinks. The water chapter explores soups and stews, while the fire chapter delves into cooking meat over heat and the earth chapter takes a deep dive into vegetables. The aether chapter contains tonics, spirits, and other great-for-you drinks, dips, nibbles, and stocks.

As in Cortney's award-winning cookbook *Bar Tartine*, there's a larder section of several dozen building-block recipes: simple sauces, infused vinegars, toasted seed mixtures, and pickles that enliven any dish, from a baked sweet potato to a bowl of sliced cucumbers.

This book provides a springboard for home cooks to bring all of their life experiences to their cooking. We tear up roots. We reroot. We turn to the stove. We nourish ourselves home.

NOURISH ME HOME

NOURISH ME HOME

125 SOUL-SUSTAINING, ELEMENTAL RECIPES

CORTNEY BURNS

Photography by
HEAMI LEE

Illustrations by
MARY MITCHELL

Recipe collaboration with Remy Robert and
editorial collaboration with Hannah Davitian

CHRONICLE BOOKS
SAN FRANCISCO

Library of Congress Cataloging-in-Publication Data

Names: Burns, Cortney, author. | Lee, Heami, photographer. |
    Mitchell, Mary (Illustrator), illustrator.
Title: Nourish me home : 125 soul-sustaining, elemental recipes /
    Cortney Burns ; photographs by Heami Lee ; illustrations by Mary Mitchell.
Description: San Francisco, CA : Chronicle Books, 2020. | Includes index. |
Identifiers: LCCN 2019054969 | ISBN 9781452175850 (hardcover) |
    ISBN 9781452177465 (ebook)
Subjects: LCSH: Cooking, American--New England style. | Cooking, American—
    California style. | Cooking. | BISAC: COOKING/Comfort Food | LCGFT:
    Cookbooks.
Classification: LCC TX715.2.N48 .B89 2020 | DDC 641.5973—dc23
    LC record available at https://lccn.loc.gov/2019054969

Manufactured in Italy.

Prop styling by Rebecca Bartoshesky.
Food styling by Cortney Burns.
Design by Vanessa Dina.
Typesetting by Frank Brayton.

10 9 8 7 6 5 4 3 2 1

Chronicle books and gifts are available at special quantity discounts to corpora-
tions, professional associations, literacy programs, and other organizations. For
details and discount information, please contact our premiums department at
corporatesales@chroniclebooks.com or at 1-800-759-0190.

Chronicle Books LLC
680 Second Street
San Francisco, California 94107
www.chroniclebooks.com

I dedicate this book to JP, for holding space as we push the boundaries of what is possible within this container of life and beyond. And to the young people in my life—Lucia, JJ, Javier, Hunter, and Jaden—never let anyone steal your magic.

Chapter 4:
Larder

Chapter 5:
Weaving Maple into Silk

INTRODUCTION

This is a book about uprooting in order to reroot. It's about self-discovery, the search for home, and nourishing one's heart and soul. From the garden to the kitchen, and everywhere in between, shadows and all, these are the methods and recipes that make me feel healthy, strong, and nourished.

Cooking is often an autobiographical performance, and this book sketches my last few years. These recipes weave together childhood flavors from growing up in a Jewish family in the suburbs of Chicago with knowledge I gathered through travel, as a professional chef, and as a student of naturopathy and herbology. Here, too, are my musings on New England and the type of cross-cultural pollination I imagine could have happened here as worlds and cultures collided into a new harmony over centuries.

My hope is that this book is an inspiring guide, letting you adopt my cooking techniques into your own repertoire, mixed and matched according to the season and your cravings. I invite you to dive back into your imagination and honor your creativity. Both can provide a road map to cooking honest, healthful, soulful food that helps you connect to your surroundings or yourself in a new way. If you let it, the kitchen can be a sacred place and a wise teacher.

I encourage you to think of this book as a choose-your-own-adventure guide. Fill your table with a sauce from one recipe and a vegetable technique from another. Satisfy your cravings and desires by customizing the plate. The recipes in this book tell my personal journey, but, more importantly, they capture my arsenal of cooking techniques, my "culinary armor," if you will. No matter which direction the winds of change blow, these are the methods I turn to again and again.

CASTING A CIRCLE

For most of my adult life, cooking has been a spiritual and artistic practice and the kitchen has been one of my sacred gathering places. So I begin this book by inviting you to join me here, as I cast a circle around you and me—us.

Every time I enter the kitchen, I cast a circle, infusing the space with energy and creating a ring of protection around it as I set my creative intentions for the day. This ritual grounds me in the here and now. Creativity breeds vulnerability, so I take solace in the physical act of cooking along with the more spiritual mode of connection that I gain from it.

While casting this circle, I take a moment to honor the four cardinal directions and their corresponding elements. The calling of elemental powers represents our connection with the forces of the outside world. After all, the kitchen is a place where alchemy abounds, and alchemy is, by definition, the interplay between mind and matter, self and the world. Cooking is my way of uniting the powers of nature with my own, creating something delicious and nourishing while forging a deeper bond with what's around me. So, as you hold this book, my hope is that it helps you do the same. While you cook through these recipes, let them become your own portal to a place of imagination and creation.

THE JOURNEY

I have been an itinerant for much of my adult life. Before the kitchen beckoned, I was a nomad of sorts, traveling from here to there, moving from one place to the next, a bit uncertain of my path. I've always found there's an expansiveness when you look beyond your physical and emotional borders. It's the act of looking out in order to look in that facilitates growth.

My wanderlust led me to the kitchen. At the University of Wisconsin-Madison, I studied cultural anthropology and South Asian studies with a focus on the Tibetan language. Eager to take my learnings from classroom to country, I spent a year living in Nepal and India, traveling throughout Thailand and Mongolia. It was there that my love of travel and food officially converged. I visited Ayurvedic and Tibetan medicine clinics, first out of necessity, then because I was entranced by their teachings. As I began to look deeper, I found that herbalism, plants, and food were the bedrock of these healing practices. Within these medicines, there was a reverence for the land, ingredients, and the body that I'd never encountered before.

After graduating college, I moved to Australia for a year, where I cooked in restaurants in far North Queensland in the Daintree rain forest. After cooking for a few months, I took my 1971 Ford Falcon, dubbed "Spacey Gracey," and puttered across the country with not much more than my passport and a one-way ticket to Dharamshala. Then 9/11 hit and the whole world took a deep inhale. I flew home to Chicago. I started focusing on photography, with the hope of getting an MFA and working for *National Geographic*. But when I wasn't accepted into my top program, I packed up my car with a backpack full of clothes, some vinyl records, and a mountain bike, and drove to California to begin cooking in earnest.

I often think that I could have chosen any creative, tactile profession. I'm content so long as I'm making something. There's a rawness to cooking that exhilarates and terrifies me each time I put on an apron. It's as if I'm showing someone my journal and inviting them in with a magnifying glass. But the truly mesmerizing thing about food is that it brings together culture and history, science and medicine, the outside with the inside. It allows me to tap into layers beneath my consciousness—flavor memories of my own making and those I can only imagine. It allows me to become introspective, to learn something new about myself.

I never went to culinary school, but rather learned to cook through the hum of service and by poring over cookbooks, food memoirs, Eastern medicine manuals, and herbalism treatises. I realized early on that food has powerful healing properties if used properly. In my twenties, I struggled with digestive issues and when Western medicine offered little relief, I turned once more to the East. It was at a naturopath's suggestion that I started fermenting foods—first water kefir, then sauerkraut; then I began sprouting nuts, seeds, and legumes, the healthy properties a welcomed addendum to new flavors and textures. It was at this moment that a visceral link between food and health came into focus.

I spent the next ten years cooking my way across the United States in professional kitchens. I was a line cook, a sous chef, a private chef, and a teacher. I did product development and cooked behind the scenes for television shows. In the spring of 2011, I found myself at Bar Tartine in San Francisco's animated Mission district. As the story goes, I came in to the restaurant one day to butcher a goat and never left, which is more or less true. I immediately dove into the processing kitchen and began making everything by hand. We became known as the place that redefined "cooking from scratch" by utilizing a seasonless larder: The bounty of one season was preserved for the next. Our food seemed to transcend geography in an eclectic yet choreographed way.

At Bar Tartine, I honed what would become my cooking style: using history as a springboard for creativity while drawing on my own culinary knowledge and nutrient-rich approach to lead the way. Nick Balla, my then-life and cooking partner, and I ran the kitchen together for the better part of seven years. During that time, we wrote our cookbook, *Bar Tartine*; launched a line of probiotic drinks; and mentored countless chefs, helping them bring their own culinary voices to the rest of world.

It was in late 2016 that Nick and I decided to leave Bar Tartine. At the same time, as if the wind was listening, I was approached by an eclectic hospitality group opening a forty-eight-room boutique hotel in North Adams, Massachusetts, an old mill town in the western part of the state. The idea was to integrate hospitality, design, music, art, and food into a new type of travel destination. My charge was to create a food program and restaurant with the Bar Tartine ethos, but tethered to New England. Fast-forward five months, and I was headed to a place I didn't know, with farmers I hadn't met and a rich history I had only heard whispers of. As I packed boxes from one coast destined for the other, I realized I was in a liminal space of not quite belonging in either locale. The land, people, and history of Massachusetts were all new to me. With little more than my desire to explore, New England became my culinary muse.

The history of New England is rich with stories of immigration, warfare, land disputes, deforestation, and reforestation. Miles of farmland are bound by a minimal growing season and a strong tradition of preservation. I found myself drawn to the region's deep histories and the many communities that called it home—the indigenous peoples, Chinese, Lebanese, Irish, and Eastern Europeans. On the plate, I set out to unravel history, so to speak, but to give it my own twist. And while the vision was poetic, practice proved much rockier.

I spent the first two months in the Berkshires, tripping over my own feet. I had no restaurant kitchen or even a home kitchen. If cooking is a mode of self-discovery, then the kitchen is the nexus, and without either, I felt vulnerable and lost. In truth, the act of uprooting in order to reroot is often more of a study in emotional tenacity than pure geography. In New England, I knew I had to find my own voice. Nick and I had cooked side by side for so long that our creativity was enmeshed. He'd start a dish and I'd finish it as if we could tap into some kind of collective palate. But in many respects, I had forgotten what it was to cook alone—cooking solely from a place within myself, trusting only my own instincts.

This erstwhile mill town, somewhat sleepy and forgotten, became a field for self-discovery, the kind of introspection that forces you to peel back layers of identity and live, for a while at least, in the rawness of the unknown. I began to ask myself, *Who was I without my restaurant and where was home?* Knowing that I needed a place to cook, I built a kitchen in a four-bay garage and put my head down, perhaps not really picking it back up until two years later, when I was uprooted yet again to New Hampshire. At the beginning of my time in North Adams, I started meeting farmers, studying the history of the land in the library at neighboring Williams College, digging through the database on immigration patterns at the local Historical Society, foraging in the surrounding forests, and building my New England pantry. Always an anthropologist, I couldn't stop delving deeper into these stories and how I could represent them through food.

I spent two years immersed in creating a seasonless larder, working with the local agricultural community, testing recipes, designing a restaurant, and gearing up for our summer 2018 debut. The hotel, Tourists, opened, but the restaurant, Loom, never did. Change is constant; the restaurant world has taught me this truth time and again. So when things shift course unexpectedly, I know to accept the current with grace. From openness comes opportunity.

When I started dreaming up and writing this book, I imagined it would, in a way, codify Loom's genesis. Since then, much has changed, including my approach to cooking. I'm no longer in a restaurant kitchen from sun up until sun down, and professional-grade equipment isn't at the ready, so I understand the need for simplification. As I now spend my time between the mountains of New Hampshire and the coast of Massachusetts, with my partner and his children, part of my journey within these pages has been realizing what it's like cooking for a family on a Tuesday night after a full day of activities.

While I must confess that many of these recipes still tilt toward a multi-ingredient style of cooking, each demonstrates a technique, component, or flavor combination that I'll often pull out to use in my everyday cooking. When not destined for the more-involved Summer Bean Soup with Tomato Brown Butter (page 25), baking Romano beans into oblivion makes a delicious side dish to grilled chicken or adds a toasty note to a bowl of steamed rice. And while the Autumn Chowder with Corn and Smoky Potatoes (page 47) provides an electric taste of the season, the smashed potatoes are a weeknight go-to no matter the month.

While I continue to consult on restaurants, my world is no longer defined by their walls. For my entire adult life, I cooked for others, for thousands of diners. There's a real sense of pride in creating a special meal for someone marking an anniversary, a wedding, or just a high note in an otherwise long and exhausting day. But I rarely ever cooked for myself at home. Funny how that works.

Now, for the first time in a long time, I cook at home for my family. Food is less about pushing my culinary boundaries and more about that happy medium where creativity collides with practicality. I'm beginning to understand what my world means outside of the kitchen, appreciating the culinary projects as much as simple, quiet dinners at home.

FINDING HOME

I call my journey east "my reverse migration," leaving the youngest part of the country, California, for the oldest, New England, but I didn't realize that in these rolling pastures and never-ending winters, I'd actually find myself. In many ways, I grew up in the kitchen. As a chef, I thought of the restaurant as home. After all, I spent most of my waking hours there. I found solace amid the spurts of sizzling oil and the clanging of pots and pans. I became a teacher, mentoring my cooks on how to butcher chickens and ferment pounds of peppers, and sometimes helping them navigate the messier personal life stuff. Most importantly, I learned to be gentle and respect myself amid the adrenaline-pumping backdrop of professional cooking. It took yanking me from the familiar kitchen in California into the silence of Western Massachusetts for me to fully understand what "home" means.

Home isn't a place, in the tangible sense, but rather it's a state of mind. I have learned that whenever life feels transitory, I can create a sense of constancy no matter where I am in the world by cooking. I lean on a few key culinary principles to help foster a sense of place and familiarity.

MY CULINARY ARSENAL

Food as medicine for the body and soul

The world's first medicines were created from the plant kingdom. Whenever I cook, I'm searching for deliciousness but also looking at how best to feed my body, mind, and soul, rather than just my appetite. Now more than ever, I realize the power of food to nourish in all senses of the word. I ferment for probiotics, use

spices and herbs for their countless benefits, and dry-char or slow-roast instead of using high heat, which often oxidizes fats.

But healthy food doesn't have to mean bland or boring. For me, it's about wearing two hats, that of the curious naturopath-herbalist and that of the chef. When these worlds collide, food leaps from the plate. But it's not just the food itself that heals; it's also the way the food is prepared that can have a lasting effect on overall health. It may sound overly romantic, but I truly believe we infuse emotions into what we cook. Food is a spiritual gesture, and the deepest form of love and nurturing.

Place as muse

As an anthropologist, I often think of myself as a collector. I collect what's around me, both metaphorically and physically, as a way to root myself in a certain time and space. I find much creativity by digging deep into the history of my surroundings, a jumping-off point for my own creative freedom.

In this book, I explore New England's multilayered heritage: the indigenous peoples who originally walked these lands; the Italian, Welsh, Dutch, Irish, and Chinese immigrants who called it home in the nineteenth century; the Lebanese communities who created a thriving restaurant industry; the Polish, Eastern European Jews, and Scots who moved here in the first half of the twentieth century. I reinterpret all these layers through my own eclectic and modern way of cooking, wholesome and healthful. Though New England is my starting place, this book is about distilling disparate cultures and cuisines into layered, honest cooking. It's about the multiplicity of food—how it satiates body and mind while also telling stories of the land, communities, and ourselves.

Batch process

It takes a bit of effort every season, but investing in a larder is how I build intensity of flavor. True, it takes time, and sometimes you have to wait for things to ferment or work your way through large quantities of ingredients, but there are great rewards. You'll have an arsenal of building blocks, like sauces, dips, spice blends, and infusions, at your fingertips to elevate weeknight cooking. A quick swoosh of Green Tahini Sauce (page 72), for example, can transform a simple meal of rice and eggs into something quite extraordinary. Use the larder section as inspiration, but improvise! It's all part of the fun.

Herbs as vegetables

For millennia, humans have been using herbs for flavor and wellness. In this spirit, I reach for herbs by the bushel. My salads at home are often one part herbs to one part whatever else. I take a bowl to the garden and snip away. Spindly dill or slender spears of tarragon, for example, add unique flavors and textures. They bring a whole new sense of vivacity when used with gusto. A tangle of fresh herbs offers a grassy promise and acts as a flavorful digestive or curative (as in Charred Lettuces with Green Tahini, page 71), while a bit of heat subdues their singularity and turns everything into an entirely new type of savoriness (as in Green Eggs with All the Leaves, page 129). Many recipes in this book call for an assortment of herbs, which, for the most part, can be used interchangeably. Learn which greens you enjoy most and do save the stems. Most of the time, tender stems, which often have a more pronounced flavor, can be finely chopped up alongside their leaves. Try it with parsley, cilantro, and the tips of dill, but steer clear of woody stems, such as mint, tarragon, or rosemary.

Spices as ingredients

Spices have traditionally been used as therapeutic foods. I use them for flavor but also for their healing properties—crushing saffron into broths or teas for its floral note, as well as its benefit of preserving dopamine and serotonin levels in the brain, or turning to star anise for its warm fire and infection-fighting properties. Ever since my time in Southeast Asia, I've considered spices ingredients. As I cook, I add them in layers. The motion is rhythmic: Sauté alliums (onions, garlic, and the like), then blend in freshly ground spices,

letting them bloom in the oil to create an intoxicating base flavor (as in the nettle-spinach soup, page 43).

Harnessing natural sweetness

There are natural sugars everywhere. Most fruits are sweet, of course, but many vegetables contain natural sugars, too: sweet potatoes, beets, onions, green peas, sweet corn, pumpkins, winter squashes, rutabagas, carrots, and tomatoes to name a few. Onions and carrots lend their sweetness to soups while fruit purées sweeten many of my desserts without the addition of outside sugars (see Date and Preserved Lemon Balls, page 221).

I use little to no refined sugar in my everyday cooking, but when I do want more intensity, I reach for unrefined syrups, such as honey or maple syrup, or their powdered counterparts (page 203). I look to these natural versions to bring a more complex sweetness to my food, one that might also impart floral, toffee, or musky notes to dishes.

Cooking in tune with the seasons

Choosing food that is local and in season connects me to a specific place and time. Each region of the world has a specific growing season, soil, and heritage all its own. All of these layers determine what is grown and when it is at its peak. Since fresh foods taste most intensely of themselves, it's best to cook in accordance with the seasons.

Not only do the seasons dictate what I eat but also how I eat. The tender new growth of spring and juicy summer months make me crave fresh, bright flavors, while the chill of fall and winter has me cozying up to richer foods. The natural cycle of the plant world has a rhythmic way of guiding my kitchen.

Preserving the seasons

I preserve foods to create a seasonless sensibility. I always want access to an array of buzzing flavors. The beauty of building a larder that captures each season's bounty is that it harnesses time. The ripe flavors of ingredients at their peak are distilled to their essences—and you can use them all year long. Leaning on a few techniques—spirit infusions, oil curing, drying, preserving in honey, fermenting—I'm able to capture fleeting bounties, as with Oil-Preserved Eggplant (page 192), and ensure that nothing goes to waste while also coaxing out nuances that go unnoticed in the fresh form, like the sweet tang of Lacto-Fermented Corn (page 184) or the herbal aroma of Tomato Leaf Oil (page 194).

Cooking with pickles and preserves

I never think of vinegary pickles or funky lacto-ferments as condiments to be stashed in a jar in the back of the fridge. Pickles add a punchy contour to all the other fixings. For me, cooking is a balancing act of sweet, salty, sour, and funky, and the world of sour can be much more than the typical collection of vinegars, citrus juices, yogurts, and tomatoes (though I do love all of these ingredients). Try reaching for brine the next time you want a squeeze of lemon, or use pickled and fresh versions of a vegetable in the same dish to create an uncanny depth where the flavors echo one another, but are still somewhat elusive (as in the Fermented Carrot Borscht, page 33).

Meat on the side

Most of the time, I think of meat as a side dish and not the meal's principle component. I mainly look to meat to round out a feast, acting as a layer of umami to intermingle with vegetables on the table. It adds density, depth, and a little extra protein to a meal, which can be very satiating. But in shifting away from meat as the centerpiece, I find the spectrum of flavors within vegetable cookery expands exponentially. When vegetables take the leading role, the diversity of tastes, textures, and techniques broadens. Take, for instance, cauliflower. When whole-roasted (page 103), it is tender yet burly, but when used in the Chicken Potpie with Creamed Cauliflower and Fennel (page 157), it melts into a silken sauce.

Cooking with intention

For me, cooking for people is one of the deepest ways I know to show love. It's my secret language, and each time I put on my apron, I aim to cook mindfully and with grace. I believe it is my duty to try to be a little bit better every day, to be a better steward of the land and my community. For a long time, I have been telling my cooks that the kitchen is a forum for growth. It's the place we come not just to cook, but also to do our human work.

The home kitchen offers the same type of introspection, a call to be present. The mindfulness you bring to the kitchen can transcend to other arenas in life, and the energy put into cooking transfers to a finished dish. A meal made when you're upset rarely tastes as good as one made when you're happy. There's a link between the head, heart, and hand, and tapping into it can be a powerful experience.

ABOUT THIS BOOK

Since my larder is the backbone of my kitchen, I've created an entire section devoted to different preservation techniques. My hope is that these base recipes will teach you methods that inspire your own seasonal creations. Find comparable substitutions at the farmers' market or grocery store if you want to make a dish but don't have time for the larder element. Don't let it dissuade you; let it be a catalyst for creativity.

In a handful of these recipes, I provide seasonal variations, helping you foster a nimbleness in the kitchen throughout the year. In these instances, the general essence and technique of a dish stays the same, but the dish adopts a slightly different look and taste.

A handful of other recipes have a section for simplifying. This is my way of breaking down some of the more complex dishes into components that more than shine on their own.

FILLING
THE
POT

CHAPTER 1

Notes on Looking West to Honor the Element of Water

Water in the spiritual realm

West, the direction of the setting sun, represents the element water and the power of love, cleansing, and purification. There is a fluidity and flowing nature encouraging us to tap into the power of our subconscious and connect to everything around us. Pulsing through our bodies, water allows us spiritual buoyancy by forming our physical body as the container for expansion and growth. It's a superconductor, long revered as a sacred cleanser, igniting the production of life and mirroring our internal reflection.

Water in the physical realm

Water is a mysterious gift of nature that supports and holds life on Earth. On the surface, water is food, transportation, and recreation, an element for cleansing, purification, and initiation in cultural ceremonies. But under the surface it is the most important element on Earth. It moves rocks and dirt, shifts land into mountains and valleys, and nourishes the soil we plant our food in. Water makes life possible.

In cooking, water is the base for almost everything. It's indispensable in the kitchen, allowing us to make broth, tea, wine, and beer; to steam, simmer, poach, boil, blanch, braise, and ferment. It's a solvent, ideal for extracting and carrying flavors. In the physical realm, water is responsible for triggering all of the natural chemical processes in baking and pastry through hydration, steam formation, gluten activation, fermentation, and a host of other indispensable interactions.

Since water sustains life on Earth, and since, throughout history and across the world, broth-based dishes have been revered as nourishing, calming, and rooting, starting with a chapter on soups and stews seems like the humblest way to begin. Every culture has a go-to soup that's valued for its medicinal properties, for curing all that ails us, from a chill deep in the bones to a broken heart.

SPRING CHOWDER WITH PEAS AND CLAMS

I'm not generally a chowder person. I've never been one. In fact, there's really only one place, Bob Chin's Crab House in Wheeling, Illinois, where I'd gladly slurp up a bowl. Every year growing up, the day after my birthday, my family would pile into the car and drive there for king crab legs, blue crab claws, and steaming cups of their thick and chunky stew. I couldn't get enough. My version takes all the touchpoints of a traditional chowder but lightens it up to something I now crave frequently. The broth base is an homage to bourride, a Provencal fish soup that I first learned to make when I worked at Café Rouge in Berkeley, California. There, we'd whisk aioli into a fortified fish broth, a technique that gave it density, creaminess, and a wallop of garlic. Knowing the French influence in these parts of the East Coast by way of Canada, it only felt right to adopt the technique here.

Makes 4 servings

2½ lb [1.2 kg] clams (about 24 clams), such as cherrystone or littleneck

1 Tbsp cornmeal

2 leeks (about 1 lb [455 g])

6 cups [1.4 L] Kombu Dashi (page 207) or fish stock

2 Tbsp grapeseed oil

12 oz [340 g] small fingerling potatoes, halved

Kosher salt

½ lb [230 g] slab bacon, cut into ½ in [12 mm] lardons

1 lb [455 g] English peas, shelled (7 oz/1¼ cups after shelled)

Aioli (page 204)

Clam "Kimchi" (page 185) and pea shoots for garnish

Place the clams in a large bowl with the cornmeal, which helps to remove sand and grit. Cover completely with water and set aside in the refrigerator for at least 20 minutes and up to 1 hour while you prepare the other components.

Preheat the oven to 300°F [150°C]. Lop the dark green tops from the leeks (reserve the rest to cook a bit later in the recipe), rinse thoroughly, and combine them with the Kombu Dashi in a large saucepan. Bring to a gentle simmer—monitor it so there's very little movement in the pot—and gently steep the leeks in the broth while you prepare the rest of the chowder.

Set a large, lidded, ovenproof skillet over medium heat and warm the oil until it's shimmering. Add the potatoes, cut-side down, in a single layer. Season with salt and allow to cook on the stovetop until they form a light golden crust. Transfer the pan to the oven and bake until tender, about 20 minutes. Remove the potatoes from the pan and set aside.

Add the bacon to the same skillet. Cook over medium-low heat, stirring occasionally, slowly rendering most of the fat. When the bacon is tender and gently browned, remove and set aside.

CONTINUED

Cut the reserved light-colored leeks into ½ in [12 mm] slices and rinse thoroughly, keeping the rings intact. Arrange the slices in the skillet with the bacon fat. Increase the heat to medium until the bottoms are lightly caramelized. Splash about ¼ cup [60 ml] of water into the skillet, immediately cover with the lid, and steam until tender but not completely melted, 30 to 45 minutes. Push the leeks to one side of the pan, then add the bacon and potatoes alongside; cover and place back in the oven to rewarm in unison.

Remove and discard the leek tops from the Kombu Dashi and bring the broth to an active simmer. Drain and thoroughly rinse the clams, then add them to the broth, cover, and steam over medium heat to coax them open. Check on them after 4 minutes; as the shells open, use a slotted spoon to remove them and to divide them among the serving bowls. Re-cover the pan and continue cooking until all are opened up. (Discard any that stay clamped shut.)

Add the peas to the broth and cook, uncovered, for 2 to 3 minutes, until tender, then use the slotted spoon to divide them among the bowls, followed by the potatoes, bacon, and leeks. Whisk 1 cup [240 ml] of the broth into the aioli until incorporated, then pour this back into the pan. Cook, whisking regularly, until the broth thickens slightly, 4 to 5 minutes; ladle it into each of the serving bowls. To serve, top with the kimchi and pea shoots.

Seasonal Variations

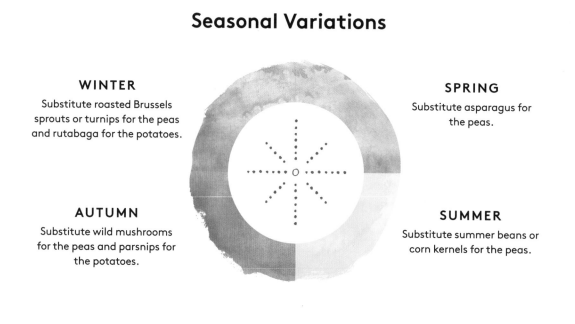

WINTER
Substitute roasted Brussels sprouts or turnips for the peas and rutabaga for the potatoes.

SPRING
Substitute asparagus for the peas.

AUTUMN
Substitute wild mushrooms for the peas and parsnips for the potatoes.

SUMMER
Substitute summer beans or corn kernels for the peas.

Soups and Stews

The fable of stone soup begins with hungry strangers arriving in a village with nothing more than a cooking pot. They ask the villagers for some food, and when they're refused, they go to the river to fill their pot with water and stones. Then they light a fire. Propelled by curiosity, the villagers gather to see what is brewing. The travelers tell them they're making a soup of water and stones, but need a little something extra to make it delicious. One by one, the villagers bring ingredients from their gardens, cupboards, and stores to go into the pot. Soon enough, gentle trickery turns into a feast for both the travelers and the villagers.

It's an enchanting tale, but for me it shows the magic of food and how it can bring us together. After all, food is the great equalizer and the soft entry point to culture. It's said that when you share a meal with people you love, the body takes in more nutrients. In company, we eat less, more slowly, and usually in a more healthful way. Of course, a big celebration can feel quite the opposite, but it's the joy in the room that will carry you on.

When it comes to broths, nothing, or at least as little as possible, goes to waste in my kitchen. Bones and vegetable scraps—fennel and leek tops, celery and carrot ends, parsnip butts, herb stems—are stored in the freezer until my stash of frozen stock runs low or my freezer fixings run high. Then into the pot they go, destined for a heady elixir.

Here in New Hampshire, I make big batches of broth on our wood-fired stove. It simmers for hours with ingredients going in and out of the pot in an almost rhythmic choreography: vegetables pulled the moment they collapse, a dash of vinegar to help extract more nutrients hibernating in the bones. Sometimes the brew bubbles for six hours, sometimes twelve, depending on the bones and the intensity we're after. Then we strain the broth and let it cool, a step we often leave to the snow during the winter months. In the morning, the movements begin again: Over heat it simmers once more, but this time we wilt seaweed, then add bonito flakes off the heat. After straining it again, we steep herb stems off the heat so we don't lose their delicate aromatics. Broths have humble beginnings and are often sketches in resourcefulness (like stone soup, anything goes!), but the result is not only one of the most flavorful building blocks in the kitchen, but also a variety of deeply restorative tonics.

This chapter has soups for every season, from a chilled apple soup (page 31) for the dawn of autumn to a spring clam chowder (page 21) lightened with dashi, kimchi, and aioli in lieu of cream. The larder section showcases some of my favorite oil infusions, which not only preserve fleeting, or at times wilting, ingredients, but also create a boost of flavor that easily intensifies otherwise simple meals—especially soups. And the brilliance of infusions is that they don't take much effort, but their rewards are lasting.

SUMMER BEAN SOUP WITH TOMATO BROWN BUTTER

Baked beans, with their sweet, meaty elixir and mahogany complexion, are somewhat of an edible manifesto in New England. Bean stew, a perfect dish to let simmer unattended throughout the day, provided ballast to colonial life and remains a culinary cornerstone in these parts of the woods. So with baked beans on my mind, I set out to create my own version, which, in all honesty, strays quite far from tradition. Unlike its sweeter original form, this variation is deeply savory, with anchovies, bacon, and a brown butter–tomato sauce anchoring the whole thing. Forever a seeker of acidic bursts and layers of crunch, I decided to add a dilly salad plus salty feta. While it began as a playful ode to baked beans, the dish quickly turned into a celebration of the vast range and life cycle of beans themselves—from runners to shelling, fresh to dry.

Makes 4 servings

Bean Soup

8 oz [230 g] dried beans, such as flageolet or navy, or fresh shelling beans

2 in [5 cm] square dried kombu

2 large tomatoes

2 celery ribs

1 carrot

1 leek, white and light green parts only

6 shallots, skins intact

6 garlic cloves, minced

4 oil-packed anchovy fillets

6 Tbsp [90 ml] extra-virgin olive oil

2 Tbsp maple syrup

1½ Tbsp kosher salt

1 Tbsp red pepper flakes

1 tsp whole-grain mustard

TO MAKE THE SOUP: Combine the dried beans and kombu in a large container and cover with plenty of water to soak for at least 4 hours or overnight; skip this step if using fresh beans.

Drain the beans and kombu and add them to a large pot with enough water to cover by about 1 in [2.5 cm] (if using fresh beans, add the kombu now). Bring to a boil over medium-high heat; meanwhile, halve the tomatoes and cut the celery, carrot, and leek into about 3 in [7.5 cm] pieces. As soon as the water boils, decrease the heat to medium-low and add the vegetables to the pot, along with the whole shallots and minced garlic. Continue to cook at a gentle simmer until the beans are very creamy, 60 to 90 minutes for dried beans and about half that for fresh.

Remove the pot from the heat and use a slotted spoon to reserve the tomatoes; remove and discard the other vegetables.

Set up a sieve over a heatproof container and strain the beans (there should be about 3 cups [480 g]), reserving all the cooking liquid.

In a blender, combine 1 cup [160 g] of the cooked beans with 2 cups [480 ml] of the cooking liquid, plus the tomatoes, anchovies, oil, maple syrup, salt, red pepper flakes, and mustard. Purée until extremely smooth, pour into a large bowl, and fold in the reserved cooked beans by hand. At this point, you can serve it right away or transfer to an airtight container and refrigerate for up to 3 days, gently rewarming over medium-low heat when you're ready to serve.

CONTINUED

Baked Beans

8 oz [230 g] bacon

8 oz [230 g] Romano beans or green beans, chopped into 1 in [2.5 cm] pieces

2 shallots, thinly sliced

1 tsp red pepper flakes

Zest and juice of 1 lemon

1 garlic clove, grated

TO MAKE THE BAKED BEANS: While the bean soup is cooking, preheat the oven to 325°F [165°C]. Cut the bacon into ¼ in [6 mm] lardons; reserve 3 whole beans for garnish and cut the rest into 2 to 3 in [5 to 7.5 cm] pieces.

In a medium saucepan or Dutch oven, spread the bacon in an even layer and cook over medium-low heat until it starts to turn golden and crisp, about 10 minutes. Use a slotted spoon to remove the pieces but leave the fat behind.

Increase the heat slightly, and sauté the shallots until translucent, 5 to 10 minutes. Stir in the chopped beans, bacon, and red pepper flakes. Cover with a lid or a tight layer of foil and bake until the beans are very soft, 60 to 90 minutes. Stir in the lemon zest, juice, and garlic as soon as the beans come out of the oven and cover again; the residual steam will cook the garlic.

TO MAKE THE BROWN BUTTER: Place the tomato in a blender and purée, then strain through a fine-mesh sieve; you should get about ½ cup [120 ml].

Add the butter to a large skillet and gently cook over medium heat until it starts to brown and smell nutty. Stir in the smooth tomato purée (be careful; it might spatter) and simmer for another minute or so. You're looking to slightly cook the purée but keep its brightness. The mix won't emulsify, which is fine. Season with salt and pepper and set aside.

TO MAKE THE SALAD: Thinly slice the pickled green beans on the bias. Combine with the cherry tomatoes, oil, and vinegar.

To serve, ladle the bean soup into bowls with a big spoonful of the baked beans on top. Garnish with the pickled green bean mix, a swirl of tomato brown butter, crumbled feta, and torn fresh herbs. Leftovers can all be refrigerated in separate airtight containers, though the green bean salad is best on the day it's made, when the beans are most crisp and the tomatoes are fresh.

Tomato Brown Butter

1 large tomato (about 8 oz [230 g])

½ cup [120 g] unsalted butter

Kosher salt

Freshly ground black pepper

Green Bean Salad

12 pickled green beans (see Basic Wet Salt Method, page 180)

9 cherry tomatoes, quartered

2 tsp extra-virgin olive oil

1 tsp sherry vinegar

Crumbled feta, parsley leaves, and marjoram leaves for garnish

Simplify It

SOUP BASE	• Serve the soup on its own with a simple green salad. • Use the soup as a base, adding to it any seasonal charred roasted vegetables or wilted greens. • Add shredded chicken, pulled pork, or chunks of Oil-Preserved Shallots with veggies (page 193) for a heartier dish.
BAKED BEANS	• Chop them up and fold them into steamed rice. • Serve as a side dish over quickly grilled green beans for a green bean duo. • Add to a sandwich with Fresh Ricotta (page 204) and a fried egg. • Serve with corn cakes (page 235) and roast chicken.
TOMATO BROWN BUTTER	• You'll have plenty of the tomatoey brown butter left over, which is perfect swirled into pasta or cooked shelling beans, or spooned over roasted vegetables. • Spoon over Coddled Eggs (page 113), fried eggs, or Gift-Wrapped Fish (page 135).
PICKLED GREEN BEAN MASHUP	• Add raw, charred, or steamed green beans for a more robust vegetable side. • Spoon over warm hummus and serve with corn cakes (page 235).

KITCHEN NOTE

When you think the flageolets are done, blow on a bean to see if the skin bursts and peels back like dried glue flaking from childhood fingertips. Meanwhile, braise the Romano beans until they surrender all resistance and become a densely flavored tangle. It's somewhat daunting to let them cook for so long, but trust the process. You'll be left with the most deliriously concentrated jumble of beans that, if you're like me, you'll be hard-pressed not to eat straight from the pot.

LATE HARVEST GAZPACHO

Late in summer, on the cusp of autumn, as the light changes and the days shorten, I find tomatoes are at their best. Having soaked up summer's warmth, they become deliriously sweet and juicy. Or perhaps it's their fleeting nature that fuels my love affair. I make this soup to honor the seasonal shift from light to dark, warm to cold. It's my favorite way to take in and celebrate summer's final hurrah.

Makes 4 servings

2 lb [910 g] late-season tomatoes (about 4 large)

4 sweet red bell peppers

9 oz [255 g] Lacto-Fermented Cucumbers (page 184) or store-bought dill pickles

½ cup [6 g] lightly packed parsley leaves, chopped, plus more for garnish

2 Tbsp lightly packed cilantro leaves, chopped, plus more for garnish

2 Tbsp lightly packed dill leaves, chopped, plus more for garnish

¼ Preserved Lemon, diced (page 185)

1 large shallot, minced

4 oil-packed anchovy fillets, minced

2 garlic cloves, grated

½ serrano chile, grated

2 Tbsp sherry vinegar

1 Tbsp kosher salt

1 tsp coriander seeds, toasted and ground

1 tsp freshly ground black pepper

½ cup [120 ml] pickle brine

¼ cup [60 ml] extra-virgin olive oil

Herby Yogurt (page 204)

16 cherry tomatoes, quartered, for garnish

Fresh herbs, such as basil, tarragon, chives, or bronze fennel, for garnish

Set a metal grate directly over a gas burner or heat a grill to medium-high. Set the whole tomatoes over the flame and wait for the skins to blister, then flip and repeat; this should take only a minute or two per side. When the tomatoes are cool enough to handle, peel away their skins, remove their cores, and cut them into quarters.

Char the red peppers over the flame, giving a little more time for their skins to become mostly black all over. As you did with the tomatoes, wait for them to cool before peeling away their skins and any papery char (it's OK if a bit of char lingers), then remove the stems, scrape out the seeds, and dice.

Dice the cucumbers and reserve about ¼ cup [30 g] in an airtight container for the garnish. Add the rest to the bowl of a food processor along with the tomatoes, peppers, parsley, cilantro, dill, preserved lemon, shallot, anchovies, garlic, serrano, vinegar, salt, coriander, and pepper. Pulse until all of the vegetables are mostly incorporated but still retain a rustic consistency.

To make the soup extra-smooth, ladle half of it into a blender along with the pickle brine and purée until very smooth. With the blender (or food processor) still going, stream in the oil. Transfer all of the soup to an airtight container and refrigerate until completely chilled, at least 1 hour and up to 3 days.

To serve, divide the soup among serving bowls. Top with a giant spoonful of the yogurt, the cherry tomatoes, reserved cucumbers, and torn fresh herbs.

KITCHEN NOTE:

Salt-brined pickles and the citrus funk of preserved lemon give this soup a slight fermented acidity and depth that doesn't overwhelm the freshness of the rest of the vegetables, but fresh ingredients can be substituted for their preserved counterparts, using fresh cucumbers for the pickled ones and 2 Tbsp lemon juice in place of the preserved lemons.

CHILLED EARLY HARVEST APPLE SOUP

I remember my first apple harvest in the eastern United States: freshly fallen leaves crunching under the truck's wheels, the thumping of apples into buckets, echoes of constant laughter, and the dusky glow of autumn. But it wasn't until I moved to New Hampshire that I got two prolific apple trees of my own. In spring, the rangy branches shake off winter's white veil just in time for tiny green buds to sprout and blossoms to bloom. The real magic is watching the boys run beneath the trees and collect fallen apples for applesauce, cider, and their first homemade apple pie. This soup is one of my favorite ways to honor the season's first fallen fruit. The flavor is crisp. Served cold, it is a nod to the famous fruit soups of Eastern Europe. The heated version will warm you on a brisk day.

Makes 4 servings

½ lb [230 g] golden beets, greens attached

3 large tart apples, such as Granny Smith or Honeycrisp (about 1½ lb [680 g])

1 fennel bulb

2 tsp fresh lemon juice

1 small russet potato (about 4 oz [115 g]), peeled

2 leeks, white and light green parts only

2 garlic cloves

2 Tbsp unsalted butter

2 Tbsp extra-virgin olive oil

1 Tbsp kosher salt, plus more as needed

1 tsp coriander seeds, ground

1 tsp fennel seeds, ground

½ tsp freshly ground black pepper, plus more as needed

2½ cups [600 ml] Kombu Dashi (page 207) or vegetable stock

1⅓ cups [320 ml] buttermilk

⅔ cup [160 ml] apple cider or apple juice

2 Tbsp sesame tahini

5 Tbsp [75 ml] apple cider vinegar

3 oz [85 g] bacon

1 Tbsp sesame oil

Fennel Oil (page 194) for garnish

Preheat the oven to 375°F [190°C]. Trim, chop, and reserve the beet greens.

Place the beets in a roasting pan and cover with a lid or tightly wrap with foil. Roast until very tender and easily pierced with a fork, but not mushy, 40 to 60 minutes. When they're cool enough to handle, peel and cut a quarter of them into a small dice (about ¼ in [6 mm]) and reserve for the garnish; chop the rest.

Core the apples. As you did with the beets, dice half of 1 apple for garnish and chop the rest. Remove the fennel's tough outer layers and core it; dice one-quarter of the bulb and thinly slice the rest. To make the garnish, toss the diced fennel with the diced apples, the diced beets, and lemon juice; refrigerate until you're ready to serve, up to 1 day ahead of time. Lemon juice will keep your apples from browning.

Chop the potato, thinly slice the leeks, and smash and chop the garlic. Combine with the sliced fennel and chopped apples and set aside.

CONTINUED

Combine the butter and olive oil in a large pot and melt over medium heat. Add the apple–potato mixture and salt and cook, stirring occasionally, until the apples start to soften. Stir in the coriander, fennel seeds, and pepper and allow them to bloom for a minute or so. Add the beets, Kombu Dashi, buttermilk, cider, and 1 Tbsp of the tahini. Increase the heat to medium-high until the mixture comes to a simmer, then reduce the heat to medium-low and continue cooking until all of the vegetables are very soft, 20 to 30 minutes. Remove from the heat and allow to cool for about 10 minutes before puréeing.

Set up a fine-mesh sieve or chinois over a large bowl. Working in batches, purée and strain the soup. Swirl ¼ cup [60 ml] of the vinegar into the soup, plus more salt if needed. Transfer to an airtight container and refrigerate until completely chilled, up to 2 days.

Before you serve the soup, cut the bacon into roughly ½ in [12 mm] pieces. In a large skillet, cook the bacon over medium-low heat, stirring occasionally, until it renders all its fat. Use a slotted spoon or spatula to transfer it to a bowl, leaving the fat behind, then add the reserved beet greens and toss gently to coat; sauté just until wilted. Add the greens to the bowl with the bacon and toss with the remaining 1 Tbsp of tahini. Set aside.

Separately, toss the reserved apples, beets, and fennel with the sesame oil and the remaining 1 Tbsp of vinegar; season with salt and pepper.

To serve, ladle the soup into individual bowls. Divide the bacon and greens over the top, followed by the apple, beet, and fennel mix. Finish with a swirl of fennel oil and serve immediately. Leftover soup and garnish can be refrigerated in separate airtight containers; the leftover bacon mix is best eaten day of, when the bacon is crisp. If made ahead, gently rewarm each component.

FERMENTED CARROT BORSCHT

My Lithuanian grandmother, Ethel, made borscht the old-fashioned way, with a *rössel* (that's Yiddish for fermented beets), but Mom refused to eat it as a child since pink foods were enjoyed only as ice pops. Because Mom shunned the soup, I only found and fell in love with it in adulthood.

My love affair with traditional borscht is the soul of this dish, but my desire to reinvent it brings us to this golden version, perhaps one even Mom will like. Fermented carrots imbued with ginger and turmeric bolster the soup, its traditional crimson complexion giving way to something a bit more electric. But, just like Grandma's, it's that lactic funk that helps ground the sweetness of the roots. To me, the dish holds three generations in one bowl.

Makes 4 servings

6 Tbsp [90 g] unsalted butter

10 Tbsp [150 ml] extra-virgin olive oil

4 or 5 Lacto-Fermented Carrots (page 181) (about 12 oz [340 g])

2 tsp ground turmeric

1½ tsp fennel seeds, ground

1 tsp caraway seeds, ground

1 tsp coriander seeds, ground

1 tsp freshly ground black pepper

⅛ tsp cumin seeds, ground

8 small carrots (about ½ lb [230 g]), chopped

5 shallots (about 6 oz [170 g]), thinly sliced

1 golden beet (about 4 oz [110 g]), chopped

1 fennel bulb, chopped

4 garlic cloves, minced

One 3 in [7.5 cm] piece fresh ginger, minced

3 Tbsp diced dried apples

Zest of 1 lemon

1 Tbsp kosher salt, plus more as needed

6 cups [1.4 L] chicken or vegetable stock

6 Tbsp [90 ml] apple juice

1 Tbsp honey

Wilted spinach, for garnish

¼ cup [60 g] strained full-fat Greek-style yogurt

1 tsp urfa biber or Aleppo pepper

In a medium pot, combine the butter and 6 Tbsp [90 ml] of the oil and warm gently over medium heat until the butter is just starting to sizzle, 3 to 4 minutes. Grate ¼ cup [40 g] of the fermented carrots and reserve in the refrigerator for garnish; chop the rest the same size as the other vegetables.

Add the turmeric, fennel seeds, caraway, coriander, pepper, and cumin to the pot and bloom for a couple of minutes. When the spices are very fragrant, add the fermented and fresh carrots, shallots, beet, fennel bulb, garlic, ginger, apples, lemon zest, and salt. Cook, stirring occasionally, until the shallots are translucent and the other vegetables are slightly softened, 12 to 15 minutes.

CONTINUED

Add the stock, apple juice, and honey; increase the heat to high until the soup simmers, then decrease to medium-low and gently simmer until all of the vegetables are completely tender, 25 to 35 minutes. Remove from the heat and let cool slightly before puréeing.

Set a fine-mesh sieve or chinois over a large bowl. Working in batches, use a blender to purée the soup until very smooth, then strain. Season with more salt as needed. At this point, you can serve the soup right away or transfer to an airtight container and refrigerate for up to 3 days, gently rewarming over medium-low heat when you're ready to serve.

To serve, warm a medium skillet over medium-low heat. Warm 1 Tbsp of the olive oil, add the spinach, and wilt. Season with salt. Combine the yogurt with the remaining 3 Tbsp of oil and the urfa biber. Ladle the soup into bowls and garnish with the yogurt, spinach, and reserved, shredded fermented carrots.

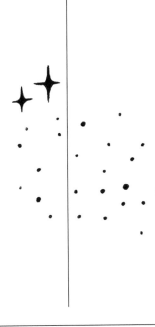

SHALLOT SOUP WITH CHARRED BROCCOLINI AND ROMAN GNOCCHI

Think of this soup as an Italian stracciatella colliding with the Far East. Gossamer eggs float in a fortified chicken broth with kombu and soy adding a deep savoriness. Flakes of bonito (smoked and dried tuna) provide a taste of the earth and a gentle aroma of the sea.

When I worked at Boulettes Larder in San Francisco, we'd often make corn bread in corn-shaped cast-iron molds—there was always something captivating about reassembling ingredients to mimic their original forms. Here, I fill those pans with polenta before charring them under the broiler, making them look as if a fire has singed the cobs. Then I douse everything with a shallot-infused oil. Side note: Shallots are the most nutrient dense of all alliums, so I like to lean on them for an onion kick.

Makes 6 servings

Roman Gnocchi

¾ cup [180 ml] whole milk

1 tsp kosher salt

½ cup [70 g] dry polenta

1 egg yolk

2 Tbsp finely grated hard cheese, such as Piave or Parmesan

1½ Tbsp unsalted butter

Freshly ground black pepper

TO MAKE THE GNOCCHI: Brush a light coat of olive oil inside individual cast-iron molds (approximately ¼ cup [60 g] each) or an 8 in [20 cm] square baking dish. In a medium saucepan over medium heat, combine the milk and salt with ¾ cup [180 ml] of water. Warm until the surface is steaming but not yet simmering.

Whisk the polenta into the pan and reduce the heat to medium-low. Cook, stirring regularly with a wooden spoon or spatula, for 45 to 60 minutes, until the polenta is very thick with tender grains. Remove from the heat.

Stir in the egg yolk, cheese, and butter until fully incorporated; season with pepper. Evenly distribute the mixture among the prepared molds or pour into the baking dish. Smooth the tops and refrigerate until fully cool. Gently unmold using a butter knife or small offset spatula. If you let it set in a baking dish, cut the cooled mixture into 4 in [10 cm] squares. Proceed with the soup right away or refrigerate the polenta in an airtight container for up to 3 days.

CONTINUED

Shallot and Broccolini Soup

3 qt [2.8 L] chicken stock

5 in [12 cm] square dried kombu

1 cup [25 g] tightly packed
bonito flakes

2 Tbsp white soy sauce

8 oz [230 g] flowering broccolini or
broccoli florets

2 Tbsp extra-virgin olive oil

4 to 8 Oil-Preserved Shallots
(page 193), plus their oil for serving

1½ tsp fresh lemon juice

½ tsp fish sauce

¼ tsp kosher salt

3 eggs

¼ cup [20 g] finely grated
Parmesan cheese

TO MAKE THE SOUP: Pour the stock into a large pot and bring to an active simmer. Allow it to reduce to 2 qt [2 L] before adding the kombu; reduce the heat to medium-low and continue to simmer gently until you have about 1½ qt [1.5 L] stock. By this point, the kombu should be tender but not falling apart. Discard it and add the bonito flakes off the heat. Steep for 5 minutes, then strain through a fine-mesh sieve and add the soy sauce. Proceed right away or refrigerate the fortified stock in an airtight container for up to 3 days.

The day you're serving the soup, fill a large pot with 1 to 2 in [2½ to 5 cm] of water and fit a steamer inside, making sure the water isn't high enough to seep into it. Bring the water to a simmer over medium-high heat.

If you're using smaller broccolini, taste a piece of the stems to see if the skin is tender; if you're using a head of broccoli, cut it into florets so that each piece has a wide, flat side. Slice tender stems (peel them first if necessary) and steam everything until bright green but still crisp.

Heat a cast-iron skillet or a grill to medium-high heat. In a large bowl, toss the broccolini with 1 Tbsp of the oil to lightly coat. Separately, halve the shallots along their equators. Sear the vegetables in batches, with the flat sides down, until they're nicely golden with a warm, roasty flavor, 3 to 5 minutes per batch.

Reserve the shallots and return the broccolini to the bowl. Toss with the lemon juice, fish sauce, salt, and the remaining 1 Tbsp oil. Set aside.

If you prepared the gnocchi, preheat the oven to 325°F [165°C] with one rack 4 to 6 in [10 to 15 cm] beneath the heating element. Place the broccoli and the reserved shallots on one baking sheet and the gnocchi on another; bake until everything is completely warmed through. Pull the vegetables from the oven and broil the gnocchi on the top rack for a couple of minutes, just to build some color (like grilled corn) and a little crispness.

Meanwhile, bring the fortified stock to a gentle simmer in a pot or saucepan. Beat the eggs and Parmesan in a medium bowl. With a whisk, stir the stock vigorously in one direction and pour the egg mixture into the pot while the water swirls around like a whirlpool. The egg mixture will cook as it moves around in the broth.

To serve, place 1 gnocchi, 2 shallot halves, and a few broccolini florets in the bottom of each bowl. Ladle the stock over the top and garnish with a spoonful of shallot oil.

Simplify It

ROMAN GNOCCHI

- Use the polenta mixture as a base for pizza-like toppings. Spread into a pan, chill, then load it up with your favorite toppings. Bake and broil the cheese to finish. Serve in wedges with a simple salad.
- Serve as a side with roasted meats, fish, or platters full of grilled summer vegetables.

SOUP BASE

- Shred leftover roast chicken or vegetables into the soup.
- Add a scoop of leftover rice or legumes to add heft, or throw in a handful of spinach at the last minute to wilt.

OIL-PRESERVED SHALLOTS (PAGE 193)

- Chop and add to quick pan sauces.
- Pulse into an allium relish with herbs and spices for grilled meats, fish, or vegetables.
- Warm in the oven and broil gently. Serve with sautéed mushrooms for a quick side dish.

EGGPLANT SOUP WITH WALNUT DUMPLINGS

Charoset has always been my favorite Passover dish. I'd beg Mom to let me hold a big bowl of the nubbly mix in the car ride to Seder, as if keeping it closer meant I'd get first dibs at dinner. That may not have been the case, but I did get to sneak a few bites along the way. Even as a kid, I was less interested in its initial sweetness and more drawn to its bitter undercurrent, the wine and walnuts leaving me with a cat-tongue sensation. For these dumplings, I soak walnuts in red wine à la charoset. The dumplings are an homage to my dear friend and culinary anthropologist Darra Goldstein and the walnut dumplings from her lauded book *The Georgian Feast*. Eggplant works well for a creamy soup since its texture turns to custard with a bit of heat, but the flavor never overpowers. Have fun with the halloumi. It's a funny cheese that kind of squeaks on your teeth, but the brilliance is in its inability to melt. Think of it here as croutons with a little bit of bounce.

Makes 4 servings

Ginger-Walnut Dumplings

2 cups [240 g] walnuts

2 cups [480 ml] red wine

2 tsp lightly packed cilantro leaves, chopped

1 tsp lightly packed dill leaves, chopped

1 tsp caraway seeds, toasted and ground

1 tsp kosher salt

2 eggs

2 dates, finely chopped

1 garlic clove, grated

½ in [12 mm] piece fresh ginger, grated

Zest of 1 lemon

Freshly ground black pepper

TO MAKE THE DUMPLINGS: Combine the walnuts and wine in a bowl and let soak for 1 hour. Drain the walnuts. In a food processor, pulse a few times to break them up, then add the cilantro, dill, caraway, salt, eggs, dates, garlic, ginger, and lemon zest and process just until the mixture is uniform and finely chopped. Season with pepper.

Fill a large pot with 1 to 2 in [2½ to 5 cm] of water and fit a steamer inside, making sure the water isn't high enough to seep into it. Cover and bring the water to a gentle simmer over medium heat.

Scoop the dumplings into roughly tablespoon-size mounds and use two spoons to shape them into quenelles (ovals). Steam in batches, making sure they don't stick together, until they are firm and holding their shape, 8 to 10 minutes. Leave at room temperature if you are proceeding right away or refrigerate in an airtight container for up to 3 days. If you make the dumplings ahead, allow them to sit at room temperature for about 30 minutes before searing.

CONTINUED

Charred Eggplant Soup

2 lb [910 g] eggplant

4 or 5 scallions

4 garlic cloves

½ serrano chile

½ bulb fennel

½ red onion

3 Tbsp extra-virgin olive oil

3 Tbsp walnut oil, plus more for frying

1½ in [4 cm] piece fresh ginger, minced

2 tsp fennel seeds, finely ground

¾ tsp coriander seeds, finely ground

¾ tsp celery seeds, finely ground

¾ tsp caraway seeds, finely ground

5¼ cups [1.3 L] Kombu Dashi (page 207) or chicken broth

3½ tsp apple cider vinegar

2 tsp kosher salt

Ginger-Walnut Dumplings (recipe precedes)

8 oz [224 g] halloumi cheese

⅔ cup [90 g] rice flour

2 Tbsp lightly packed dill leaves, finely chopped

Zest of 1 lemon

3 scallions, chopped

Tomato Leaf Oil (page 194) for garnish

TO MAKE THE SOUP: Heat a grill to high heat or set a metal grate directly over a gas burner. Char the eggplant, scallions, garlic, and serrano (if using) over the flame. The eggplant is ready when it's black and ashy all over and soft throughout; the scallions, garlic, and serrano are ready when they're blistered but holding their shape. Chop the scallions and reserve for garnish.

When the eggplant is cool enough to handle, trim the stem and peel away its papery, black skin. Coarsely chop it along with the garlic and serrano and set aside.

Peel away the tough outer layers of the fennel and thinly slice it along with the onion.

In a pot or large saucepan, combine the olive oil and walnut oil over medium heat. When they are warm, add the fennel, onion, and ginger; sauté, stirring regularly, until translucent and soft with no coloration. Stir in the fennel, coriander, celery, and caraway seeds and let them bloom until very fragrant, 5 to 8 minutes.

Add the charred eggplant, garlic, and serrano to the pot, then cover with the Kombu Dashi, 1½ tsp of the apple cider vinegar, and the salt. Bring the whole pot to a simmer over medium heat and continue cooking until all of the vegetables are very tender, 20 to 30 minutes. Remove from the heat and let cool slightly. Working in batches, use a blender to purée the soup until very smooth. At this point, you can serve it right away or transfer to an airtight container and refrigerate for up to 3 days, gently rewarming over medium-low heat when you're ready to serve.

While the soup cooks, or whenever you're ready to serve the soup, line a plate or baking sheet with paper towels. Coat the bottom of a skillet with about ⅛ in [4 mm] of walnut oil and let it get very warm over medium heat. Sear the dumplings so they're crisp and golden, 2 to 3 minutes per side, then let them drain on the lined plate. Allow the oil to rewarm and add more if needed.

Tear the halloumi into rough bite-size pieces and set the flour in a wide, shallow bowl.

In a separate bowl, combine the dill, lemon zest, and a splash of walnut oil. Set aside.

Dust the halloumi in the flour, shaking off any excess, and fry in batches, leaving plenty of space between the pieces, 30 seconds to 1 minute per side. Immediately after cooking, allow the cheese to drain on the prepared plate, then toss with the lemon-dill mix (it may not want to cling to the cheese, but you should be able to lightly coat it).

To serve, ladle the soup into bowls and divide the dumplings among them. Top with the crispy cheese, scallions, and tomato oil.

CREAMED NETTLE–SPINACH SOUP WITH SUMAC OIL

As a child of the Midwest during the 1980s, I grew up on cream of broccoli soup. It always smelled like microwaved broccoli—overly sulfuric and "wet"—but an exorbitant amount of cheese hid any flaw. Its sea-foam complexion brought great comfort, if also a heaviness. I've lightened it up a bit here and looked to local wild ingredients for the soup's signature verdure. Nettles, the jagged porcupines of the plant world, grow effortlessly throughout New England, and when cooked, they have a beautiful spinach-like flavor. But take caution when holding them: Gloves work best. Or use all spinach if the prickles feel like too much to handle or if nettles are not available in your area.

Makes 4 servings

15 cups [300 g] spinach

15 cups [300 g] nettles

10½ oz [300 g] Yukon gold potatoes

1 large yellow onion, thinly sliced

4 garlic cloves, thinly sliced

1 serrano chile, thinly sliced

1½ tsp grated fresh ginger

½ cup [113 g] ghee

¼ cup [60 ml] untoasted sesame oil

2 tsp coriander seeds, ground

2 tsp fennel seeds, ground

1 tsp cumin seeds, ground

1 tsp peppercorns, ground

½ star anise pod, ground

½ tsp ground turmeric

5 cups [1.2 L] Kombu Dashi (page 207) or vegetable stock

1 Tbsp plus ¼ tsp kosher salt

1 cup [240 g] strained full-fat Greek yogurt

¼ cup [3 g] lightly packed dill leaves, finely chopped, plus more for garnish

Zest of 2 lemons

Freshly ground black pepper

Sumac Oil (page 194) for garnish

Sweet paprika for garnish

Pluck away any tough stems from the spinach and nettles and wash them well to remove any grit.

Fill a large pot with water and bring it to a rolling boil. Meanwhile, make an ice bath in a large bowl.

Submerge half the greens in the boiling water and cook until very soft but still bright green, about 1 minute. Use a spider or fine-mesh sieve to pull out the greens and immediately plunge them into the ice bath. Bring the water back to a rolling boil and repeat with the rest of the greens. Drain the greens and squeeze them well to remove as much moisture as possible, then chop them finely and reserve at room temperature or in the refrigerator.

Peel and cut the potatoes into ¼ in [6 mm] cubes and combine them in a large bowl with the onion, garlic, serrano, and ginger; set aside.

CONTINUED

In a large saucepan, warm the ghee and sesame oil over medium heat. When the fat begins to shimmer, stir in the coriander, fennel, cumin, peppercorns, anise, and turmeric and allow them to get toasty and fragrant, 4 to 5 minutes.

Add the potato mixture all at once and sauté, stirring occasionally, until the potatoes are soft enough that they can be smashed with your spoon, 45 to 60 minutes. Add the Kombu Dashi and 1 Tbsp of the salt, increase the heat to high until it comes to a simmer, then remove from the heat and allow to cool at room temperature.

While the soup cools, prepare the garnishes. Season the yogurt with the dill, lemon zest, and pepper; keep refrigerated until it's time to serve.

In a blender, purée the chopped greens and potato mixture with the remaining ¼ tsp salt, in batches if necessary. If you'd like, pass it through a fine-mesh sieve or chinois to make it completely smooth. Serve warm, garnished with the dill yogurt, sumac oil, dill leaves, and paprika.

Seasonal Variations

WINTER

Substitute kale or broccoli for the nettles.

SPRING

Substitute asparagus or peas for the nettles.

AUTUMN

Substitute charred and roasted green cabbage for the nettles.

SUMMER

Substitute watercress for the nettles.

AUTUMN CHOWDER WITH CORN AND SMOKY POTATOES

This is a chowder for that moment when summer takes its final breath and exhales into autumn. It's root-to-stalk cooking, where naked corncobs gently infuse a simple broth with their milky sweetness, nary a droplet of cream. Once blended, the soup takes on an ebullient yellow glow, perfect for fall's palette. While the fermented corn brings an extra layer of depth, the soup more than stands on its own without it. Just don't skip the potatoes, with their craggy edges cradling the herbaceous chimichurri sauce.

Makes 4 servings

1 lb [455 g] small waxy potatoes, such as fingerling or Yukon gold

1 Tbsp extra-virgin olive oil

2 Tbsp kosher salt, plus more for seasoning

4 ears corn, husked

4 heads garlic

2 qt [2 L] Kombu Dashi (page 207), chicken stock, or vegetable stock

1 yellow onion, quartered

¼ cup [60 g] unsalted butter

4 shallots, thinly sliced

½ fennel bulb, thinly sliced

1 tsp ground coriander seeds

1 tsp sweet paprika

½ tsp chili powder

½ tsp freshly ground black pepper, plus more for seasoning

Grapeseed oil for frying

Smoky Chimichurri (page 205)

Lacto-Fermented Corn (page 184) for garnish

Preheat the oven to 325°F [165°C]. In a roasting dish or on a rimmed baking sheet, toss the potatoes with the olive oil and ½ Tbsp of the salt. Roast, uncovered, until the potatoes are very soft, 60 to 90 minutes. (Save this step for the day you'll be eating if you're making the soup ahead.)

Meanwhile, cut the kernels from the corn and reserve. Peel away the papery outer layers on the heads of garlic, then halve them crosswise. Add the cobs and garlic to a large pot with the Kombu Dashi and onion. Bring to a simmer over high heat; as soon as it comes to a boil, decrease the heat to medium and continue to simmer until the stock is infused with a gentle corn flavor, about 30 minutes. Strain and discard the solids; you should have about 6 cups [1.4 L] of stock.

In a large pot or Dutch oven over medium heat, lightly brown the butter. Add the shallots, fennel, and the remaining 1½ Tbsp salt and sauté until translucent, 5 to 10 minutes. Stir in the coriander, paprika, chili powder, and pepper and let toast until fragrant, about 1 minute. Add the reserved corn kernels and continue to cook, stirring occasionally, until the kernels ever so slightly brighten in color, about 5 minutes. Add the stock and simmer for 15 minutes. Remove from the heat and let cool slightly before puréeing.

Working in batches, use a blender to purée the soup; if you'd like, pass it through a fine-mesh sieve or chinois set over a large bowl to make it extra-smooth. Season to taste. Serve right away or transfer to an airtight container and refrigerate for up to 3 days, gently rewarming over medium-low heat when you're ready to serve.

CONTINUED

To serve, line a plate with paper towels and coat the bottom of a skillet with a thin layer (about ⅛ in [4 mm]) of grapeseed oil over medium-high heat. Test the temperature by splashing a couple of drops of water into the pan; when they immediately sizzle and steam, the pan is ready. Using the heel of your hand, smash the roasted potatoes so they're flat but remain intact.

Working in batches, fry the potatoes in a single layer, leaving some space between them and decreasing the heat to medium as soon as the potatoes hit the pan. Fry until they're deeply golden with some crispy bits, 2 to 3 minutes per side, then transfer to the prepared plate to drain. Add the chimichurri to a large bowl and fold in the potatoes to coat.

To serve, ladle the chowder into bowls and top with a few potatoes plus any chimichurri still lingering in the bowl; garnish with a scoop of the fermented corn.

Simplify It

SMASHED POTATOES

- This is a great potato technique to stick in your back pocket, and it's a blank canvas for spices, herbs, and other sauces from the book. It's fast, easy, and never disappoints, creating a creamy interior and crispy edges. They're great for a brunch side dish or to serve alongside other vegetables and a salad. If you're feeling adventurous, make the Dried Beef Floss (page 92) and serve it over these potato bites. Toss them in Chutney-esque Spice Blend (page 199) with lots of chopped-up herbs, dip them into Harissa (page 187), or melt cheese on top.

FIVE-SPICE CHICKEN SOUP

As the saying goes, chicken soup is the Jewish penicillin, good for all that
ails you. It's clear that our grandparents knew the sublime wonders of bone
broth before it became a craze. Like most Ashkenazi Jews, I grew up eating
matzo ball soup—ethereal orbs (never sinkers!) bobbing in a schmaltz
(chicken fat)-cloaked broth. This is my not-so-obvious riff on the food of
my childhood, brought forward with the flavors of China's spiced broths.
Instead of matzo balls, I reimagine turnip cakes from dim sum carts,
coaxing out aromas from vegetables instead of flour.

4 servings

Daikon Dumplings

3 fresh or dried shiitake mushrooms

¾ cup [105 g] rice flour

¼ cup [35 g] corn flour

1½ tsp kosher salt

½ tsp freshly ground black pepper

2 strips (about 2 oz [60 g]) bacon,
finely chopped

4 oil-packed anchovy fillets, chopped

4 scallions, white and light green
parts only, finely chopped

2 Tbsp lightly packed tarragon leaves,
chopped

8 oz [230 g] daikon radish, coarsely
grated

3 Tbsp schmaltz or unsalted butter,
at room temperature

TO MAKE THE DUMPLINGS: If you're using dried mushrooms, cover them
with warm water and leave to hydrate for at least 1 hour or overnight, then drain.

Fill a large pot with 1 to 2 in [2.5 to 5 cm] of water and fit a steamer inside, making
sure the water isn't high enough to seep into it. Cover and bring the water to a gentle
simmer over medium heat. You'll need 8 foil cupcake wrappers (2½ in [6.3 cm]
diameter) or individual small aluminum baking tins (or, for free-form dumplings,
a layer of parchment to set inside the steamer). Finely dice the mushrooms.
Separately, combine the rice flour, corn flour, salt, and pepper and set it aside.

Add the bacon to a large skillet and cook over medium-low heat, stirring occasionally, until it renders most of its fat, 6 to 8 minutes. Add the mushrooms, anchovies,
scallions, and tarragon and cook for another 5 to 6 minutes, until the scallions are
soft. Use a slotted spoon to transfer the mixture to a large bowl, leaving behind
some rendered fat.

Add the daikon and ⅓ cup [80 ml] of water to the same pan and give it a good stir.
Sauté until the daikon is soft and translucent but before it starts to brown. Scrape
the contents of the pan into the bacon mix, along with any lingering water, and
stir in the schmaltz until it's melted and everything is incorporated. Add the flour
mixture and combine by hand or with a wooden spoon until it comes together and
resembles biscuit dough. Add 3 Tbsp of water—the dough should be soft and well
moistened but not too loose, like a cookie dough. If it's still a bit dry, add more
water, 1 Tbsp at a time.

If you're using cupcake wrappers or aluminum baking tins, divide the dough
between them in roughly ¼ cup (2 oz [60 g]) portions. If you're making free-form
dumplings, line your steamer with parchment and portion the dough into small,
thick disks, about 2 oz [60 g] each. Working in batches so they're not crowded, add
the dumplings to the steamer and tightly cover. Cook until the cakes firm up through
the center but are still a bit wet on top, 30 to 40 minutes, checking halfway through
and adjusting the heat or adding water as needed to keep the steam steadily circu-
lating. Allow to dry to the touch before frying so they don't cling to the pan or, if
you're making them in advance, refrigerate in an airtight container for up to 3 days.

CONTINUED

TO MAKE THE SOUP: Place the chicken in a large pot and cover it completely with the Kombu Dashi. Add the cremini mushrooms, leeks, carrot, fennel, garlic, ginger, and Five-Spice Blend. Bring to a simmer over medium-high heat, then immediately decrease the temperature to medium-low and continue to gently simmer until the thickest part of the chicken breast reaches 150°F to 160°F [65°C to 70°C] on an instant-read thermometer or when you see the chicken bob and float, 30 to 40 minutes. Carefully pull the chicken out of the stock and set it aside to cool.

Add 1 Tbsp of the salt to the pot and increase the heat to medium. Keep at an active simmer until it has reduced to about 2 qt [2 L], 2 hours or so. Remove from the heat and immediately add the bonito flakes. Steep for 5 minutes, then strain through a fine-mesh sieve and discard all the solids. Stir the soy sauce into the broth.

When the chicken is cool enough to handle, pull all the meat off the bone, leaving the pieces as large as possible. Toss to coat with the schmaltz and the remaining 1 tsp salt. Proceed right away or refrigerate the chicken and broth separately in airtight containers for up to 3 days.

On the day you're serving the soup, roast the wild mushrooms. Preheat the oven to 375°F [190°C]. If the mushrooms are large, cut them into floret-size pieces. Toss with a bit of grapeseed oil and season lightly with salt; roast for 15 to 20 minutes, until crispy-edged and golden. Decrease the heat to 250°F [120°C].

If you made the broth in advance, add it to a pot and gently rewarm over medium heat; meanwhile, allow the chicken to come to room temperature for about 30 minutes.

Coat the bottom of a skillet with a thin layer of grapeseed oil and warm over medium-high heat until it's dancing. Unwrap the daikon cakes if you steamed them in cupcake wrappers. Add the cakes to the oil and lower the heat to medium; working in batches, cook until crisp and deeply golden, 2 to 3 minutes per side. Transfer to the 250°F [120°C] oven for 5 to 10 minutes to finish warming; use the tip of a paring knife or a cake tester to check the center and ensure it's warmed through. Meanwhile, add the chicken to the broth to gently warm it.

To serve, place one or two dumplings in each serving bowl with the roasted mushrooms and pieces of chicken alongside them. Ladle the broth into each bowl and finish with a swirl of chili oil, scallions, and tarragon. Serve immediately.

Five-Spice Chicken Soup

1 small chicken (about 3½ lb [1.6 kg])

5 qt [4.7 L] Kombu Dashi (page 207) or vegetable stock

8 oz [225 g] cremini mushrooms (about 2½ cups)

2 leeks, roughly chopped

1 carrot, roughly chopped

1 fennel bulb, roughly chopped

20 garlic cloves, smashed

2 in [5 cm] piece fresh ginger, cut into thin slices

2 Tbsp Five-Spice Blend (page 200)

1 Tbsp plus 1 tsp kosher salt, plus more as needed

½ cup [12 g] tightly packed bonito flakes

2 Tbsp white soy sauce

1 Tbsp schmaltz or unsalted butter, plus more for frying

1 lb [455 g] wild mushrooms (about 5 cups), such as maitake, oyster, or chanterelle

Grapeseed oil

Daikon Dumplings (recipe precedes)

Tarragon Chili Oil (page 194), chopped scallions, and tarragon leaves for garnish

Simplify It

FIVE-SPICE BLEND	• Season any cut of meat, or dust over cooked eggs.
	• Bloom in oil for a bread-dipping condiment.
	• Mix into salad dressings.
	• Season dips like guacamole or labne.
DAIKON DUMPLINGS	• Serve as a side dish with roast meat or a poached egg and salad.
	• Serve on a bed of steamed and oiled kale with a fried egg.

WINTER BROTH WITH MEATBALLS, BUCKWHEAT, AND PRESERVED VEGETABLES

As a descendent of Eastern Europeans, I couldn't create a book without an homage to the humble cabbage roll. This version unites two of my favorite childhood comfort foods—plump green bundles of kasha with slow-cooked onions. I use lacinato kale for these little sausage parcels, providing an extra bit of earthiness, but cabbage or chard would work just as well.

Using dried vegetables may seem unusual, but I love their concentrated flavors. Drying strips of zucchini, planks of eggplant, cherry tomatoes, and corn is not only a fantastic way to make vegetables smaller for storing (versus other methods, such as pickling), but also a resourceful way to pack summer nutrients into a winter stew.

Makes 4 servings

Broth

1 leek, white and light green parts only, chopped

2 qt [2 L] chicken or pork stock

1 fennel bulb, chopped

5 in [12 cm] square dried kombu

1 Tbsp kosher salt

½ bunch cilantro

1 cup [25 g] packed bonito flakes

TO MAKE THE BROTH: Clean the leek thoroughly to remove any lingering sand. In a large pot, combine it with the stock, fennel, kombu, and salt. Pull the stems from the cilantro (reserving the leaves) and add them to the pot. Bring to a simmer over high heat, then immediately lower the heat to medium and gently reduce by about one-quarter, 40 minutes to 1 hour.

Remove the stock from the heat and add the bonito flakes. Steep for 5 minutes, then strain; discard all of the solids. Cover and remove from the heat if you're proceeding right away or transfer to an airtight container and refrigerate for up to 5 days or freeze for up to 1 month.

CONTINUED

TO MAKE THE MEATBALLS: Fill a saucepan with water, add the salt, and bring to a boil. Add the buckwheat and cook until tender, 8 to 10 minutes; drain. Reserve half of the cooked buckwheat for the soup.

In a small bowl, cover the dried apples with the cider to rehydrate.

In a food processor, pulse the remaining cooked buckwheat until it's mostly smooth. Add the reserved cilantro leaves from the broth recipe to the processor along with the pork, egg, scallions, garlic, ginger, serrano, and pepper. Pulse until the mixture comes together, then transfer to an airtight container and refrigerate until completely chilled, at least 1 hour and up to 3 days.

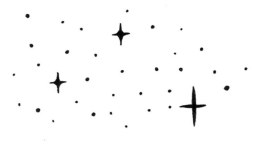

Lion's Head Meatballs

1 Tbsp kosher salt, plus more for seasoning

½ cup [90 g] buckwheat groats, toasted

2 Tbsp diced dried apples

2 Tbsp apple cider

1 lb [455 g] pork shoulder, ground

1 egg

6 scallions, minced

4 garlic cloves, grated

1 in [2.5 cm] piece fresh ginger, grated

1 serrano chile, grated

2 tsp freshly ground black pepper

Soup

½ to 1 cup [80 to 160 g] Dried Summer Vegetables (page 200) or freeze-dried vegetables

3 Tbsp unsalted butter

1 small yellow onion, thinly sliced

½ tsp kosher salt, plus more as needed

¼ cup [30 g] sauerkraut, drained

Freshly ground black pepper

Broth (recipe precedes)

Reserved cooked buckwheat (from meatball recipe)

1 bunch kale

Lion's Head Meatballs (recipe precedes)

TO MAKE THE SOUP: When you're ready to serve the soup, rehydrate the dried vegetables by covering them in plenty of warm water and set aside for 10 to 20 minutes. (They will soften but won't increase much in volume.) Remove the vegetables from the water and cut larger vegetables into smaller, bite-size pieces.

In a skillet over medium heat, melt the butter, then add the onion and salt. Sauté until translucent, 5 to 8 minutes, then add the sauerkraut and rehydrated vegetables. Season with pepper and, if needed, a bit more salt. Set aside. If you made the broth in advance, gently rewarm it in a large saucepan over medium-low heat. Separately, allow the reserved cooked buckwheat to come to room temperature.

Meanwhile, fill a large pot with 1 to 2 in [2.5 to 5 cm] of water and fit a steamer inside, making sure the water isn't high enough to seep into it. Cover and bring to a gentle simmer over medium heat.

Use a paring knife to stem the kale so the leaves stay intact at the top; you'll need 8 large leaves. Steam just until tender, about 30 seconds, then pat the leaves dry and lay them flat. Cover the pot and reduce the heat to medium-low, keeping the water at a low simmer.

Divide the meatball mix into eight even mounds, then place each mound at the top of a kale leaf. Starting from the top, roll the kale around the meatball, tucking the ends of the leaf around the sides of the parcel to secure. (If they still won't stay put, use a toothpick.) Make sure there's enough water actively simmering in the pot and steam the meatballs, covered, until they are firm but still tender, 20 to 30 minutes. Set aside at room temperature.

To serve, divide the reserved buckwheat and rehydrated vegetable medley among individual serving bowls. Add two meatballs to each bowl and ladle the broth over them. Serve right away.

WEAVING ROOTS

CHAPTER 2

Notes on Looking North to Honor the Element of Earth

Earth in the spiritual realm

North, the place of greatest darkness, represents the element earth and the power of the physical and spiritual body. It's this inherent physicality that allows us to feel the world around us. Earth, unlike flowing water or transient air, is nurturing and stable, solid and firm, full of endurance, fertility, and strength. It guides the changing of the seasons and the cyclical nature of time: life emerging from the ground and then decomposing back into the soil. Earth is the basis for all the other elements. We are rooted to her through our feet, allowed to expand outside our feeling bodies into the aether without floating away. Her stability facilitates our outward expansion.

Earth in the physical realm

In nature, earth forms rock, clay, sand, and soil, but Mother Earth is not just the land we walk on; it gives life to everything around us. It's a delicate living ecosystem where everything must hang in balance to coexist.

I connect to the earth by foraging in forests and growing food. Gardens are where humanity and nature converge, where we give and take in reciprocity. Here, on my little plot in New Hampshire, I cooperate with forces beyond my control. I nurture seeds into nourishing plants as winds, storms, and disease test our perserverance. In the spring of 1993, I was fourteen years old, and I dug up a patch of manicured grass from my parents' suburban lawn to plant a vegetable garden. The mint was unruly, the cucumbers grew as long as my arm, and the summer squash seemed to triple in quantity overnight. I had taken care of dogs and fish as pets, even a frog who jumped from his cage and became taxidermy before I found where he had hopped off to, but I had never tended to something quite like this before, where I began the life cycle myself. To sow seeds (with love and water) was entirely new, and I was entranced.

In early spring, I begin planning my garden for the year. Even the act of planning connects me with the earth—what new life do I want to see grow? Then I get dirty and sink my hands into the black soil, depositing seeds like I might broadcast spices atop a dish. Moon phases guide my planting schedule, as the moon's gravitational pull dictates the available moisture in the soil. Whether in the kitchen or garden, I like to think of myself as a conductor of sorts, helping bring disparate elements together in a harmonious way. It's quite breathtaking when you take a moment to realize the concert of parts; I'm one element among many.

It's this mindfulness and respect that I try to bring from the outside in. When I check in with what my body needs, what it *actually* craves, the answer is almost always vegetables. Packed with phytonutrients, those naturally occurring compounds that not only give them their brilliant colors but also help reduce risk of disease, vegetables nourish me in the most profound way. They make my body sing and give me the most energy. Plus, exploring the breadth of vegetable cookery feels boundless, a pretty exciting thing when you're in the kitchen. Root-to-stalk cooking is often an exercise in delicious creativity. Just take the "Eggplant Parm" Dip (page 63). Here, different techniques coax out a myriad of flavors from the eggplant, giving the dish continuity and depth. Don't get me wrong, I do enjoy meat, and we'll encounter plenty of it in the next chapter, but for now, I choose to put vegetables at the center of my plate.

The Wheel of the Year

My year is marked by eight, not four, moments that not only guide my table but also my interior world. In many ways, the bounty of the seasons reflects the cadence of the year. In winter, I reach for rich foods, all the better to satiate my need to hibernate. Spring, with its verdant promise, lets me exhale with a renewed spirit and sense of freedom. I think of each season as two distinct periods since the flavors and feelings in those initial months are markedly different from those found in its final moments. In the kitchen, I like to use this tempo as my guide.

The waning winter is when we begin to go into the cold stores of the garden, and warm ourselves with rich, flavored foods. From the shortest days, we move closer to the waxing spring, and from the darkness of midwinter comes light, longer days, and shorter shadows. As the sun shines, we rev our internal engines for waning spring when the birds come back out, green emerges from the ground again, and the outside world awakens.

It's a slow roll from waning spring onto the shoulder of waxing summer, where the first harvests grace our tables, peaking during the height of summer: blazing hot days, late summer storms. Waxing autumn slides into the fields of auburn light where a literal cornucopia spills forth. Waning arrives quietly, gracefully into the arms of waxing winter, her dense rooted vegetables guiding the way from lightness into dark.

WAXING SPRING

The harmony between light and dark means new beginnings, yet when the equinox arrives the air still feels a lot like winter. My cellared vegetable stores run low. The greenery of spring has yet to arrive, so I continue to sprout microgreens, mung beans, and lentils for fresh crunch. In the preservation kitchen, I catalog what's left from winter and begin to plan what new things to put in the crocks. I sow a few seeds indoors and look for daylily stalks and ramps in my usual spots, even if I know it's too soon, retracing old steps to be sure I remember where to go.

WANING SPRING

I think of waning spring as high spring, a time for renewal, growth, and expansion. It's a time to plant seeds, clean the house, and let go of winter's baggage. I ready the garden, turn the soil, start seedlings, plant bulbs outdoors, and tidy the patio for alfresco dining. My cooking turns lighter. Fresh green vegetables—asparagus, peas, artichokes—replace the heavier root dishes. I snatch the last of sweet overwintered carrots. In the preservation kitchen, I infuse spirits and syrups with spring flowers; gather nettles, ramps, and fiddleheads; and dunk fleeting vegetables into brine to keep for later months.

WAXING SUMMER

With the peak of spring and beginning of summer comes the first harvest. We can literally eat the rainbow. I crave raw foods in the heat, and snip bowlfuls of herbs and edible flowers, baby fennel and gem lettuces. In this moment of abundance, I make infused herb oils and summer tisane blends with dried herbs and flowers. I pick young beets and quickly cook their greens, collect tender baby pine cones destined for honey, salt underripe blueberries for "capers," turn elderflowers into tonics, and pickle carrots while tossing their tops into green eggs.

WANING SUMMER

We honor the longest day of the year. I start to cook with heat again, grilling corncobs, eggplants, and sweet peppers over the open fire. I bite into tomatoes as if they were apples, shell mottled beans from their pods. As the bounty overflows, I pickle, dry, infuse, steep, and repeat, filling the larder with jars of this and that to sustain me for when the cold comes: pepper pastes, cucumber pickles, cucumber blossom infusions, tomato paste, half-dried tomatoes, tomato syrup, nasturtium salt, rose salt, eggplant pickles, coriander capers, fennel capers . . . the list goes on and on.

WAXING AUTUMN

Summer's sweet bounty collides with the earthier notes of fall. I roast the last of the peppers and tomatoes, and begin to forage mushrooms in the forest, to cook with kale gathered from the garden. During this time, I ferment the last of the season's corn, make a final batch of late-harvest tomato paste, and throw every remaining squash, pepper, or onion into a crock to ferment. I pick the first of the season's apples, smoke crab apples for tinctures, pull roots from the garden, and oil-cure as many mushrooms as I can collect.

WANING AUTUMN

The chill of autumn sets in, and with it comes cabbage, cauliflower, chard, leeks, and other vegetables that benefit from a cool snap. Excitement about the return of the rich, dense foods of fall feels magnified by the excitement of the holiday season. To get as much preserved as possible, I make kraut; plop turnips, beets, and carrots into a salt brine; reduce apple cider into a syrup; and turn pears and quince into rich pastes.

WAXING WINTER

With a chill in the air and frost on the ground, I gravitate toward grounding, warming foods. All shades of roots—carrots, parsnips, rutabagas—become mainstays on the table, as do slow-cooked meats and rib-sticking stocks. The holidays ease us into the depth of the season: spirits are high with friends and family, tables abound with festive treats, and laughter fills the rooms. It's beautiful commotion and then, just like that, the new year glides me into the quiet of winter. It's this time of year that I fill crocks with shaved Brussels sprouts for kraut, infuse honey with garlic, and pause to see all the jars in every nook and cupboard from my year in the preservation kitchen.

WANING WINTER

The days are short, the nights are long, and the season often feels never-ending. I find myself retreating inward, becoming more introspective, and reaching for denser foods, like roots, winter squashes, tubers, and cabbage. There's an inherent sweetness in these foods, which balances winter's cold. It's this time of year when I find myself sprouting as many legumes as possible and growing microgreens on top of the refrigerator for some much-needed freshness. My body craves broths, braises, and roasts, but the wish for something green and vegetal is never far behind. In the preservation kitchen, I ferment cabbage in innumerable ways and pickle beets, carrots, and Brussels sprouts, balancing their hearty sweetness with a punchy brine that will carry me through the coming months.

HERBY SMASHED SARDINE DIP WITH CRUDITÉS

I am always looking for ways to feed my brain and body, to have as much energy as possible. I seek foods that are both delicious and full of bioavailable nutrients. Sardines are one of nature's powerhouse foods: an excellent source of choline, vitamin B12, selenium, phosphorus, omega-3 fatty acids, protein, and vitamin D. They also happen to be one of the most sustainable fish in our waterways. While a sardine dip may sound unusual, the oily texture of sardines makes a great base, the natural fats helping to disperse flavors and aromas. My go-to mix has always been sardines with avocados, handfuls of herbs, and a seed mix swirled throughout. But since avocados aren't as plentiful on the East Coast, I decided to use Yukon gold potatoes for their requisite fluffiness and readily available carbohydrates. And if, like me, you're on the move and need an especially quick bite, feel free to use plain tahini in place of the green version (page 72); just be sure to fold in extra herbs at the end.

Makes about 2 cups [480 ml]

4 oz [115 g] Yukon gold potatoes

8 oz [230 g] oil-packed canned sardines or Oil-Poached Fish (page 133)

¼ cup [30 g] finely diced kohlrabi or celery

¼ cup [40 g] Spiced Seed Mix (page 197), plus more for garnish

3 Tbsp Green Tahini Sauce (page 72)

3 Tbsp Aioli (page 204) or mayonnaise

2 Tbsp Green Coriander Capers (page 186) or store-bought capers

2 Tbsp lightly packed cilantro leaves, chopped, plus more for garnish

1 Tbsp lightly packed parsley leaves, chopped, plus more for garnish

1 Tbsp lightly packed dill leaves, chopped, plus more for garnish

1 Tbsp fresh lemon juice

Zest of 1 lemon

½ serrano chile, grated, or ½ tsp red pepper flakes

Black pepper and fresh coriander flowers for garnish

Seeded Herb Crackers (page 232)

1 lb [455 g] mixed raw vegetables, such as radishes, cherry tomatoes, young carrots, Persian cucumber, fennel, or endives, or blanched vegetables, such as asparagus, green beans, or romanesco, cut into slices or wedges if necessary

Preheat the oven to 375°F [190°C]. Pierce the potatoes a few times with a fork and bake on a sheet pan until they're very tender, about 1 hour. While they cook, add the sardines with their oil to a large bowl and use the tines of a fork to gently break them up.

When the potatoes are cool enough to handle, peel away the papery skin and smash them into the sardines until well mixed but still a bit coarse. Allow to cool to room temperature. Then work in the kohlrabi, seed mix, green tahini, aioli, green capers, cilantro, parsley, dill, lemon juice and zest, and serrano until well incorporated but not completely homogenous. If you're not eating it right away, cover and refrigerate for up to 3 days.

To serve, transfer the dip into a bowl and garnish with cilantro, parsley, dill, more seed mix, a couple twists of freshly cracked black pepper, and coriander flowers. Serve with plenty of seeded crackers and/or crudités.

"EGGPLANT PARM" DIP

Here I mimic the flavors of a classic Italian-American dish. While I set out to make a tart, I quickly turned to a less fussy interpretation, one that is best eaten with your hands. In cold parts of the country, canning summer's bounty feels like a mandatory rite to get us through the many frosty months. Curing eggplants in oil is one of my favorite techniques: The flesh becomes silky and the vinegar marinade ensures explosive flavor. My nod to the classic breading is these feta crisps, which tilt toward a grown-up Cheez-It and are equally addictive. Don't discard those tomato leaves—packed with flavor and loads of nutrients, they're an underutilized powerhouse that gives an herbal aroma to the dish.

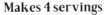

Makes 4 servings

Tomato Leaf Pesto (page 205)

Oil-Preserved Eggplant (page 192)

Oil-Preserved Tomatoes (page 193)

Torn fresh herbs (mint, basil, parsley, or marjoram) for garnish

Feta Crisps

5 Tbsp [50 g] flaxseeds

1½ Tbsp dried basil

1 Tbsp dried thyme

1 cup [120 g] crumbled feta

1 cup [140 g] brown rice flour, plus more for rolling

½ cup [70 g] white rice flour

½ cup [120 ml] ice-cold water

¼ cup [60 g] unsalted butter

¼ cup [60 g] store-bought tomato paste

2 tsp baking powder

¼ tsp kosher salt

Zest of ½ lemon

TO MAKE THE FETA CRISPS: Combine the flaxseeds, basil, and thyme in a spice grinder or mortar and pestle and grind to a fine powder. Add them to a food processor along with the feta, brown rice flour, white rice flour, water, butter, tomato paste, baking powder, salt, and lemon zest. Pulse until the dough starts to pull into a ball; it will feel like cookie dough. Divide the dough in half and shape each half into a rectangle about the size and shape of a paperback book. Tightly wrap them individually in plastic wrap and refrigerate for at least 1 hour.

Preheat the oven to 300°F [150°C]. Dust two silicone baking mats or sheets of parchment paper with rice flour and place a block of dough on top of the floured mats. Dust a bit more flour over the tops of the dough and on a rolling pin, then roll each ball into a thin sheet no thicker than ⅛ in [4 mm]; use a bench scraper to straighten any fraying edges, and scatter flour over the dough and rolling pin as needed to keep the dough from sticking.

Cut the dough into squares or rectangles to make the crackers and separate them just enough for air to circulate all around as they bake. Prick the tops of each cracker with the tines of a fork and bake until completely dry and golden on the top, 40 to 50 minutes, rotating the pan every 15 or 20 minutes. Cool completely; they'll continue to crisp as they cool. Serve right away or store in an airtight container at room temperature for up to 14 days. If the air is really humid in your kitchen, either add a desiccator packet to the crackers or spread them in an even layer and re-toast in a 200°F [95°C] oven for just a few minutes to crisp them back up.

CONTINUED

Feta Mousse

1 Japanese eggplant
(about 6 oz [170 g])

2 Tbsp fresh lemon juice

2 Tbsp strained, full-fat
Greek-style yogurt

2 tsp lightly packed mint leaves,
chopped

1 tsp lightly packed thyme leaves,
chopped

1 tsp lightly packed parsley leaves,
chopped

½ tsp freshly ground black pepper

½ tsp kosher salt, plus more for
seasoning

Zest of 1 lemon

1⅓ cups [160 g] crumbled feta

¼ cup [60 ml] extra-virgin olive oil

TO MAKE THE FETA MOUSSE: Heat a grill to high heat or set a metal grate directly over a gas burner. Char the eggplant directly over the flame until it's black and ashy all over and soft throughout, with a custardy texture. (If it's not totally soft when the exterior is charred, finish cooking in a 375°F [190°C] oven.) When it's cool to the touch, trim the stem end, peel away the papery, black skin, and set aside.

Pour the lemon juice and yogurt into a blender, followed by the eggplant, mint, thyme, parsley, pepper, salt, and lemon zest and purée. When the mixture is smooth, add the feta in batches, and finally stream in the oil. Blend until very smooth and light. The feta is salty on its own, but season with more salt if needed. This can be refrigerated in an airtight container for up to 3 days.

To serve, spread the mousse in a wide, shallow bowl and spoon pesto in pools all over. Chop or tear the eggplant into bite-size pieces and arrange them with the oil-preserved tomatoes over the top. Garnish with torn fresh herbs and serve the crisps on the side.

Simplify It

OIL-PRESERVED EGGPLANT	• Make these en masse when summer is at its peak. Use on any antipasto platter. • Layer in a sandwich. • Pulse into tahini for a pickle-spiked baba ganoush. • Warm gently and serve with rice and grilled meats or fish. • Smash a few into wilted greens and serve with roast chicken.
FETA CRISPS	• These have a terrific shelf life if stored in a sealed container. Make a double batch to have on hand for a quick cheese platter. • The dough freezes well, so consider making an extra batch to pull out and bake.
FETA MOUSSE	• Use as a base for a tomato-cucumber salad or roasted carrots with seeds. • Spread on toast with wilted greens and soft-boiled eggs.

VERNAL EQUINOX SALAD

The name of this salad can be a bit misleading since many of the ingredients are not ready when the spring equinox hits. But it is about this time that I start stirring, ready to shed winter's clasp, and start craving this salad in anticipation of spring. During the darker, colder months, pea and sunflower sprouts grown indoors help hint at the grassiness that awaits, so when the first asparagus and radishes arrive at the markets, I fold everything into a bright salad. While most everything is left raw, a few cooked elements keep me cozy during the final cool weeks.

Makes 4 servings

2 Tbsp plus ¾ tsp kosher salt, plus more for cooking

4 eggs, at room temperature

3 cups [480 g] cooked or drained canned beans, such as garbanzo or cannellini

½ cup [120 ml] extra-virgin olive oil, plus more for garnish

2 Tbsp fresh lemon juice

½ tsp red pepper flakes

Zest of 1 lemon

Freshly ground black pepper

2 fennel bulbs, halved

4 Tbsp [60 ml] grapeseed oil

1 lb [455 g] asparagus, trimmed

1 bunch radishes, such as French Breakfast or Cherry Bomb

Sorrel-Anchovy Vinaigrette (page 206)

4 oz [115 g] sunflower greens or pea shoots

Toasted sunflower seeds, dill leaves, and Dry Fennel Seed Capers (page 186) for garnish

Fill a medium saucepan with 2 qt [2 L] of water and 2 Tbsp of the salt. Meanwhile, make an ice bath in a large bowl. Bring the pot of water to a rolling boil, then gently lower the eggs into the water and cook for 6½ minutes. Drain, then immediately transfer to the ice bath. Once the eggs are completely cool, peel. (Soft-boiled eggs can be made up to 1 or 2 days ahead; just wait to peel until you're ready to serve.)

Rinse the beans well. In a medium bowl, toss to combine with 6 Tbsp [90 ml] of the olive oil, the lemon juice, the remaining ¾ tsp of salt, the red pepper flakes, and lemon zest; season with pepper. Allow the beans to marinate at room temperature while you prepare the rest of the ingredients.

Preheat the oven to 325°F [165°C]. Trim away any brown bits or tough outer layers of the fennel bulbs. Reserve half of 1 bulb and cut the others into quarters, then halve, leaving the core intact all the while. Gently toss to coat with 3 Tbsp of the grapeseed oil.

Cut the reserved half fennel bulb into very thin slices, about ⅛ in [4 mm] thick. Slice a quarter of the asparagus into similarly thin coins, followed by a quarter of the radishes (it's best to halve them lengthwise first so they lie evenly on the cutting board). In a medium bowl, toss the sliced vegetables with just enough vinaigrette to coat, about ¼ cup [60 ml], and set aside.

Set a cast-iron skillet over medium-high heat or prepare a grill with a medium flame. When the pan is almost smoking, add the remaining asparagus, working in batches so the spears don't crowd the pan. When they're lightly browned in places but still firm and bright green, remove from the skillet or grill, season with salt, and set aside; when cool enough to handle, cut into 2 to 3 in [5 to 7.5 cm] pieces.

Halve the remaining radishes lengthwise and toss them with the remaining 1 Tbsp of grapeseed oil. Cook in the same skillet, flat-side down, giving them a gentle press with your spatula to encourage even browning. After 2 to 3 minutes, while still al dente but warmed through, remove them from the pan and season with salt.

CONTINUED

Working in batches, arrange each of the slices of oil-tossed fennel in the hot skillet so they're not crowded. Cook until deeply golden with frizzled edges and tender interiors, about 2 minutes per side.

Set an ovenproof skillet over medium heat until it's warm. Spread the beans in an even layer and warm them for about 30 seconds. Transfer the pan to the oven and cook until warmed through and creamy, 5 to 10 minutes. Use the back of a spoon to coarsely mash half of the beans, then fold in the remaining 2 Tbsp of olive oil.

To serve, spread the warm beans over individual plates or on the bottom of a platter, then top with the thinly sliced raw vegetables, sunflower greens and seeds, dill, and fennel seed capers. Arrange the browned asparagus, radishes, and fennel over the top and gently tear the eggs in half, tucking each half around the vegetables. Salt the runny yolks and finish with olive oil. Serve immediately.

Seasonal Variations

WINTER

Swap cooked sweet potato for the radish and wilted kale for the asparagus.

SPRING

Swap snap peas for the asparagus.

AUTUMN

Swap roasted beets for the radish, and cooked and raw turnips for the asparagus.

SUMMER

Swap tomatoes for the radishes and zucchini for the asparagus.

SUMMER SQUASH SALAD

Summer days in North Adams, Massachusetts, were long, humid, and warm. Summer squash began to take over my garden, its lily pad–like leaves and gangly stems conspicuously stretching in every direction. This explosion of squash happened next to an equally prolific plant, the daylily. I plucked the plants, knowing that they were edible, and started playing, determined to transform squash's lackluster reputation and over-abundance into something tempting by combining these two ingredients. Paired with the cooling dressing, mole-like pumpkin seed sauce, and gently floral buds, squash transcends its typical humdrum stance. Try it with simply grilled fish, roast chicken, or Silver Dollar Corn Cakes (page 235).

Makes 4 servings

4 small summer squash or zucchini (about 1½ lb [680 g])

½ red onion

Kosher salt

8 Vinegar-Pickled Daylilies (page 189), plus their pickling liquid for serving and blossoms for garnish

¼ cup [3 g] lightly packed dill leaves, plus more for garnish

Freshly ground black pepper

Pumpkin Seed and Cilantro Sauce (page 206)

Buttermilk Dressing (page 204)

¼ cup [40 g] pumpkin seeds, toasted, for garnish

1 tsp extra-virgin olive oil, plus more for garnish

⅛ tsp sweet paprika for garnish

Preheat the oven to 350°F [180°C]. To prepare the fluted squash, set one chopstick along either side of the squash so the squash rests snugly between them. Cut ¼ in [6 mm] slices down the length of two of the squash, stopping your knife about ½ in [12 mm] before it cuts all the way through, so the pieces stay intact with thin layers like pages of a book. The chopsticks will halt your knife. Cut the onion into 4 wedges, leaving the root end intact.

Set a cast-iron skillet or heavy-bottomed pan over high heat until it's hot. Add the onion wedges flat-side down and cook until they're nicely charred, 1 to 2 minutes per side. Cook the squash, fluted-side down, until deeply browned.

Cover the pan and transfer to the oven to finish cooking, until the onions and squash are tender enough to pierce with a knife, 10 to 15 minutes. Remove from the oven, season lightly with salt, and portion the squash into approximately 1½ in [4 cm] pieces. Cool to room temperature or refrigerate in an airtight container for up to 1 day.

Meanwhile, use a mandoline, vegetable peeler, or knife to cut the remaining 2 squash lengthwise into very thin slices. Get the cast-iron skillet smoking hot once again and, working in batches, lay the squash slices flat. Cook just until they build a little color but before they begin to fall apart or dry out, 1 minute per side. Your goal is to release some of the squash's natural sugars, while cooking it gently enough to leave it a bit al dente. Once all the slices are cooked, line them side by side on a cutting board vertically for ease of rolling if you're proceeding right away. These can also be made 1 day in advance and refrigerated in an airtight container.

Thinly slice the daylily buds in ¼ in [6 mm] rounds and lightly scatter them over half of the squash ribbons along with some torn dill leaves; season with salt and pepper. Top each one with another ribbon to make "sandwiches" and, starting at one end, roll each one into a little spiral.

To serve, spread the pumpkin seed sauce over a platter or four individual plates. Add the rolled squash, spiral-side up, the squash chunks, and charred onion petals. Spoon the dressing over and garnish with pumpkin seeds tossed with the olive oil and paprika. Scatter with more fresh dill and pickled daylily blossoms. Finish with pepper and a bit more olive oil; serve right away.

CHARRED LETTUCES WITH GREEN TAHINI

This salad feels much like an expanded crudité platter. After all, what makes a salad anyway? Charring the lettuce adds texture and smoke, but if you're worried about soggy greens, feel free to chop the tips off and fold them in fresh. The core of the lettuce can hold up to the heat. If you decide to sear the whole heads, make sure the pan is piping hot and don't wait long before eating. This salad doesn't reward patience.

Makes 4 servings

Salad

4 heads Little Gem lettuce or 2 heads romaine lettuce

1 head Chioggia radicchio

2 Persian cucumbers

4 watermelon radishes (about 6 oz [170 g]), peeled

Green Tahini Sauce (recipe follows)

1 cup [60 g] Spiced Seed Mix (page 197)

¾ cup [180 ml] Lemon-Dill Vinaigrette (page 207)

Cilantro, dill, and mint leaves for garnish

TO MAKE THE SALAD: Remove the tough outer leaves from the lettuce and radicchio. Keeping their cores intact, quarter them lengthwise, then cut each wedge in half. Halve the cucumbers lengthwise, then cut each piece in half. Quarter and thinly slice the radishes, then set them aside.

Set a cast-iron skillet over medium-high heat or prepare a grill with a medium flame. Dry-char the cucumbers, flat-side down, giving them a little press with your spatula to help them brown; remove them from the heat while they are still very crisp. Season with salt and cut into 1 in [2.5 cm] triangles, then combine them in a small bowl with the radishes and toss with 2 to 3 Tbsp of the tahini sauce.

Lightly brush the lettuce and radicchio wedges with oil and char them as you did the cucumbers, until lightly golden in places but still very bright and crisp.

To serve, spread a generous spoonful of the tahini sauce over the bottoms of individual plates or on one large platter. Place the Spiced Seed Mix in a wide, shallow dish. Toss the greens very delicately in the lemon vinaigrette, then dredge them in the seed mix. Arrange the greens on the plates or platter, then spoon the dressed cucumbers and radishes around them. Garnish with the cilantro, dill, mint, and more seed mix.

CONTINUED

Green Tahini Sauce

¼ cup [60 ml] grapeseed oil

5 garlic cloves

¼ yellow onion, julienned

1½ tsp coriander seeds,
toasted and ground

1½ tsp fennel seeds, toasted and
ground

½ tsp caraway seeds, toasted and
ground

½ tsp cumin seeds, toasted and ground

1 cup [12 g] lightly packed cilantro
leaves

½ cup [6 g] lightly packed parsley
leaves

½ cup [6 g] lightly packed dill leaves

½ cup [6 g] lightly packed mint leaves

1 Tbsp lightly packed tarragon leaves

½ serrano chile

¼ cup [60 ml] fresh lemon juice

2 Tbsp apple juice

2 Tbsp apple cider vinegar

1½ tsp kosher salt

¾ cup [165 g] sesame tahini

1½ tsp honey

TO MAKE THE SAUCE: Warm a medium skillet over medium-low heat. Add the oil. Add the garlic and onion and sauté, stirring occassionally, until tender and browned. Increase the heat to medium and add the coriander, fennel, caraway, and cumin. Heat until fragrant, about 1 minute. Remove from the heat and cool to room temperature.

Coarsely chop the cilantro, parsley, dill, mint, and tarragon. In a blender, combine the herbs with the cooled onion mixture, the serrano, lemon juice, apple juice, vinegar, and salt and purée. When the mixture is smooth, add the sesame tahini and honey and purée again until fully combined. Use right away or refrigerate in an airtight container for up to 2 weeks.

Simplify It

CHARRED LETTUCE	• If you want to have a new lettuce technique in your arsenal, get comfy charring some lettuce and dressing it your way. You can go raw and cooked for added nuances and texture. Try it the next time you make a Caesar or throw a poached egg on it with some crispy bacon and a warm mustard dressing.
GREEN TAHINI SAUCE	• Use this "dressing" as a dip with raw vegetables or seed crackers.
	• Add a swoosh beneath roasted sweet potatoes, cauliflower, chicken, or lamb meatballs and top with a scoop of yogurt, herbs, and seeds.
	• It freezes beautifully, so make a big batch and freeze in 1 cup [240 ml] containers or little baggies so it thaws easily.

Moon-Cycle Planting

The dance of the sun and moon lights my path to the garden. I find my gardening rhythms mirror the rhythms of the moon. Just as the moon influences the tides in the oceans, it also gently tugs water underground, causing the moisture in the soil to rise and fall as it waxes and wanes.

Planting in harmony with the different moon phases, I look to the natural ebb and flow of the land, its silent gravitational pull, to dictate when and what I plant. During the new moon, I plant crops with aboveground blooms that seed separately from their fruiting parts, such as spinach, celery, and cauliflower. With longer moonlight comes balanced leaf-to-root growth. As we approach the full moon, the light is at its strongest and lengthens, encouraging robust leaf growth. It's then that I plant aboveground seed crops, fruit that contains its seed within, such as beans, peppers, and tomatoes.

Right after the full moon, I plant root vegetables and bulb flowers, such as beets and perennial bulbs. The soil is once again moist, but the waning moonlight promotes the development of a strong root system. During the last quarter, when the moonlight is shortest, I avoid seed planting altogether. Instead, I work on garden maintenance, such as amending, weeding, or transplanting.

SPROUTED LENTIL SALAD WITH HARISSA VINAIGRETTE

I started sprouting legumes in 2008 after seeing a naturopathic doctor. I first became hooked on sprouted mung beans, then I was sprouting everything. There was a real sense of freedom in being able to eat fresh things I only ever thought were destined for the pan, especially in the dead of winter when my body always craves crunch. Sprouting mimics nature by providing water (i.e., rain), igniting the growing cycle and allowing nutrients, which have been packed into seeds, to become more bioavailable. If you don't have time to sprout, you can still make this dish with regular cooked lentils; you'll just forgo a slight grassy flavor and a bit of crunch. For me, this salad is a mix of inspiration—the whole herb and feta platters that start Persian meals; a classic French endive salad, the kind I remember eating on the rue-de-somewhere amazing in Paris; and California's "hippie" food.

Makes 4 servings

¼ cup [50 g] dried beluga lentils

1 cup [120 g] chopped walnuts

Zest of 2 limes

1 tsp extra-virgin olive oil

Kosher salt

3 lb [1.4 kg] fava beans, shucked

1 fennel bulb

2 endive heads

4 watermelon radishes, peeled

4 Medjool dates, pitted

Harissa Vinaigrette (page 207)

¾ cup [90 g] crumbled feta

½ cup [6 g] cress

½ cup [6 g] lightly packed cilantro leaves

¼ cup [3 g] lightly packed parsley leaves

¼ cup [3 g] lightly packed dill leaves

2 Tbsp lightly packed mint leaves

1 Tbsp plus 1 tsp lightly packed marjoram leaves

Freshly ground black pepper for serving

Cover the lentils in three parts water to one part bean. Let soak at room temperature for 12 hours. Drain, rinse, cover with cheesecloth, and let the drained beans stand at room temperature. Over the course of 2 or 3 days, rinse the lentils with cold water three times a day. When all of the beans have grown small tails, give the sprouts a final rinse, dry them quickly on a clean towel, and transfer to a sealed container. Use immediately or refrigerate for up to 1 week.

To cook the lentils, fill a medium saucepan with gently salted water and bring to a boil; have a colander or sieve ready, since the cooking happens quickly. Reserve about a quarter of the sprouted lentils to use raw as a garnish; add the rest to the water and cook for 1 to 2 minutes, just until tender but not soft. Drain and set aside.

Preheat the oven to 325°F [165°C]. Toast the walnuts until fragrant, 8 to 10 minutes; when they're still warm, toss them with the lime zest and oil. Season with salt and set aside to cool completely.

Set a cast-iron skillet over medium-high heat until it's smoking, then add the fava beans and lightly char on both sides. Remove from the pan and, when they're cool enough to handle, peel away their skins; season with salt.

Trim the root end, browned bits, and tough outer leaves from the fennel, then dice. Trim the endives, too, and give them a rough chop. Quarter and thinly slice the radishes. Lightly grease your knife with oil and finely dice the dates. In a large bowl, combine the cooked lentils, charred fava beans, fennel, endive, radishes, and dates and set it aside.

CONTINUED

To serve, add about half of the vinaigrette to the lentil-fava mixture and toss to coat; gradually add a bit more until it's as you'd like it. Add the walnuts and feta, tear the cress and herbs into the bowl, and fold once or twice just to incorporate.

Spread a generous spoonful of the vinaigrette over the bottoms of individual plates or on a large platter and scoop the salad on top. Garnish with the reserved raw sprouted lentils and black pepper and serve right away.

Seasonal Variations

WINTER

Substitute cooked dried or canned beans for the fava beans and Oil-Preserved Shallots (page 193) or roasted carrots for the radishes.

SPRING

Substitute asparagus, sugar snap or English peas, or artichokes for the fava beans.

AUTUMN

Substitute roasted mushrooms for the fava beans and roasted beets for the radishes.

SUMMER

Substitute charred summer beans or raw corn kernels for the fava beans, and cucumbers or raw cherry tomato halves for the radishes.

CUCUMBER CATTAIL SALAD WITH BUTTERMILK BAGNA CAUDA

This is the type of salad I would sneak away to a closet just so I could eat it all by myself, though it really is a perfect dish for a feast. It's crispy, funky, spicy, and creamy while still feeling fresh. Being in dairy country, I bolster the Northern Italian sauce with buttermilk, giving it a Caesar-like piquancy.

Makes 4 to 6 servings

Buttermilk Bagna Cauda

Makes 2 cups [480 ml]

2 Tbsp unsalted butter

2 Tbsp extra-virgin olive oil

20 oil-packed anchovy fillets, chopped

10 garlic cloves, grated

1 Tbsp grated fresh ginger

1 tsp red pepper flakes

2 cups [480 ml] buttermilk

2 Tbsp rice vinegar

1 tsp freshly ground black pepper

¼ tsp kosher salt

Zest of ½ lemon

2 Tbsp celery leaves, finely chopped

TO MAKE THE BAGNA CAUDA: In a medium saucepan, lightly brown the butter over medium heat. When the butter smells nutty, add the olive oil and warm. Stir in the anchovies, garlic, ginger, and red pepper flakes. Simmer, stirring, until the anchovies dissolve. Add the buttermilk and bring to a gentle simmer, stirring occasionally. Reduce by about one-quarter. Set aside to come to room temperature. Transfer to a blender and add the vinegar, pepper, salt, and lemon zest. Purée until smooth. Stir in the celery leaves.

CONTINUED

Salad

¼ cup [40 g] unsalted peanuts, finely chopped

2 tsp poppy seeds

2 tsp black sesame seeds, toasted

1 tsp celery seeds, toasted

1 tsp caraway seeds, toasted and finely ground

8 Persian cucumbers (or 1 English cucumber)

1 small daikon radish or large kohlrabi (about ¾ lb [340 g])

6 young cattail shoots

10 Oil-Preserved Hot Peppers (page 192)

8 inner celery stalks, plus leaves for garnish

Vinegar-Pickled Red Onions (page 189)

Buttermilk Bagna Cauda (recipe precedes)

1 tsp kosher salt

¼ cup [60 ml] fresh lime juice

Zest of 1 lime

Celery leaves and freshly ground black pepper for garnish

TO MAKE THE SALAD: In a small bowl, combine the peanuts, poppy seeds, sesame seeds, celery seeds, and caraway seeds. Set aside.

Halve the cucumbers lengthwise and cut them into 1½ to 2 in [4 to 5 cm] pieces. Lay the flat side on your cutting board and use the side of your knife to gently crush each piece without splitting them.

Peel the daikon (trim the stems and leaves first); cut it into ⅛ in [4 mm] slices, then cut those slices into ⅛ in [4 mm] matchsticks.

Trim away the dark green tops of the cattails and remove any tough or loose outer leaves. Slice the hearts into thin rounds, thinly slice the hot peppers, and then slice the celery stalks thinly on the bias.

Combine the cucumbers, daikon, cattails, peppers, and celery in a large bowl with all of the pickled red onions. Toss with the bagna cauda, salt, lime juice and zest, 2 Tbsp of oil from the hot peppers, and 2 Tbsp of brine from the pickled red onions. Allow to marinate for about 1 hour before serving.

To serve, garnish with the celery leaves and pepper. This is best eaten the same day, but any leftovers can be stored in the refrigerator for up to 1 day.

KITCHEN NOTE:

Cattails grow abundantly in the neighboring ponds near my home. Their flavor and texture veer somewhere between celery and hearts of palm. While I do hope you'll pull up your sleeves and do a bit of foraging, if you can't find the stalks, heart of palm or celery root are lovely substitutions.

BEET SALAD WITH PARSNIP SKORDALIA

While I'm a chef by trade, I like to think of myself more as an anthropologist. Cooking has always been a way for me to tell stories about cultures. I love imagining the culinary collision between the Chinese, Lebanese, and Eastern Europeans in New England.

This dish began as an homage to Szechuan potato floss salads that come chilled and covered in chili oil. I love how the fiery pepper lingers on your tongue long after the meal has concluded. But here, loamy beets and nose-busting horseradish take center stage as parsnips and feta get whipped together into a creamy base. The sauce lends a sweet refrain to the earthiness of the sautéed vegetables. Enjoy everything together or each on its own as little side dishes, like Korean *banchan*, the small bites lining the table before the feast, buzzing with salt, funk, and just a touch of sweetness.

Makes 4 servings

Parsnip Skordalia

8 oz [230 g] parsnips

¾ cup [90 g] crumbled feta

¼ cup [60 ml] fresh lemon juice

2 Tbsp hazelnuts, toasted and finely chopped

¼ serrano chile, grated

2 garlic cloves, grated

½ cup [120 ml] extra-virgin olive oil

TO MAKE THE SKORDALIA: Preheat the oven to 375°F [190°C]. Place the parsnips in a medium baking dish or ovenproof pan, cover with a lid or tightly wrap in foil, and dry-roast until very soft and mashable like a baked potato, about 60 minutes. Allow to cool slightly.

Use a food processor to purée the feta, lemon juice, hazelnuts, serrano, and garlic. When the parsnips are cool enough to handle, peel off the outer skin and coarsely break them into the bowl and process until incorporated. With the processor still going, stream in the oil and allow the processor to run until the dip is extremely smooth and light. Use right away or refrigerate in an airtight container for up to 3 days; it will thicken as it cools.

CONTINUED

Horseradish Gremolata

¼ cup [30 g] walnuts, toasted and chopped

2 Tbsp lightly packed dill leaves, finely chopped

1 Tbsp lightly packed mint leaves, finely chopped

1 Tbsp lightly packed tarragon leaves, finely chopped

1 Tbsp lightly packed cress leaves or arugula, finely chopped, plus more for garnish

1½ tsp coriander seed, toasted and finely ground

1 tsp dill seeds, finely ground

¼ tsp kosher salt

½ shallot, minced

One ½ in [12 mm] knob of horseradish, grated, plus more for garnish

½ garlic clove, grated

Zest of ½ lemon

TO MAKE THE GREMOLATA: On the day you're making the salad, combine the walnuts, dill, mint, tarragon, cress, coriander, dill seeds, salt, shallot, horseradish, garlic, and lemon zest in a bowl. Refrigerate in an airtight container until you're ready to serve.

TO MAKE THE BEETS: Lay each beet flat on its side and cut it into ⅛ in [4 mm] slices, then cut those slices into ⅛ in [4 mm] batons. Prepare the fermented beets the same way. (You can place the fresh beets in a bowl of cool water as you work to help prevent discoloration; just be sure to drain and dry them thoroughly before cooking.)

Separate the greens from the bulbs of the spring onions, thinly slice the greens into rounds, and set aside. Halve the onions lengthwise, then again across the middle, and thinly slice them into batons about the same size as the beets.

Heat 2 Tbsp of the oil in a large skillet over medium heat. When it starts to dance, sauté the onions until they've just begun to take on color, then stir in the anchovies, and cook for a minute or two until they break down and become almost melty. Set aside.

In the same skillet, heat more oil and cook the yellow beets in batches, just for a few minutes, until cooked, but al dente in mouthfeel. Combine everything—the cooked beets, pickled beets, and onions and their greens—in the pan and sauté for a minute or two to warm them through and fold them into one another. Season with the lemon juice, salt, and pepper.

To serve, spread the skordalia on individual plates or over the bottom of a large serving platter. Layer the beets on top and garnish with a generous spoonful of gremolata, more grated horseradish, and cress.

Slivered Beets

1½ lb [680 g] yellow beets, peeled and halved

4 oz [115 g] Lacto-Fermented Beets (page 184)

2 spring onions, or substitute 2 shallots and 1 bunch scallions

6 Tbsp [90 ml] extra-virgin olive oil

5 oil-packed anchovy fillets, chopped

3 Tbsp fresh lemon juice

Kosher salt

Freshly ground black pepper

Simplify It

SKORDALIA	• You can substitute potato, Japanese sweet potato, rutabaga, or cauliflower for the parsnips. • Use as part of a dip spread with raw vegetables and crackers. • Use as a sandwich spread. • Toss pasta in it. • Use it as the base for any roasted vegetables.
HORSERADISH GREMOLATA	• Substitute any nut for the walnuts. • Use it as a crunchy, herbaceous topping for roasted vegetables. • Fold it into salads or cooked rice. • Scatter it over Slow-Cooked Pork Steak (page 169).
SLIVERED BEETS	• Serve these as a side dish or with cooked grains, such as Simplest Rice (page 294) or Buckwheat Dumplings with Cabbage and Hasselback Squash (page 99).

Seasonal Variations

WINTER
Add a large scoop of roasted winter squash, shaved turnips, or shaved cabbage to the beet mixture.

SPRING
Add ½ cup [55 g] cooked peas, favas, or asparagus to the beet mixture.

AUTUMN
Add ½ cup [100 g] roasted wild mushrooms or roasted Brussels sprouts to the beet mixture.

SUMMER
Add ½ cup [80 g] halved cherry tomatoes or julienned roasted peppers to the beet mixture.

STUFFED SQUASH BLOSSOMS WITH HARISSA RATATOUILLE

It's not every day that we get the opportunity to eat vegetables from flower to fruit, unless we grow our own food or connect with farmers that share in the magic of it with us. The flowers are the keepers of growth potential. For some vegetables, without the flower there would be no fruit, while for others, a second crop depends on flowering. But because the flowers are often quite delicate, we rarely get to enjoy them. This is a flower-to-fruit dish spotlighting the zucchini. There's a moment in summer when bounty turns to overabundance, and any farmer, home gardener, or green-thumb enthusiast will attest to zucchini's brazen nature. It waits for no one. Diced zucchini gets folded into a ratatouille that blankets the plate for its stuffed blossoms. Millet, an ancient grain consumed extensively in arid parts of the world like India but rarely enjoyed here, reminds me of couscous, but with a more prominent nutty flavor. It adds a bit of heft to the stuffing and a nice crackle to the coating.

Don't feel like stuffing? The ratatouille is great on its own with some crumbled feta, shakshuka-fied, or slathered on toast with goat cheese and a fried egg.

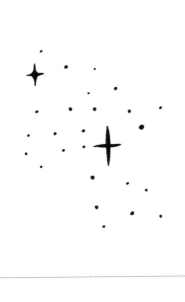

Makes 4 servings as a side dish

Ratatouille

2 Tbsp extra-virgin olive oil

½ yellow onion, diced

1½ tsp kosher salt

1 lb [455 g] zucchini (about 3 small), diced

2 garlic cloves, minced

¼ cup [60 g] Harissa Vinaigrette (page 207)

Freshly ground black pepper

1 Tbsp lightly packed parsley leaves, chopped

2 tsp lightly packed thyme leaves, chopped

2 tsp lightly packed mint leaves, chopped

1 tsp lightly packed marjoram leaves, chopped

TO MAKE THE RATATOUILLE: In a large skillet, warm the oil over medium heat. Sauté the onion with the salt until tender, then add the zucchini and garlic and continue to cook, stirring occasionally, just until the zucchini has let off some of its crunch but still has some tooth left, 5 to 7 minutes. Stir in the harissa, and cook for another minute or so, until incorporated. Season with pepper.

Use a food processor to purée about a quarter of the ratatouille, which gives the overall dish a lusciousness. Add the purée back to the pan and fold it together with the parsley, thyme, mint, and marjoram. At this point, proceed right away or refrigerate in an airtight container for up to 5 days.

CONTINUED

Squash Blossoms

⅓ cup [30 g] millet, toasted

1 egg

½ cup [60 g] crumbled feta

2 Tbsp Vinegar-Pickled Squash Blossoms (page 189), finely chopped

1 Tbsp lightly packed parsley leaves, chopped

1 Tbsp lightly packed thyme leaves, chopped

1 Tbsp lightly packed mint leaves, chopped

1 garlic clove, minced

1¼ tsp kosher salt, plus more as needed

¼ tsp red pepper flakes

¼ tsp sumac powder

¼ tsp freshly ground black pepper

Zest of 1 lemon

12 large squash blossoms

⅓ cup [45 g] rice flour

⅓ cup [45 g] millet flour

1 egg white

½ cup [120 ml] club soda

Olive oil for frying

Black sesame seeds for garnish

TO MAKE THE SQUASH BLOSSOMS: In a small saucepan, bring 1 cup [240 ml] of water to a simmer. Stir in the millet and cook, covered, for 15 to 20 minutes, until the water is fully absorbed. Remove from the heat, fluff with a fork, and let cool completely.

In a medium bowl, combine the cooled millet with the egg, feta, Vinegar-Pickled Squash Blossoms, parsley, thyme, mint, garlic, ¾ tsp of the salt, the red pepper flakes, sumac, pepper, and lemon zest.

Trim the stems from the fresh squash blossoms, leaving 2 in [5 cm] attached to the flower. Very gently separate the petals at the top of the flower (you can blow air inside to help them open up) and use one finger to remove the stamen from the inside, trying not to tear the petals as you work.

Delicately, gradually, fill each blossom with 1 to 2 Tbsp of the millet mixture, just up to where the petals separate and the green becomes orange. Twirl the tops to secure; set aside.

To make the batter, pulse the rice flour in a spice grinder or food processor to get it very fine. In a medium bowl, combine with the millet flour and the remaining ½ tsp of salt. Add the egg white and club soda and whisk until smooth.

Coat the bottom of a skillet with about ⅛ in [4 mm] olive oil and warm it over medium-high heat until it's shimmering. Line a plate or cooling rack with paper towels.

Working in batches, hold onto the blossoms' stems as you dip them to coat in the batter. Allow excess batter to drip off, then fry in the warmed oil, leaving plenty of space around the blossoms so you don't overcrowd the pan, which causes the oil to cool too quickly and leaves your battered delicacies soggy. Use a spoon to baste the tops with oil as they cook and fry for 3 to 4 minutes per side, until they're a deep golden brown. Transfer to the lined plate, season with salt and scatter with black sesame seeds, and repeat with the rest of the blossoms.

To serve, spread the ratatouille on plates or a large serving platter, or transfer it to a bowl. Perch the fried blossoms on top. Serve immediately.

BEAVER TAIL MUSHROOMS WITH BONE MARROW

European trappers of the seventeenth century considered beaver tail a delicacy. Its high fat content made it a powerful fuel source for those traveling in the wild, and the pelts provided warmth for the many cool East Coast nights. In fact, New England cooks used beaver tail all the way up until the 1940s. The most common preparation included scoring the tail crosshatch style, charring it directly over a fire, and then peeling back the skin to expose its pearlescent fat. Almost completely devoid of actual meat, the white tail fat is delicate, rich, and creamy, much like bone marrow. With this tale on my mind, I set out to create something reminiscent but not altogether literal. A bracingly piquant salsa verde, studded with fermented ramps and brine, helps frame the rich flavors of marrow and mushrooms, scored and seared until meaty and toothsome.

Makes 4 to 6 servings

6 beef marrowbone halves, 6 to 8 in [15 to 20 cm] long

1 lemon, halved

12 baby artichokes or 4 large artichokes

6 porcini mushrooms

¼ cup [60 ml] extra-virgin olive oil

Kosher salt

½ cup [6 g] lightly packed mint leaves

4 thyme sprigs

Ramp Salsa Verde (page 205)

½ cup [6 g] lightly packed cress leaves

Freshly ground black pepper for serving

Light as a Feather Brown Bread (page 241), toasted, or something crusty for serving

The day before you plan to cook, place the marrowbones in ice-cold, gently salted water (about 1 Tbsp per quart) and refrigerate for 12 hours, draining and refreshing the water after about 6 hours. (This step helps leach out any blood.)

When you're ready to cook, remove the marrowbones from the water. Preheat the oven to 350°F [180°C].

Fill a large bowl with water and squeeze the juice of half the lemon into it. Thinly slice the other lemon half and set it aside.

Clean the artichokes of all outer leaves (if you're using large artichokes, lop off the tops as well); reserve the leaves for artichoke tincture (page 273) and snip the remaining stems to about 1 in [2.5 cm]. Using a peeler, trim away the stems' outer green layers to reveal the tender inner core, then halve lengthwise. Use a spoon to scoop out the prickly chokes and purple inner leaves. Place the artichokes in the lemon water to prevent browning.

Cut the mushrooms lengthwise into ¼ in [6 mm] slices. With a sharp knife, shallowly score one side of each slice in a crosshatched pattern. Set a large cast-iron pan over medium heat and warm the oil until it begins to shimmer. Making sure not to overcrowd the pan, sear the mushrooms for a few minutes per side, until bronzed. Remove from the heat and season with salt while they're warm.

CONTINUED

Add the lemon slices, mint, and thyme to the same pan, plus more salt, and give them a moment to soften and toast. Reserving half of the artichokes in the lemon water, layer the rest, cut-side down, in one even layer in the pan and allow to cook, undisturbed, until they begin to brown, about 5 minutes. Transfer to the oven and roast until tender, 10 minutes more. Set aside until cool enough to handle. Increase the oven's heat to 400°F [200°C].

To make the artichoke salad, thinly slice the reserved raw artichokes lengthwise, about ⅛ in [4 mm], following the shape of the artichoke, or shave on a mandoline. Cut the roasted artichokes into wedges and coarsely chop the lemon. Toss them all together in a bowl with 2 to 3 Tbsp of salsa verde to coat. Season with more salt if necessary and set aside.

Arrange the marrowbones, cut-side up, in a roasting dish, bolstered by crumpled sheets of foil to keep them faceup without rolling. Season with salt and roast until the marrow is warmed, freckled brown, and starting to sizzle, 20 to 30 minutes. If you have a broiler, feel free to give the marrow a quick last-minute broil to caramelize the fat.

To serve, toss the cress with the marinated artichokes. Place 1 or 2 marrowbones with mushrooms atop the bones on individual plates or arrange on a large platter. Top with the marinated artichoke salad, more salsa verde, coarse salt, and pepper. Place the toasted bread in the center of the table with the remaining salsa verde.

Seasonal Variations

WINTER

Substitute shiitake mushrooms for the porcinis, wilted kale or spinach for the artichokes, and minced shallots for the raw ramps in the salsa verde.

AUTUMN

Substitute maitake mushrooms for the porcinis, kale wilted down and chopped up for the artichokes, and minced shallots for the raw ramps in the salsa verde.

SPRING

Substitute morels for the porcinis and asparagus for the artichokes.

SUMMER

Substitute chanterelle mushrooms for the porcinis, cooked corn and raw sweet peppers for the artichokes, and minced shallots for the raw ramps in the salsa verde.

GRILLED CORN WITH DRIED BEEF AND SMOKED BUTTER

During the last thirteen years, I have had the opportunity to attend my brother-in-law's family sweat lodge ceremonies. Each chance to connect with family and the creator in this setting has been a powerful one, healing us and nourishing growth. On a couple of occasions, after the ceremony concluded, the four sacred foods were brought into the lodge: water, corn, buffalo meat, and raw berries. After praying, we consumed each of the foods my brother-in-law's ancestors once ate. This dish is my way of honoring these memories and the many medicines of Mother Earth.

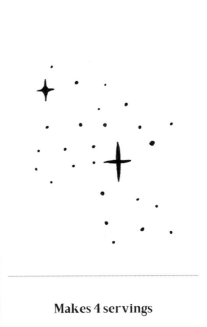

Makes 4 servings

Blueberry Butter

2 Tbsp freeze-dried blueberries

6 Tbsp [90 g] unsalted butter, at room temperature

¼ tsp fine smoked salt

¼ tsp freshly ground black pepper

Corn

4 ears of corn

Blueberry Butter (recipe precedes)

Dried Beef Floss (recipe follows)

TO MAKE THE BUTTER: Use a spice grinder or mortar and pestle to finely grind the blueberries, then stir them into the butter with the salt and pepper. Set aside at room temperature or refrigerate for up to 3 days; allow to come back to room temperature before serving.

TO MAKE THE CORN: Remove the husks or tie them in a knot at the base of the ear; strip away all the silks. Heat a grill with a high flame or set a metal grate directly over a gas burner set to high.

Grill the corn directly over the flame, turning occasionally, until it's lightly charred all over. Spread the butter over the cobs and dust the beef floss all over the cobs in an even layer so it sticks to the butter. Serve right away.

CONTINUED

Dried Beef Floss

Makes 1 cup [65 g]

4 oz [115 g] lean beef or buffalo, such as tenderloin or sirloin

4 in [10 cm] square dried kombu

¼ yellow onion

1½ tsp kosher salt

¼ cup [15 g] coriander seeds, toasted and ground

1½ tsp fennel seeds, toasted and ground

½ tsp cumin seeds, toasted and ground

¼ tsp lemon powder (see Drying section, page 196)

⅛ tsp freshly ground black pepper

¼ cup [60 ml] buttermilk

½ shallot, chopped

¼ jalapeño or serrano chile, chopped

2 garlic cloves, chopped

½ cup [6 g] lightly packed parsley leaves

Grapeseed oil for frying

¼ tsp Maple Sugar (page 203)

TO MAKE THE FLOSS: Trim the meat of any sinew or fat and cut it into 2 in [5 cm] chunks. Place it in a saucepan with the kombu, onion, and 1 tsp of the salt; cover with 1 qt [1 L] of water. Bring to a boil, then reduce the heat to medium and continue to simmer, uncovered, until the beef is very tender and easily pierced with a knife, 1½ to 2 hours. Drain and reserve the beef.

While the meat cooks, combine the coriander, fennel, cumin, lemon powder, and black pepper in a medium bowl.

In a blender, purée 1 Tbsp of the buttermilk with the shallot, jalapeño, and garlic; add the parsley and continue to blend until smooth. Add the mixture to the spices and mix to make a thick paste.

When the meat is cool enough to handle but still warm, lightly pound it with the bottom of a pot or a meat tenderizer to break up the grain. Use a fork and your hands to finely shred the meat, going with the grain. Add all of the meat to the bowl with the spiced paste and use your hands to thoroughly incorporate. Refrigerate in an airtight container for at least 2 hours or overnight.

Thinly coat the bottom of a wok or a large Dutch oven with oil and warm it over medium heat. When the oil starts to shimmer, add the marinated beef and stir to coat with the oil. As it cooks, the beef will become very aromatic, deeply browned, and crumbly; stir frequently so it doesn't scorch, and use a spoon or metal spatula to break apart larger pieces. This can take 30 to 40 minutes.

Decrease the heat to low and add the remaining 3 Tbsp of buttermilk, the remaining ½ tsp of salt, and the maple sugar. Continue to stir for 20 to 30 minutes, until very dry, light, and almost fluffy. Allow the meat to cool to room temperature before transferring to an airtight container; store at room temperature for up to 3 days or freeze for up to 1 month before serving.

Simplify It

DRIED BEEF FLOSS	• Stores really well, so it can be made in big batches.
	• Use on rice.
	• Use on top of corn chowder (page 47) or as garnish for any brothy or noodle soup.
	• Garnish curries along with lots of fresh herbs.
	• Use on top of roast veggies for a meaty punch.
BLUEBERRY BUTTER	• Serve with corn cakes (page 235), poached fruit, and maple syrup, crepe style.
	• Use on toast with nut butter or jam, spread on a muffin, or use on pancakes and waffles.
	• Serve with your favorite corn bread.

CARROT-RICOTTA CUSTARD

As a young cook at Quince restaurant in San Francisco, I made countless versions of a savory vegetable custard, which is known in Italian as *sformato* (its literal translation means "to unmold"), furiously whisking the béchamel sauce for the base. But here, I use fresh farmer's cheese or ricotta in its place, since it tastes like pure, sweet milk and has enough heft to bind everything together into something that lingers between a soufflé and a pudding.

While many vegetables can be used in the base, I urge you to seek out red or purple carrots whenever possible. They are the oldest recorded carrot variety and have a concentrated source of antioxidants. Not to mention that they give this custard a delightful lavender complexion.

**Makes 6 muffin-size custards
or 1 larger custard**

Custard

¼ cup [60 g] unsalted butter, plus more for the molds

10½ oz [300 g] small carrots, purple or red if you can find them; otherwise, substitute orange ones

1 tsp fennel seeds, toasted and ground

1 tsp kosher salt

2 Tbsp Queen Anne's Lace Vinegar (page 188) or champagne vinegar

1 cup [240 g] Fresh Ricotta (page 204), drained

2 eggs

½ cup [60 g] grated hard cheese, such as clothbound Cheddar, Piave, or Parmesan

½ tsp onion powder

¼ tsp ground cayenne pepper

½ tsp fennel pollen (if available) or ground fennel

¼ tsp freshly ground black pepper

Gluten-free flour for the molds

TO MAKE THE CUSTARD: Preheat the oven to 350°F [180°C].

In a medium ovenproof sauté pan with a fitted lid, warm the butter over medium heat until it begins to brown and lets off a nutty aroma. Add the carrots whole (halve or quarter them lengthwise if they're on the larger side), season with the fennel seeds and ½ tsp of the salt, and toss to coat well. Sauté until light golden brown all over, about 15 minutes. Add the vinegar and allow it to reduce for about 2 minutes.

Add 2 Tbsp of water to the pan, quickly cover it, and transfer to the oven. Cook the carrots until mashable, 50 to 60 minutes. Remove from the heat and allow to cool to room temperature before proceeding with the next steps as they are too hot at this point to be mixed with raw eggs.

In a blender, purée the carrots with the ricotta, eggs, grated cheese, onion powder, cayenne, fennel, pepper, and the remaining ½ tsp of salt until very smooth. Transfer the mixture to an airtight container and refrigerate until completely chilled.

Preheat the oven to 350°F [180°C]. Butter and flour the molds, then fill them with the custard. Rap each filled mold firmly on your work surface to dislodge any air bubbles. Bake for 30 to 40 minutes. (A single larger custard will require a longer time, 40 to 45 minutes.) When the custards are done, they will be firm, slightly risen, and starting to pull away from the sides of the molds. These custards are best when eaten right from the oven; however, you can bake them up to 2 hours before you use them. They will be fine at room temperature until then.

CONTINUED

FOR THE MEDLEY: If you find yourself with an extra 20 minutes and a sunny day, put your mushrooms in the sun before cooking them, since they have an uncanny ability to take in vitamin D$_2$ and retain 90 percent of it after cooking.

Heat a medium sauté pan over medium heat until a drop of water flicked on the surface sizzles gently on contact. Add the butter to the pan and immediately follow it with the shallots, garlic, fennel, and salt. Cook, stirring occasionally, until the vegetables begin to soften, about 10 minutes. Add the mushrooms and stir gently, allowing them to marry with the other ingredients. Turn the heat to low and cover the pan for 8 minutes before checking to see if the mushrooms are cooked all the way through. If not, continue in 5-minute increments until they are tender but not mushy. Add the vinegar and let stand until you are ready to serve.

To serve, gently reheat the custards (if you made them in advance) for about 10 minutes at 350°F [180°C] until warmed through. Slip a butter knife or small offset spatula along the sides to loosen the edges.

Finish the parsley sauce by gently warming the cultured butter in a small saucepan. When it has just begun to bubble and foam, gradually whisk in the parsley sauce; season with more salt if necessary.

Evenly spoon the sauce onto the middle of individual warm plates (if you made small custards) or over a serving platter (if you made 1 large custard). Invert the custards and place them atop the sauce, draping the mushroom medley over and around it. Garnish with parsley and pickled carrots. Serve warm. Leftovers can be refrigerated in separate airtight containers; rewarm them gently in a low oven, with the custards in a covered container and the mushroom medley on a baking sheet. Leftover parsley sauce can be gently reheated in a saucepan over medium-low heat.

Mushroom Medley

8 oz [230 g] mushrooms, such as button, maitake, oyster, or chanterelle

2 Tbsp unsalted butter

3 medium shallots, thinly sliced

4 garlic cloves, thinly sliced

½ small fennel bulb, thinly sliced

2 tsp kosher salt

1½ tsp Queen Anne's Lace Vinegar (page 188) or champagne vinegar

Parsley Sauce (page 205)

3 Tbsp unsalted cultured butter for finishing the sauce

Kosher salt for finishing the sauce

Chopped fresh parsley for garnish

Vinegar-Pickled Red Carrots (page 189) for garnish

Seasonal Variations

WINTER

Substitute winter squash for carrots. Peel and cut 10½ oz [300 g] winter squash, such as butternut or kabocha, into 1 in [2.5 cm] chunks. Sauté in butter, then bake, covered, at 350°F [180°C] until tender. Garnish with lemon thyme and chopped hazelnuts.

AUTUMN

Substitute celery root or parsnips for carrots. Peel and cut 10½ oz [300 g] celery root into 1 in [2.5 cm] chunks, sauté in butter, and bake, covered, at 350°F [180°C] until tender. Garnish with a chiffonade of sage.

SPRING

Substitute English peas for carrots. Blanch and shock 10½ oz [300 g] shucked English peas, then gently warm them in the butter before puréeing. Garnish the custards with torn mint.

SUMMER

Substitute corn for the carrots. Gently cook 10½ oz [300 g] shucked corn kernels in the butter before puréeing. Garnish the custards with cherry tomatoes and basil.

ROOT VEGETABLE FRITTERS WITH FARMER'S CHEESE SAUCE

Mom used to let me grate the potatoes for latkes. We had an old-school box grater, all one piece of metal, gently rusting where it turned over onto itself. Mom would peel the potatoes and leave them bobbing in cold water until we were ready to cook. I would clutch the icy flesh, swiftly moving them up and down, praying the grater holes wouldn't claim a nick or two from my knuckles. I remember milky starch dripping off of the potatoes before they turned to confetti. Like the latkes of my childhood, or Indian *pakora*, fritters are a great back-pocket recipe to have when you're craving something crisp and warm. Think of this more as a guide than a recipe. Swap out different lacto-fermented vegetables (page 180) or keep it all fresh, though you'll forgo that extra bit of tartness, which I find helps balance the richness of the fry. Another option is to play with different legumes as the binder. So long as the total net weight is the same, the ingredients are interchangeable.

Makes 4 servings

Root Vegetable Fritters

Makes about 24

1 Japanese sweet potato
(about 7 oz [200 g])

½ lb [230 g] lacto-fermented root vegetables (page 181), such as carrots, beets, or turnips

½ cup [70 g] rice flour

1 Tbsp kosher salt

1 tsp red pepper flakes

1 tsp caraway seeds, toasted and ground

1 tsp coriander seeds, toasted and ground

1¼ cups [210 g] cooked or drained canned beans (from one 15 oz [430 g] can), such as cannellini or garbanzo, rinsed

1 egg

2 Tbsp lightly packed dill leaves, chopped

2 garlic cloves, grated

1 serrano chile, grated

Zest of 2 lemons

Grapeseed oil for panfrying

TO MAKE THE FRITTERS: Preheat the oven to 375°F [190°C]. Prick the sweet potato a few times with a fork (this helps to release steam) and bake until very soft and mashable. Meanwhile, coarsely grate the fermented vegetables and use a few layers of cheesecloth or a clean dish towel to wring out some (but not all) of their moisture.

In a separate bowl, combine the flour, salt, red pepper flakes, caraway, and coriander.

CONTINUED

When the sweet potato is cool enough to handle, peel away and discard its skin. In a large bowl, use a fork or potato masher to smash the potato with the beans and egg until roughly combined. Stir in the grated vegetables, dill, garlic, serrano, and lemon zest; use your hands or a wooden spoon to mix well until evenly incorporated. It should feel like a wet dough.

Coat the bottom of a skillet with about ⅛ in [4 mm] of the grapeseed oil and warm it over medium-high heat; it's ready when a drop of water immediately sizzles and evaporates on contact. Line a plate or cooling rack with paper towels.

Working in batches, shape the fritters into cakes about 3 in [7.5 cm] across and ½ in [12 mm] thick and add to the pan. Immediately decrease the heat to medium. Be sure to leave plenty of space between each one so you don't cool the oil down, causing your fritters to get soggy instead of crispy. Cook, undisturbed, until the bottom is deeply golden and releases easily from the pan, 3 to 4 minutes. Flip and repeat on the other side. Transfer to the lined plate to drain and repeat with the rest of the batter.

Serve the fritters right away (if necessary, keep them warm in a 200°F [95°C] oven) with the cheese sauce.

TO MAKE THE SAUCE: In a small saucepan over medium heat, melt the butter. Add the onion, garlic, and potato and cook, stirring occasionally, until the onion is translucent, 5 to 10 minutes.

Add the Kombu Dashi to the pan, increase the heat to medium-high, and bring the mixture to a simmer. Immediately decrease the heat to medium-low, and continue to cook gently until nearly all of the liquid has been reduced and the potatoes are very tender, 25 to 35 minutes. Remove from the heat and allow to cool for 5 to 10 minutes.

Transfer the cooked vegetables to a blender; add the farmer's cheese, salt, coriander, and pepper; purée until very smooth. If you're making this in advance, refrigerate in an airtight container for up to 3 days, gently rewarming over low heat when you're ready to serve.

Stir the parsley into the warm cheese sauce just before serving.

Farmer's Cheese Sauce

Makes 1½ cups [360 ml]

2 Tbsp unsalted butter

1 yellow onion, thinly sliced

4 garlic cloves, minced

½ medium russet potato (about 3 oz [85 g]), peeled and diced

½ cup [120 ml] Kombu Dashi (page 207) or vegetable stock

1 cup [240 g] farmer's cheese or drained ricotta

1 Tbsp kosher salt

2 tsp coriander seeds, toasted and ground

2 tsp freshly ground black pepper

¼ cup [3 g] lightly packed parsley leaves, chopped

BUCKWHEAT DUMPLINGS WITH CABBAGE AND HASSELBACK SQUASH

By the late 1880s, there was an influx of Jewish immigrants to Western Massachusetts, with most of them coming from Russia, Hungary, Lithuania, and Poland. They, along with Lebanese immigrants, were among the first shopkeepers and restaurant owners in Massachusetts's small mill town, North Adams. I think of my own maternal grandparents who emigrated from Lithuania and Poland and their love of schmaltz, kasha, and dill. I can't help but imagine how in this corner of New England, the Eastern European flavors I grew up with may have mingled with those farther afield. This squash purée, with its sesame and spices, looks to the Levant and is my take on the type of boundary blending that may have occurred here over a century ago.

Makes 4 servings

Buckwheat Dumplings

1½ cups [250 g] buckwheat groats

4 oz [175 g] Fermented Squash and Sesame Purée (recipe follows), plus 16 oz [700 g] for serving

2 Tbsp drained ricotta

1 egg

2 tsp kosher salt

Buckwheat flour for rolling

Roasted Cabbage and Hasselback Butternut Squash (recipe follows)

Mushroom Medley (page 95)

Ghee or grapeseed oil for cooking

Toasted pumpkin seeds, dill leaves, freshly ground black pepper, and extra-virgin olive oil for garnish

TO MAKE THE BUCKWHEAT DUMPLINGS: Cover the groats in 3 cups [720 ml] of water and soak at room temperature for about 30 minutes. Drain.

Fill a medium saucepan with water and bring to a boil. Cook the buckwheat until tender, 8 to 10 minutes. Drain and rinse with cold water, allowing any excess liquid to drain off. Scoop out ½ cup [80 g] and set aside.

Process the cooked buckwheat in a food processor until it becomes a tacky paste. Add 4 oz [115 g] of the Fermented Squash and Sesame Purée, ricotta, egg, and salt. Continue to process until the mixture is very smooth and uniform; it will feel sticky and wet. Scrape it into an airtight container and refrigerate for at least 30 minutes and up to 3 days.

Fill a large pot with 1 to 2 in [2.5 to 5 cm] of water and fit a steamer inside, making sure the water isn't high enough to seep into it. Cover and bring to a gentle simmer over medium heat. While you wait for the water to boil, form the dumplings. Dust a clean work surface with the flour and, working with one small handful of dough at a time, roll it into logs about 1 in [2.5 cm] in diameter, then cut each log into 1 to 1½ in [2.5 to 4 cm] pieces. If needed, dust with additional flour to prevent sticking.

CONTINUED

When the water is boiling, working in batches, place the dumplings in the steamer basket, being careful that they aren't touching. Cover and cook for 15 to 20 minutes, until the dumplings hold together and are cooked through. Transfer to a plate while you repeat with the remaining dough. The dumplings can be made up to 3 days in advance and stored in an airtight container in the refrigerator.

When you're ready to serve, preheat the oven to 200°F [95°C]. If you made the dumplings in advance, let them come to room temperature for about 30 minutes before searing. If you roasted the cabbage and squash ahead of time, arrange them on a baking sheet and gently rewarm in the oven along with the premade mushroom medley. Gently fold the reserved cooked buckwheat into the mushroom medley.

Heat the ghee in a large skillet over medium-high heat. When it starts to shimmer, decrease the heat to medium and add the dumplings in batches so you don't crowd the pan. Allow them to brown undisturbed for 2 to 3 minutes. Flip and sear the other side. Repeat with all the dumplings.

To serve, spread a generous spoonful of Fermented Squash and Sesame Purée over the bottoms of individual plates or on one large platter, about ½ cup (4 oz [175 g]) per serving, and divide the dumplings evenly over them. Trim the core from each roasted cabbage wedge to release the petals and cut the hasselback squash into roughly 1½ in [4 cm] pieces. Tuck the vegetables among the dumplings and garnish with the pumpkin seeds, dill, pepper, and oil.

Roasted Cabbage and Hasselback Butternut Squash

¼ cup [60 g] unsalted cultured butter, at room temperature

1½ tsp caraway seeds, toasted and ground

1½ tsp fennel seeds, toasted and ground

1 small head Savoy cabbage, quartered (about 1 lb [455 g])

Kosher salt

Freshly ground black pepper

½ butternut squash neck (5 to 6 oz [140 to 170 g]), peeled

TO MAKE THE CABBAGE AND HASSELBACK SQUASH: Preheat the oven to 425°F [220°C]. In a small bowl, combine the butter, caraway, and fennel. Leaving the cabbage's core intact, rub each wedge with the spiced butter. Season with salt and pepper.

Arrange the wedges on a rimmed baking sheet and roast for 15 minutes. Flip the quarters and continue to roast until very tender and deeply browned in some areas, about 15 minutes more. Remove from the oven and set aside to cool. Reduce the oven temperature to 350°F [180°C].

Halve the squash neck lengthwise so you have two long wedges. Lay the wedges on a cutting board, flat-side down, and cut ¼ in [6 mm] slices down the length of each one, stopping your knife about ½ in [12 mm] before it cuts all the way through, so the pieces stay intact with thin layers like pages of a book. It helps to do this by setting one chopstick snugly along either side of the squash since the chopsticks will halt your knife. Roast the wedges cut-side up until they're tender, 20 to 30 minutes. Both the cabbage and squash can be roasted up to 3 hours in advance and left covered at room temperature until you're ready to serve.

CONTINUED

TO MAKE THE SQUASH PURÉE: Fill a large pot with 1 to 2 in [2.5 to 5 cm] of water and fit a steamer inside, making sure the water isn't high enough to seep into it. Cover and bring to a gentle simmer over medium heat. Cut the fresh squash and sweet potato into 1 in [2.5 cm] chunks. You should have about 2 cups [260 g] of squash and ½ cup [55 g] of sweet potato, plus about 1½ cups [360 g] of Fermented Squash.

Steam the fresh and fermented squash, sweet potato, and garlic together, covered, until they're mashable. Allow to cool for about 10 minutes.

Transfer the vegetables to the bowl of a food processor and pulse a few times to break them up a bit. Add the sesame tahini, lemon juice, and spices and continue to process until smooth.

With the processor still going, slowly stream in the oil to make a silky, emulsified paste. Taste for seasoning. Let cool to room temperature. If it's not as smooth as you would like, transfer to a blender and purée to reach the desired consistency.

Fermented Squash and Sesame Purée

10 oz [280 g] fresh butternut squash, peeled

2 oz [55 g] sweet potato, peeled

10 oz [280 g] Fermented Squash (use butternut) (page 181)

2 garlic cloves

3 Tbsp sesame tahini

2 Tbsp fresh lemon juice

2½ tsp curry powder

¾ tsp hot paprika or ground cayenne pepper

½ tsp lemon powder (see Drying section, page 196) or freshly grated lemon zest

½ tsp onion powder

¼ tsp fennel pollen or fennel seed, toasted and ground

¼ cup [60 ml] extra-virgin olive oil

Kosher salt

Simplify It

FERMENTED SQUASH AND SESAME PURÉE	• This sauce freezes beautifully, so make it whenever you find yourself with a little kitchen time and you have the right ingredients on hand. Pack it in small containers to freeze and pull it out whenever you need a sauce or dip in a pinch. Carrots or beets can easily stand in for the squash if you're looking to riff and use this as a template.
	• Serve the dip with crudité or Seeded Herb Crackers (page 232) as part of an appetizer spread.
	• Use as the sauce beneath simple roasted vegetables, roast meats, or Whole Roasted Cauliflower (facing page) or in papillote fish (page 135).
BUCKWHEAT DUMPLINGS	• These work well as a grain side; sear with ghee or oil and finish with a knob of butter, lots of chopped or torn fresh herbs, a squeeze of lemon, and some grated cheese.
	• Create little patties out of the dough and crisp in a sauté pan if you don't want to roll the logs and steam them. Serve with roasted meats or veggies and a crisp green salad.

WHOLE ROASTED CAULIFLOWER WITH TURMERIC BUTTER

Roasting whole cauliflower is a lot like cooking a large piece of meat. Low and slow yields something outrageously tender and luscious, while the top florets frizzle to a deep brown. Letting the spiced butter–rubbed cauliflower rest isn't altogether necessary, but this extra bit of patience helps season the vegetable more thoroughly as everything has time to seep into the crags and craters. The long roast also means the butter turns from milky to toasty brown, a perfect foil for the hazelnuts in the spiced topping. This is an impressive, yet nearly effortless vegetarian centerpiece or side, although I bet carnivores will be equally eager for a wedge.

Makes 6 servings

Cauliflower

1 cup [225 g] unsalted butter, at room temperature

1 Tbsp kosher salt

1 Tbsp ground turmeric

1 Tbsp coriander seeds, ground

1 Tbsp fennel seeds, ground

1½ tsp sweet paprika

1 tsp sumac powder

½ tsp freshly ground black pepper

½ tsp ground cayenne pepper

¼ tsp cumin seeds, ground

1 garlic clove, grated

1 head cauliflower (1½ to 2 lb [680 to 910 g])

Spiced Hazelnuts (recipe follows)

TO MAKE THE CAULIFLOWER: In a large bowl or in the bowl of a stand mixer, combine the butter, salt, turmeric, coriander, fennel, paprika, sumac, black pepper, cayenne pepper, cumin, and garlic. Use an electric mixer or the paddle attachment of a stand mixer to whip the butter and spices together until they are completely incorporated.

Trim the green leaves and tough stem from the cauliflower and, with your hands or a spatula (you may find gloves to be helpful here, since the turmeric could temporarily dye your palms yellow), massage the butter into the cauliflower, getting it into the nooks and crannies as best you can. Place it in a deep roasting pan or Dutch oven and refrigerate for at least 1 hour or ideally overnight, allowing the butter to firm up slightly and penetrate the cauliflower.

Preheat the oven to 400°F [200°C]. Roast the cauliflower, uncovered, for 30 minutes, using a spoon to baste it with the butter halfway through, then cover and reduce the heat to 325°F [165°C]. Continue to roast until the cauliflower is very tender and the core is easily pierced with a fork, another 90 minutes or so. Remove the lid and baste it all over with the melted butter, then place under the broiler for a couple of minutes to bronze the top.

To serve, cut the cauliflower into wedges, leaving the core intact. Serve as is or, for a little extra richness and color, spoon about 1 Tbsp of the spiced butter into a pan set over medium heat. Let it get sizzly, then sear the wedges until they have a golden crust, 2 to 4 minutes per side. Garnish with the Spiced Hazelnuts and serve right away.

CONTINUED

Spiced Hazelnuts

¾ cup [90 g] hazelnuts,
toasted and coarsely chopped

2 Tbsp toasted sesame seeds

½ tsp extra-virgin olive oil

2 tsp sumac powder

1½ tsp dill powder

¼ tsp kosher salt

¼ tsp freshly ground black pepper

TO MAKE THE SPICED HAZELNUTS: In a bowl, toss the hazelnuts with the sesame seeds, oil, sumac, dill, salt, and pepper; there should be just barely enough oil to help the spices adhere to the nuts. Use right away or store in an airtight container for up to 1 day.

WOVEN RAINBOW TART

Show me a rainbow and I'll try to weave it. An impossible proclamation, I know, but there's something bewitching about the idea, for if you weave two ends together, it just might last a bit longer. In many ways, life is a colorful tapestry of moments, knit together to create something whole. I clung to this idea during my journey east. I wanted to weave the uncertainties and fears of starting anew into something beautiful, something uniquely me.

It's not often I have an idea for what I want a dish to look like even before I've tested it, but this image came clearly. A collision of color had to be center stage—an ode to my migration, of me dragging a rainbow of flavors and stories from one coast to the other. I hope, wherever you are, that you can weave the feeling of home into this dish.

Makes 6 to 8 servings

Cauliflower Crust

1½ tsp extra-virgin olive oil, plus more for the pan

2 Tbsp rice flour, plus more for the pan

1 head cauliflower (about 1 lb [455 g])

1 tsp kosher salt

⅓ cup [40 g] almond flour

⅓ cup [40 g] oat flour

1½ tsp lightly packed thyme leaves, minced

½ oz [15 g] hard cheese, such as Parmesan or clothbound Cheddar

½ oz [15 g] fresh horseradish, peeled

1 garlic clove

1 egg yolk

TO MAKE THE CRUST: Preheat the oven to 375°F [190°C]. Oil and flour a tart pan.

Break the cauliflower down into small florets and toss them to coat with the oil and ½ tsp of the salt. Roast in a single layer on a baking sheet until the florets are soft and nicely browned along the edges, 30 to 40 minutes. Cool completely (but leave the oven on).

In a food processor, pulse the florets until they are finely chopped. Transfer to a nut milk bag or line a fine-mesh sieve with several layers of cheesecloth to gently squeeze out as much excess liquid as possible. Don't worry about overdoing this—the drier, the better.

Add the cauliflower back to the food processor along with the rice flour, almond flour, oat flour, thyme, and the remaining ½ tsp of salt. Grate the cheese, horseradish, and garlic into the bowl, preferably with a Microplane grater, and add the egg yolk. Pulse a few times until everything is incorporated.

Press the crust into the bottom and up the sides of the prepared tart pan. Refrigerate or freeze for at least 15 to 30 minutes, just until it's chilled and set. If you're making it ahead, cover and keep refrigerated for up to 3 days.

Bake until set and dry to the touch, 30 to 40 minutes; cover loosely with foil if at any point you notice it starting to brown too quickly. Allow to cool completely.

CONTINUED

TO MAKE THE MOUSSE: In a large skillet, melt the butter over medium-low heat. Gently cook the shallots, stirring regularly, until they're silky but not browned, 15 to 20 minutes.

Put the egg yolks in a large bowl or in the bowl of a stand mixer. Use an electric mixer or the whisk attachment to beat on medium speed for about 30 seconds, until the yolks begin to lighten in consistency. Add the goat cheese, crème fraîche, dill, horseradish, lemon zest, salt, and pepper and continue to whip until light and airy. Refrigerate in an airtight container until you're ready to assemble the tart, up to 3 days in advance; if you've made the mousse ahead, you'll likely need to briefly rewhip it just before using to lighten the texture.

Goat Cheese Mousse

1 Tbsp unsalted butter

2 to 3 shallots (about 3½ oz [100 g]), halved and thinly sliced

2 egg yolks

6 oz [170 g] goat cheese, at room temperature

3 Tbsp crème fraîche or sour cream

1½ Tbsp lightly packed dill leaves, chopped

½ oz [15 g] fresh horseradish, peeled

Zest of ½ lemon

1 tsp kosher salt

½ tsp freshly ground black pepper

Vegetables

4 to 6 Brussels sprouts

1 Tbsp extra-virgin olive oil, plus more for the tart

¾ tsp kosher salt, plus more for the tart

Freshly ground black pepper

2 to 3 small carrots (about 3 oz [85 g]), mixed colors if possible

1 small red beet (about 3 oz [85 g])

1 tsp sumac powder

TO MAKE THE VEGETABLES: Preheat the oven to 375°F [190°C]. Fill a large pot with 1 to 2 in [2.5 to 5 cm] of water and fit a steamer inside, making sure the water isn't high enough to seep into it. Cover and bring to a gentle simmer over medium heat.

Use a mandoline or sharp knife to shave the Brussels sprouts about ⅛ in [4 mm] thick, leaving their cores intact when possible, then toss with 1 tsp of the oil and ¼ tsp of the salt; season with pepper. Spread the Brussels sprouts on a rimmed baking sheet and roast until tender and lightly browned, 10 to 15 minutes.

Meanwhile, with your mandoline or a vegetable peeler, shave the carrots lengthwise into ribbons about ⅛ in [4 mm] thick. Steam until just barely tender but still a little crisp, 4 to 6 minutes, then toss with 1 tsp of the oil and ¼ tsp of the salt.

Shave the beet into ⅛ in [4 mm] thick rounds. (If you don't have a mandoline, halve the beet first, then lay the halves flat-side down to slice as thin as you can.) Steam until tender but not fully soft, 10 to 15 minutes. Toss with the remaining 1 tsp of oil, the remaining ¼ tsp of salt, and the sumac, keeping them separate from the carrots.

TO MAKE THE TART: Preheat the oven to 350°F [180°C]. Spread the mousse in the prebaked crust. Working with one vegetable at a time, arrange the Brussels sprouts, beet, and carrots in any pattern you'd like—shingle the beet slices and Brussels sprouts in alternating bands, for instance, and weave the carrots into a lattice top. The vegetables will shrink as they bake, so it's best to overlap them a bit in whatever pattern you choose.

Gently brush the top of the tart with a bit more oil and season with salt. Bake until the mousse filling is set, 25 to 35 minutes. Allow to cool for 15 minutes, then serve warm.

OF FEATHERS, SCALES, AND FUR

CHAPTER 3

Notes on Looking South to Honor the Element of Fire

Fire in the spiritual realm

South, the direction of heat, represents the element fire and the power of creation, destruction, and transformation. In order to convert itself into smoke, ash, heat, and light, fire must consume other elements. Through the act of ingesting, melding, and exploding, the transformation into fire begins. Fire represents the realm of behavior and doing. It heals and harms, brings new life and destroys the old. In nature, fire forms flames, lightning, and electricity, while in human life, it spurs action, sometimes with great force.

Fire in the physical realm

When I was growing up in the suburbs of Chicago, our family held weekend barbecues in the summer. In the suffocating Chicago heat, we'd gather around food and share in a moment. But it wasn't until I began to travel and cook with different people and cultures that cooking with fire took on a more spiritual significance.

Fire in cooking can alter the nutritional aspect of food, coax out sugars from starch, deepen flavors through the Maillard reaction, add smoke, and penetrate an ingredient with heat all the way to its core. By cooking food, we ward off disease and bacteria. Heating breaks down collagen in meats, making them more bioavailable for the body. Heat can also soften cell walls in some vegetables, causing them to release sugars, starches, and lipids into a matrix of minerals that our bodies are ready to utilize for energy and repair.

While much of this book focuses on produce, in this chapter you will find inspiration for preparing eggs, fish, and meat with an approach that is less about fully composed dishes and more about technique—treating meat more like "side dishes" than focal points. You will find primers on the most fundamental cooking methods, such as how to fry eggs or poach fish. From there, you'll also find recipes that utilize or riff on these techniques—my suggestions for presenting and building flavor. Meat is rich in umami, dense and savory, and wildly satiating. But with meat comes the need to source responsibly and be aware of the earthly consequences of emissions produced as a by-product of raising animals for slaughter. Arm yourself with the techniques herein, and use them to round out a meal. Of course, there are a few recipes that celebrate meat as the main event, like Mom's Pot Roast (page 163) or Salt-Baked Fish (page 139), but I often think of these dishes as festive recipes best eaten with a crowd.

Fundamental Cooking Methods: Egg Cookery

POACHED: When possible, bring eggs to room temperature for 30 minutes before cooking. In a large, deep-sided skillet or pot, add enough water to come 2 in [5 cm] up the side, plus 1 tsp of kosher salt and 2 tsp of white vinegar. Bring to a gentle boil over medium-high heat. Crack an egg into a small cup or ramekin, making sure no shell is present. With a spoon, swirl the water in one direction to make a whirlpool at the center. Drop the egg into the middle of the swirl, turn off the heat, and cover for about 5 minutes. Do this for up to 4 eggs at a time, depending on the size of your pot; just make sure to drop them in a few seconds apart, creating a new whirlpool for each egg. After 5 minutes, check for doneness by lifting the egg with a slotted spoon; the whites shouldn't feel watery, but the yolk should still be tender. If you're making these in advance, you can move the eggs to an ice bath and refrigerate for up to 8 hours, then gently reheat in warm water just before serving.

SCRAMBLED: In a nonstick or well-seasoned cast-iron pan, warm 1 Tbsp of the fat of your choice (butter, olive oil, chicken or bacon fat, etc.) over medium-low heat. Crack 2 eggs into a bowl along with ¼ tsp of salt and lightly mix with a fork, just until the yolks are broken up to create long ribbons among the whites. Pour the eggs into the pan and wait for the edges to begin to set; tilt the pan and, starting at the most set edge, drag your spatula straight across so that the wet eggs flood into the empty space. Again, wait until they start to set, then repeat, starting from a different edge. Continue until you have long ribbons that look pillowy and just set. Use your spatula to make one cut from center to edge, as if you were slicing a pie. Tilt the pan toward your plate and allow the eggs to fall gently, one cut edge and then the other. Season with flaky salt and freshly ground black pepper.

FRIED: Heat a dry nonstick pan or well-seasoned cast-iron skillet over medium-low heat. Once it's warm, add 1 Tbsp of butter, and when the foaming subsides, crack in the eggs, taking care not to overcrowd the pan. Season with salt and cook until the whites are set, then use a spatula to flip and continue to cook as long as you'd like: just a few seconds to leave the white soft on top and the yolk still quite runny ("over easy"), 10 to 20 seconds to leave the white solid but the yolk soft ("over medium"), 30 seconds to 1 minute to leave the yolk solid ("over well"), and over 1 minute to cook the yolk completely through ("over hard").

SOFT-BOILED: Bring a large pot of salted water to a boil. Meanwhile, prepare a lightly salted ice bath. Carefully pierce the large end of the eggs with a pin or needle; this pierces the air cell in the egg, allowing the air to escape, which prevents a flat spot from forming on the large end of the egg during the cooking process. It also helps make the eggs easier to peel after cooking. Gently lower the eggs into the boiling water and cook for exactly 6½ minutes, then transfer to an ice bath to stop the cooking.

ONSEN: Traditionally, these eggs were slowly cooked in Japanese *onsen* hot springs, which are approximately 170°F [75°C]. The steady, gentle heat produces an egg with a silky, custard-like white and firm but creamy yolk. The easiest way to achieve the same results at home is by setting an immersion circulator to 167°F [75°C] and cooking eggs in their shells for 13 minutes. Alternatively, you can clip a candy thermometer to the side of a pot filled with salted water. Bring the water to approximately 167°F [75°C], add the eggs, and monitor the flame on your stove to keep it between 175°F [80°C] and 180°F [82°C] for 13 minutes. If you go any longer, your eggs will overcook. Alternatively, you can use the same technique at 145°F [63°C] for 45 minutes.

CODDLED EGGS WITH SALAMI AND MUSHROOMS

My mom used to sauté slices of hard salami until their edges ruffled and fire-engine-red oil pooled. Then came the eggs, softly scrambled in that bright, funky fat. We mainly ate the meal at night for a quick dinner—no fuss, just salami and love. In this rendition, coddled eggs get gussied up with sauce, herbs, and mushrooms, but it's less about the ingredients and more about the technique. Use whatever is on hand and, most of all, have fun with it. Feeding ourselves is supposed to be playful and enjoyable.

Makes 4 servings

8 oz [230 g] mushrooms, such as button, maitake, oyster, or chanterelle, quartered

Grapeseed oil

¼ cup [3 g] lightly packed fresh herbs, such as chives, chervil, tarragon, and parsley, plus more for garnish

½ cup (120 g) Fresh Ricotta (page 204), drained

Kosher salt

Freshly ground pepper

4 tsp unsalted butter

4 to 8 thin slices cured meat, such as salami or prosciutto

8 eggs

½ cup [120 ml] heavy cream

Flaky salt for garnish

Extra-virgin olive oil for garnish

Sweet paprika for garnish

Preheat the oven to 375°F [190°C]. Toss the mushrooms with a bit of grapeseed oil, salt them, and roast until deeply brown, 15 to 20 minutes. Reduce the heat to 275°F [200°C]. Finely chop the herbs and add them to the ricotta; season lightly with salt and pepper.

Divide the butter among four coddlers or 4 oz [115 g] ramekins, followed by the ricotta, and nestle 1 or 2 slices of cured meat inside.

Gently crack 2 eggs into each coddler, being careful to keep the yolks intact. Scatter the mushrooms around each egg and top each with 2 Tbsp of the cream. Season lightly with salt and pepper.

Top the coddlers with lids or wrap very tightly in foil. Place them in a baking dish and pour enough hot water to come halfway up their sides. Bake until the whites are just set and the yolks are runny, 30 to 40 minutes, or until done to your liking.

Carefully remove the coddlers from the baking dish (the water will be hot) and top with fresh herbs, flaky salt, pepper, oil, and paprika. Serve immediately from the coddler.

KITCHEN NOTE:

I like to add a spoonful of Harissa Vinaigrette (page 207) or pesto (page 206) to the bottom of the coddler with the ricotta.

CONTINUED

Seasonal Variations

WINTER

Add roasted winter squash, Oil-Preserved Shallots (page 193), or wilted kale.

SPRING

Add asparagus, peas, or radish greens.

AUTUMN

Add roasted Japanese sweet potato chunks, any oil-preserved summer veggies (page 192), or wilted spinach.

SUMMER

Add fresh tomatoes or Oil-Preserved Tomatoes (page 193), shaved charred zucchini, corn, charred pepper, or wilted chard.

GRILLED MAPLE EGGS

When I was a kid, weekend breakfast often meant pancakes and scrambled eggs. Inevitably, a rush of maple syrup would cascade down the pancakes and flood the eggs as if a dam had broken. I loved those sweet sticky bites. When I got to the East Coast, I was lucky to participate in tapping a maple tree for syrup, watching their sap reduced to an amber elixir I'd only ever seen come from a jug, and I couldn't help but fall more deeply in love with the ingredient. When it comes to meals in sugar shacks, I quickly discovered that all bets are off and anything goes: Eggs get boiled directly in the vat of reducing sap and cooked bacon is dipped inside. This snack compresses time and space for me, uniting two experiences in an unexpected bite.

Makes 6 eggs

---

2 strips (about 2 oz [60 g]) bacon, diced

6 eggs

2 Tbsp white soy sauce

1 Tbsp minced chives

2 tsp maple syrup

¾ tsp smoked paprika

½ tsp kosher salt

⅛ tsp ground cayenne pepper (optional)

⅛ tsp freshly ground black pepper

Grapeseed oil for grilling

Preheat the oven to 200°F [95°C]. Line a plate or cooling rack with paper towels.

Cook the bacon in a medium skillet over medium-low heat until crispy, about 10 minutes. Transfer to the lined plate until completely cool.

Remove the top of the egg carton and cut the carton to hold 6 eggs. (This carton will be baked, so it should be made of cardboard, not plastic or Styrofoam.) Set an egg in each well with the wider end pointing up. Use a toothpick or metal pin to poke a tiny hole in each egg right at the top, applying very firm but even pressure until the toothpick breaks through the shell. Flip the eggs and do the same thing on the narrow end.

Now you need to pull away pieces of the shell to create a slightly bigger (½ in [12 mm] or so) hole at the top (narrow end) of the egg for filling. To do this without cracking the whole thing, dip the very tip of your toothpick back into the hole you made on the narrow end and gently angle it upward to shatter tiny bits of shell that you can pull away.

This next part feels like magic, or at the very least, a little bit silly. Working over a small bowl, purse your lips around the smaller hole of one egg. Blow air into the egg (steadily, as if you're trying to blow bubbles in a thick smoothie) until the yolk and white come through the other end and fall into the bowl. If you see any stray bits of shell, push the eggs through a fine-mesh sieve to remove them. Once you've done this with all of the eggs, gently rinse each shell with water and stand them back in the carton with the larger hole facing up.

Whisk the eggs together with the soy sauce, chives, syrup, paprika, salt, cayenne (if using), and pepper; mince the bacon as small as you can and add it, too. Pour the mix into a cup or pitcher with a spout (or use a small funnel) and fill the eggs, leaving about ¼ in [6 mm] of space at the top.

CONTINUED

Set the entire egg crate into a deeper container, cover with a lid or foil, and bake. After 90 minutes, use a toothpick to check the filling; if it's not completely set, continue to bake in 15-minute increments.

At this point, you can gently crack the eggs open and spoon the warm filling directly from their shells. Otherwise, allow them to cool in the refrigerator for at least 1 hour before peeling, or, if you're grilling the eggs, refrigerate them overnight in an airtight container so they can firm up a bit in their shells.

To char the eggs by grilling, broiling, or cooking over a gas burner, peel them carefully and allow them to come to room temperature for 30 minutes. Gently thread the eggs on skewers. Place a slotted grill pan or metal rack directly over a medium flame. If using the broiler, place a rack approximately 4 in [10 cm] beneath the heating element and preheat. Coat your palms with a bit of oil and use your hands to lightly coat the eggs. Grill or broil until the eggs have slight markings all over, rotating every minute or so. Serve immediately.

KITCHEN NOTE:

This process might feel daunting at first, but it's really not challenging or super technical—patience is more important than anything. If you're worried about breaking an egg, buy a dozen so you have a little leeway for practicing and then just scramble the ones that don't work for your lunch. Since you'll place the eggs back in their carton for cooking, make sure yours is cardboard, not plastic or Styrofoam. Baking the eggs low and slow ensures a custardy texture that is lovely on its own, warm, but if you want to grill them Cambodian-street-food style, they'll gain a tempting smokiness; just note, they'll need to be baked 1 day in advance to chill in their shell.

PICKLED SCOTCH EGGS

The Scotch egg is like a miniature treasure chest—the coating a blanket of textures and flavors revealing a world of wonderment inside. The Pennsylvania Dutch are known for pickled eggs, but it is believed that the delicacies originally came from Manchester, England, my partner's hometown.

Pickling eggs preserves them for long periods of time while also infusing more flavor within. With today's farming techniques, it's hard to believe that eggs were at one point a seasonal food just like fruits and vegetables. The cold winter temperatures were not conducive to developing chicks, nor was there enough food during those lean months for chickens to produce eggs in the first place. Today, we can have eggs all the time, but real pastured eggs are still a struggle in the frozen months. Serve these eggs with Feta Mousse (page 64), Parsnip Skordalia (page 81), Green Tahini Sauce (page 72), Fermented Squash and Sesame Purée (page 102), Aioli (page 204), or whatever you wish! These can be made with soft-boiled eggs, too, for a quicker version of the dish.

Makes 6 eggs

Turmeric Pickled Eggs

1 Tbsp kosher salt, plus more for cooking

6 eggs, at room temperature

3 shallots, thinly sliced

1 Tbsp black peppercorns

1½ cups [360 ml] apple cider vinegar

½ cup [120 ml] Kombu Dashi (page 207) or water

1 Tbsp ground turmeric

2 Tbsp Maple Sugar (page 203) or ¼ cup [80 g] maple syrup

TO MAKE THE PICKLED EGGS: Fill a saucepan with well-salted water and bring to a boil. Meanwhile, prepare a salted ice bath.

Gently lower the eggs into the boiling water and cook for exactly 6½ minutes. Immediately drain and transfer the eggs to the ice bath to halt the cooking. Separately, combine the shallots and peppercorns in a large jar that has a tight-fitting lid and space for all the eggs. When the eggs are completely cool, peel and place them in the jar atop the shallots.

In a small saucepan, combine the vinegar, Kombu Dashi, turmeric, maple sugar, and 1 Tbsp of salt. Gently warm everything in the saucepan, stirring just until the sugar and salt have completely dissolved. Pour the brine over the eggs, secure the lid, and gently rotate to disperse the shallots. Refrigerate for at least 5 days and up to 2 weeks, rotating every few days to move around any settled spices.

CONTINUED

TO MAKE THE CREPES: Combine the flours, Kombu Dashi, brine, eggs, oil, salt, and fennel pollen in a blender; mix until well incorporated. Set aside at room temperature for about 30 minutes or refrigerate overnight.

Just before you cook the crepes, whisk the batter well one last time in case any of the flour settled at the bottom. Finely chop the herbs and stir them in by hand. Preheat the oven to 200°F [95°C].

Heat a 10 in [25 cm] nonstick skillet or crepe pan over medium-high heat; it's ready when a drop of water skitters across the pan. Add a thin slice of butter and let it melt to coat the pan. Working quickly, use a small ladle or pitcher to pour 2 to 3 Tbsp of batter into the pan and use your other hand to swirl the entire pan so the batter spreads out. You're aiming for a very thin, even layer, but don't worry if it's not perfect; the first crepe especially might be an odd shape or a bit too thick, but it will still be delicious.

Cook the crepe, undisturbed, until tiny bubbles appear all across the top. Thin crepes just need a quick flip to finish cooking; thicker ones will still feel a bit raw or wet in the center and should cook a bit longer on the other side. Loosen the edges with a rubber spatula and slide it out of the pan onto a plate, then proceed with the rest of the batter, stacking each crepe between pieces of parchment or paper towel as they finish. Keep warm in the oven until ready to serve.

Corn Flour Crepes

¾ cup [105 g] white rice flour or gluten-free flour mix (such as Cup4Cup or Bob's Red Mill 1-to-1)

¾ cup [105 g] corn flour or fine cornmeal

¾ cup [180 ml] Kombu Dashi (page 207), vegetable stock, or water

6 Tbsp [90 ml] pickle brine from lacto-fermented vegetables (page 180) or store-bought salt-brined pickles

2 eggs

2 tsp grapeseed oil

1 tsp kosher salt, plus more for seasoning

½ tsp fennel pollen or ground fennel seed

2 Tbsp lightly packed fresh tarragon or dill leaves

Unsalted butter for cooking

Steamed Eggs

1 Tbsp sesame or grapeseed oil, plus more for the dish

1 medium ear corn

½ yellow onion

2 garlic cloves, minced

5 eggs

½ cup [120 ml] Kombu Dashi (page 207) or vegetable broth

1 Tbsp kosher salt

½ tsp ground turmeric

½ tsp freshly ground black pepper

Toasted sunflower seeds and fresh dill, tarragon, mint, and/or parsley for garnish

TO MAKE THE EGGS: Lightly grease a small, round casserole dish or 8 in [20 cm] square baking pan with a thin layer of sesame oil. If you have a steamer large enough to hold the dish, set it up inside a large pot filled with 1 to 2 in [2.5 to 5 cm] of water. Otherwise, fill a large pot with 1 to 2 in [2.5 to 5 cm] of water and place a clean can or inverted heatproof bowl in the bottom; this will hold your eggs aloft so they don't make contact with the hot water. Cover and bring the water to a gentle simmer over medium-low heat.

Meanwhile, cut the kernels off the corn; you should have ¾ to 1 cup [105 to 120 g]. Slice the onion paper-thin—a mandoline makes this easy, but if you don't have one, do your best with a sharp knife—and mix together with the corn and garlic.

Whisk the eggs with the Kombu Dashi, salt, turmeric, and black pepper, then stir in the vegetables. Pour the mix into the greased pan and, once the water is gently simmering, set the pan inside the steamer or pot. Cover and cook until the eggs are just set and still fluffy; check after 15 minutes, and if they're not done, cover and check back every couple of minutes for up to 30 minutes.

To serve, let the eggs cool in their dish for a few minutes, then loosen the edges and invert onto a plate. Slice the eggs. Swaddle the egg slices in the crepes; garnish with a palmful of sunflower seeds and torn fresh herbs of your choosing. Serve with the brown rice.

ORANGE EGGS WITH PUMPKIN, KALE, AND SAFFRON

Eggs have this chameleon-like way of transforming into different types of meals with vastly varying textures. This dish of "orange eggs," in the form of a classic Spanish tortilla, is loaded with pumpkin and kale in lieu of potatoes, plus wisps of saffron that dye everything a brilliant orange color and lend its distinct metallic-meets-floral flavor, which becomes more subtle if you give the tortilla a day of rest. I like serving wedges with Pumpkin Spice Mix (page 199) for a bit of crunch.

Makes 6 to 8 servings

1 small butternut squash neck (10 to 12 oz [280 to 340 g]), peeled

6 Tbsp [90 ml] grapeseed oil

1 Tbsp kosher salt, plus more as needed

¼ tsp saffron threads

1 Tbsp hot water

1 yellow onion, thinly sliced

2 cups [30 g] lightly packed curly kale leaves, torn

12 eggs

2 Tbsp extra-virgin olive oil

1 Tbsp lightly packed tarragon leaves, chopped

Pumpkin Spice Mix (page 199)

Aioli (page 204)

Preheat the oven to 350°F [180°C]. Halve the squash neck lengthwise and cut it into slices about ⅛ in [4 mm] thick. Lightly toss with 2 Tbsp of the grapeseed oil and season with salt. Spread in a single layer on a rimmed baking sheet and bake until tender, 15 to 20 minutes. Cool completely at room temperature and decrease the heat to 250°F [120°C].

In a small bowl or cup, combine the saffron with the water and set aside to steep.

In a 10 in [25 cm] nonstick, oven-safe pan or cast-iron skillet, warm the remaining ¼ cup [60 ml] of grapeseed oil over medium heat. Sauté the onion, stirring occasionally, until translucent and soft, 5 to 10 minutes. Add the kale in batches and keep cooking until it's very tender, about 10 minutes longer. Gently fold in the roasted squash and decrease the heat to low.

Crack the eggs into a large bowl and whisk in the olive oil, tarragon, and the saffron infusion along with the salt. Pour into the skillet with the vegetables, bring the heat back up to medium, and leave undisturbed for about 1 minute so the eggs start to set. Drag a rubber spatula across the center of the pan, gently dispersing the vegetables and allowing the eggs to fill in the space around them. Continue to check and scrape every 30 seconds to 1 minute, just until about half the egg mixture is cooked and the rest is still wet and runny.

Transfer the pan to the oven and bake for 40 to 50 minutes, until the center is barely set. It will still feel a bit soft to the touch. Allow to cool for a few minutes before inverting onto a plate or platter. Serve warm or at room temperature, topped with a handful of the spice mix and a scoop of aioli, or refrigerate in an airtight container for up to 3 days, bringing it completely to room temperature or rewarming gently before eating.

RED EGGS WITH TOMATOES, RED LENTILS, AND HIBISCUS PESTO

When I first moved to the East Coast, I didn't know many people and my home kitchen, the place I've always retreated to when times are trying, was under construction. Life's equilibrium felt a bit off balance to say the least. One evening, my friend Lisa invited me over for dinner. She was nervous to cook for a chef—don't be, we love the generosity!—so she decided to make her favorite dish. Using some harissa I had given her, she sautéed onions, simmered tomato sauce, and cracked eggs into a glorious shakshuka, which I tucked into with such gusto that it looked like I hadn't eaten for weeks . . . This dish forever tastes like true friendship and laughter.

Makes 3 to 6 servings

2 lb [910 g] tomatoes (4 large) or a 28 oz [794 g] can of San Marzano tomatoes

½ lb [230 g] sweet red peppers, such as bell (about 2 small), or 5 oz [150 g] store-bought roasted red peppers

2 Tbsp extra-virgin olive oil

1 large red onion, chopped

1½ Tbsp kosher salt

¼ cup [60 g] Harissa Vinaigrette (page 207)

1 tsp freshly ground black pepper

1 tsp coriander seeds, ground

¼ tsp cumin seeds, ground

6 garlic cloves, minced

1 chile, such as jalapeño or serrano, stemmed and minced

2 cups [480 ml] Kombu Dashi (page 207) or vegetable stock

1 cup [200 g] dried red lentils

8 oz [230 g] fresh spinach (about 5 cups lightly packed)

6 eggs

Hibiscus-Za'atar Pesto (page 206)

Heat a grill to medium-high heat or set a metal grate directly over a gas burner on medium-high heat. Set the tomatoes over the fire and allow the skins to blister and slightly char; this will only take 30 seconds to 1 minute. Rotate until the skin pulls away everywhere; remove from the heat, cool slightly, discard the skins, and set the tomatoes aside to cool. Set the sweet peppers over the flame and do the same thing, this time allowing them to blacken slightly; this quick roast amplifies the pepper's sweetness while adding a tinge of smoke. When the peppers are cool enough to handle, peel away their skins as best you can. Core the tomatoes, remove the seeds and membranes from the peppers, and chop the tomatoes and peppers all together. If using canned tomatoes and peppers, chop.

In a large, deep skillet or Dutch oven, warm the oil over medium heat. Add the onion and salt and cook until translucent and starting to smell sweet, 5 to 10 minutes, then add the harissa, black pepper, coriander, cumin, and garlic. Allow everything to toast for a few minutes until very fragrant.

Stir in the chopped tomatoes and sweet peppers, then add the chile and bring to a simmer, stirring occasionally, until the tomatoes have melted and thickened into more of a sauce, 20 to 30 minutes. Add the Kombu Dashi and, once it's bubbling, stir in the lentils. Reduce the heat to medium-low, cover, and cook until the lentils are tender, 15 to 20 minutes.

Stir in the spinach, one big handful at a time, then cook for another couple of minutes until completely wilted and soft. Crack an egg into a cup or ramekin and use the back of your spoon to make a well in the sauce, then pour the egg into it. Repeat with the rest of the eggs and then, very gently, spoon just a bit of sauce over the edges of the whites.

Cover and cook until the whites are set but the yolks are still runny, 5 to 7 minutes; if the whites are still a bit soft, gently baste once more with the sauce to finish cooking. Serve immediately with the pesto spooned over the top.

GREEN EGGS WITH ALL THE LEAVES

A seemingly simple ingredient with a hidden universe beneath its shell, the egg is one of the most whole, versatile, and marvelous foods. This forest-green frittata is my version of a Persian *kuku* in which bushels of greens and herbs are gently bound by eggs. Layering so many greens causes them to surrender form and flavor, becoming a new type of savory, but the exact mix is up to you. Feel free to toss in whatever greens or herbs you might have—use all arugula or all spinach, swap in chard or kale, omit some of the herbs and increase the others—the important thing is that you have a lot (5 to 5½ cups [60 to 65 g] worth). And when it comes to cooking eggs, low and slow is always my preferred method. It ensures they stay luscious, never dry. Serve the green eggs with Herby Yogurt (page 204), Feta Mousse (page 64), or Green Tahini Sauce (page 72). Eat it as a side dish, with grilled pork, alongside a big salad, or tucked inside a corn crepe (page 123) smothered with Parsnip Skordalia (page 81).

Makes 4 to 6 servings

---

2 Tbsp dried currants

2 Tbsp sherry vinegar

3 Tbsp unsalted butter

4 shallots, thinly sliced

1 Tbsp kosher salt

2 tsp sumac powder

1½ tsp freshly ground black pepper

1 tsp coriander seeds, ground

½ cup [130 g] drained sauerkraut, chopped

1½ cups [30 g] lightly packed baby arugula

1½ cups [30 g] lightly packed baby spinach

¾ cup [9 g] lightly packed cilantro leaves

¾ cup [9 g] lightly packed dill leaves

¼ cup [3 g] lightly packed parsley leaves

¼ cup [3 g] lightly packed tarragon leaves

¼ cup [3 g] lightly packed mint leaves

6 eggs

2 Tbsp extra-virgin olive oil

Whole nutmeg for garnish

Preheat the oven to 225°F [110°C]. Combine the currants and vinegar in a small bowl and set aside.

In a 10 in [25 cm] nonstick pan or well-seasoned cast-iron skillet, melt the butter over medium heat. Add the shallots and salt and sauté until the shallots begin to soften, about 5 minutes. Stir in the sumac, pepper, and coriander, toasting them in the pan for a minute or two, then add the sauerkraut and keep cooking until the shallots and kraut melt together, just a couple of minutes more. Let cool for a few minutes.

Meanwhile, finely chop the arugula, spinach, cilantro, dill, parsley, tarragon, and mint (a food processor makes this very quick work).

In a large bowl, beat the eggs with the oil, then fold in the greens and herbs, the currants and vinegar, and the shallot and kraut mixture. Scrape the mixture back into the skillet and bake until the center is no longer wobbly, 60 to 80 minutes. Once it has cooled for a few minutes, loosen the edges and slide it onto a plate. Serve warm or at room temperature and use a Microplane to dust with nutmeg just before eating. Leftovers can be refrigerated for up to 3 days and served at room temperature or gently rewarmed.

Fundamental Cooking Methods: Fish Cookery

Whether you have a whole fish, fillets, or steaks, the size, type, and butchering of your fish all play a part in how it stands up to your cooking method of choice. Consider the thickness of the fish and its level of fat before cooking.

BAKED: Baking is one of the safest ways to cook fish, but thicker and oilier fish is ideal because it is less likely to dry out during cooking. I like to use as low an oven temperature as possible, around 175°F [80°C], which allows the fish to cook gently and evenly.

EN PAPILLOTE: Baking *en papillote* (wrapped in parchment) creates a seal that cooks the fish in its own steam and prevents it from drying out, which is why it's an excellent option for more delicate types of seafood. Figure 8 to 10 minutes total per 1 in [2.5 cm] of fillet thickness.

PANFRIED: Searing the fish in a very hot pan with a bit of fat is a good choice for delicate and flaky fish because it quickly creates a crispy crust, which is an excellent contrast to the tender center. Skin-on fillets are lovely cooked this way since the skin crisps up while also protecting the flesh from direct contact with the heat. You can flip the fish briefly to gently cook the top or place the pan in a warm oven for a few moments to finish cooking.

BROILED: This cooking method is good for sturdy fish that can handle the high heat or for small pieces that cook quickly when you're hoping for a little char on the flesh. Broiling is also an ideal cooking method when adding a glaze or marinade to your fish, as the high heat caramelizes the sauce.

GRILLED: It's ideal to set your grill to dual heat zones, one side at medium heat, which sears the skin, one side with low or indirect heat so the fish can finish cooking without a long trip over the flames. Here, you should choose a fish that won't dry out easily—think whole fish or cuts from sturdier, oilier fish—and pay close attention to the heat as you go. A good rule of thumb is 5 to 6 minutes total per 1 in [2.5 cm] of fillet thickness. To prevent sticking, oil the grill grate and/or fish well before cooking and don't flip the fish until its skin releases with little to no resistance.

POACHED: Poaching in broth or oil is excellent for light fish, as it prevents the fish from drying out and helps enhance its delicate flavor (see Oil-Poached Fish, page 133). A thermometer is helpful but not necessary for maintaining steady but low heat; the most important thing is that you monitor the heat visually, adjusting it to prevent it from getting too high. Oil will add its own flavor to the fish, and you'll need a fair bit of it to envelop the fish, so use one you like, such as olive oil, and feel free to add garlic or herbs to perfume it. Leftover oil will carry a bit of the fish's flavor but can be strained, refrigerated, and used for aioli, vinaigrette, or more poaching.

STEAMED: Steaming is a traditional cooking method for many types of shellfish, but it's also a healthy way to cook other types of fish. You can do so a few ways:

IN A STEAMER: Fill a large pot with 1 to 2 in [2.5 to 5 cm] of water or broth; if you'd like, add vegetables or aromatics, such as tea and herbs, which will impart gentle aromas to the fish. Fit a steamer inside the pot, making sure the water isn't high enough to seep into it. Cover and bring to a gentle simmer over medium heat. Lay the fish inside the steamer, cover, and cook for 8 to 10 minutes per 1 in [2.5 cm] of thickness; you'll know it's done when the flesh is opaque and flakes easily. If you used broth, don't discard it! The fish's juices drip down into it and enhance its flavor.

OVER VEGETABLES: If you don't have a steamer—or for a simple, one-pot meal—rig a steamer setup by cooking the fish directly atop vegetables. The main point is to insulate the fish from the bottom of the pot and cook with gentle, even heat. Begin by sweating onions in oil or butter, with whatever spices, and then wilt some greens or sauté any other vegetables you fancy, like tender spring peas, halved cherry tomatoes, or quartered mushrooms. A splash of wine, broth, or kimchi is always welcome. Nestle the fish over the mound of vegetables, cover, and cook over medium-low heat for 8 to 10 minutes per 1 in [2.5 cm] of thickness.

OIL-POACHED FISH

There's something full circle and humble about poaching fish, taking it out of the water and re-submerging it in another liquid. It's a grand dish—a nod to bygone banquets in which fish came out on gold platters. This is a confit of sorts, the word coming from the French word *confire*, meaning "to preserve"; just be sure that your pot is large enough to completely hold the fish. The technique can take a bit of time depending on the size of your fish, but the slow cooking method means the proteins won't seize, yielding a luscious texture, plush in its firmness. Adding aromatics to the oil gently flavors the fish. You're using a lot of oil here, but it can be used for your next batch of poaching, turned into aioli, or used in a dressing.

Makes 4 servings

1 large (2.5 lb [1.2 kg]) whole fish,
4 small (1 lb [455 g]) whole fish, or four
4 to 6 oz [115 to 170 g] fish fillets

Kosher salt

Freshly ground black pepper

4 thick (½ in [12 mm]) slices yellow
or white onion

3 to 5 sprigs fresh herbs,
such as thyme, marjoram, or dill

1½ qt [1.4 L] extra-virgin olive oil,
or more as needed to cover

Pat the fish dry, lightly season it all over with salt and pepper, and allow it to sit at room temperature for about 30 minutes. Preheat the oven to 200°F [95°C].

Line the bottom of a heavy-bottomed lidded pot with the onions and herbs (this will help insulate the fish from direct heat) and clip a candy thermometer to the side of the pot. Set the fish inside with enough oil to cover it completely. Cover with a lid.

Gently warm the oil over medium-low heat until it reaches 145°F [62°C]. Keep an eye on it, adjusting the flame as necessary so it doesn't stray too far from that temperature. Cover the pot, place it in the oven, and immediately turn the oven off so the fish continues to cook slowly and evenly in the residual heat—figure 40 to 60 minutes. Check after 20 minutes. If the temperature has plummeted, turn the oven's heat back to the lowest temperature, checking every 20 minutes or so to make sure the oil isn't too hot.

The fish is done when it registers 135°F [57°C] on an instant-read thermometer, or when the flesh is opaque and flakes easily. As the fish cooks, you may see small beads of white albumen form as the proteins seize; the lower and more gently you cook the fish, the more you'll be able to avoid this, which is why it's worth taking the time to monitor the heat.

CONTINUED

With a fish spatula, gently transfer the fish to a serving platter and serve right away. To reuse the oil, strain it a couple times through a very fine mesh sieve or a coffee filter, making sure to stop straining before you reach the bottom (where any liquid residue settles); refrigerate, covered, for up to 2 weeks. Any leftover fish can be covered in its poaching oil and refrigerated for a few days.

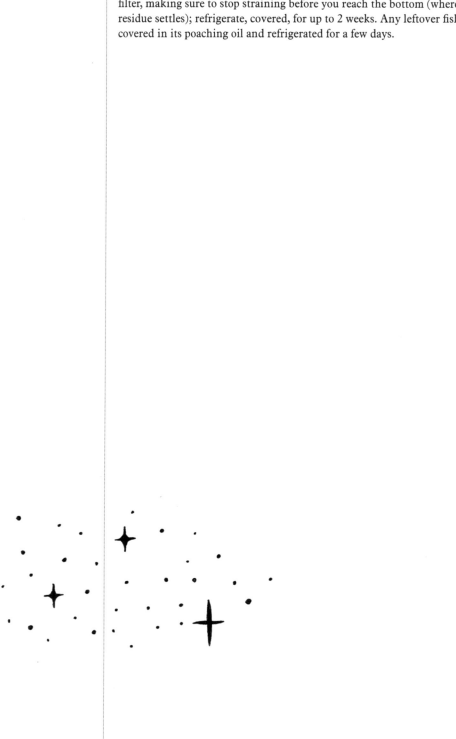

GIFT-WRAPPED FISH FOR EVERY SEASON

En papillote means "cooked in paper." It's a technique I first learned as a young cook in San Francisco. I loved all the little folding, which tested my precision and patience. Done right, it's one of the most satisfying methods. A little meticulousness up front gives way to an effortless, forgiving cooking method for delicate fish. Wrapped tightly, the papillote puffs up like blown glass, the steam swirling as it gently cooks the fish, and only deflates once the package is pierced. Think of this recipe as a template; once you master the origami-like folding, you can play endlessly with what goes inside, so long as there are enough vegetables to serve as a bed for the fish to rest atop inside the parchment.

Makes 4 servings

Mixed vegetables of your choice, enough for the fish to rest on (see Serving Suggestions)

Four 4 to 6 oz [115 to 170 g] fish fillets

Kosher salt

Freshly ground black pepper

Preheat the oven to 325°F [165°C].

Cut four sheets of parchment paper, 13 by 9 in [33 by 23 cm] each. Fold them in half lengthwise, then unfold and lay flat.

Evenly divide the vegetables among the sheets. Arrange them in small mounds, approximately the size of the fillets and abutting the crease in the paper. Set the fish directly on top and season with salt and pepper.

Fold the paper once more so the fish and vegetables are enclosed. Starting in one corner, folding it up to form a long, narrow triangle that seals the corner. Continue this way all around the packet, folding a bit of the previous triangle in each time, so the parcel is sealed. By the time you finish, it should look very much like a crimped piecrust. Tuck the last corner beneath the parcel to secure it.

Arrange the parcels side by side on a rimmed baking sheet and bake for 12 to 18 minutes; figure 8 to 10 minutes per 1 in [2.5 cm] of thickness on the fillets themselves.

To serve, have each guest tear open their own parchment parcel. Eat right away.

SERVING SUGGESTIONS: Since the vegetables and fish cook together, you'll want to choose vegetables that finish in the same time as the fish. Most vegetables are best cooked beforehand—it's necessary for heartier ingredients like potatoes, squash, or turnips, and creates better flavor with others like asparagus or tomatoes. Tender greens like spinach can be left raw, as can fresh herbs and peak-summer corn.

CONTINUED

Seasonal Variations

WINTER

Salmon or black sea bass
with Fermented Squash and
Sesame Purée (page 102) /
chanterelles—leeks—turnips.

SPRING

Scallops or halibut with
pulsed green peas—shaved
radish—baby potatoes/
spinach—peas—asparagus.

AUTUMN

Haddock or black sea bass with
Brussels sprouts—sweet potato—
oil-poached shallots/kale—Smoky
Chimichurri (page 205)—parsnips.

SUMMER

Salmon with charred peppers—
oil-roasted tomatoes—
eggplant purée/grilled corn—
green beans—leeks.

SALT-BAKED FISH

This dish riffs on the salt-baked chicken that is so revered by the Hakka people of China. But because I'm on New England's waterways, I choose to reach for fish instead of poultry. Although a seemingly astonishing amount of salt is used, it seasons lightly and seals in moisture, allowing the fish to gently steam in its own juices. Here I suggest rainbow trout or black sea bass, but any medium-size fish will do. The dipping sauce channels traditional Chinese flavors, but calls upon the sweeter, floral scent of oranges.

Makes 4 servings

---

3 lb [1.4 kg] whole fish, such as rainbow trout or black sea bass, cleaned and gutted

1 large or 2 small oranges

1 cup [12 g] lightly packed cilantro leaves

4 egg whites

One 3 lb [1.4 kg] box kosher salt

Green Onion–Citrus Sauce (page 206)

Preheat the oven to 350°F [180°C]. Line a sheet pan or baking dish with parchment paper. Using a paring knife or kitchen shears, cut the fins off of the fish. Juice 1 of the oranges (you should have about ¼ cup [60 ml]); slice the other and stuff it into the fish's belly along with the cilantro.

In a large bowl, lightly beat the egg whites just until frothy, then add the salt and orange juice. The mix should look and feel moist but not wet, like damp sand.

Using a quarter to a third of the salt mix, make a mound on your prepared baking sheet, about ⅓ in [8 mm] thick and a little bigger than the fish itself. Place the fish on top and cover it completely with the remaining mix, pressing it to ensure it is hermetically sealed.

Bake the fish for 30 minutes, until the salt crust is hardened and a nice golden brown. To check for doneness, punch the needle of a meat thermometer through the crust and into the fish, making sure you keep it shallow enough to not hit bone. The thermometer should read 130°F to 135°F [54°C to 57°C]. If it's not quite ready, continue to bake in 5-minute increments.

One nice way to showcase this technique is to present the whole fish in its crust to your guests.

To serve, use a sharp knife to cut around the circumference of the fish and remove the top crust in one piece. (Or you can do as I do and pound it gently to shatter the crust, taking care not to smash the fish itself.) Remove and discard the skin from the top of the fish and, using a fish spatula, carefully transfer the top fillet to a platter. Flip the fish over and repeat on the other side. Serve right away with the sauce spooned over the top.

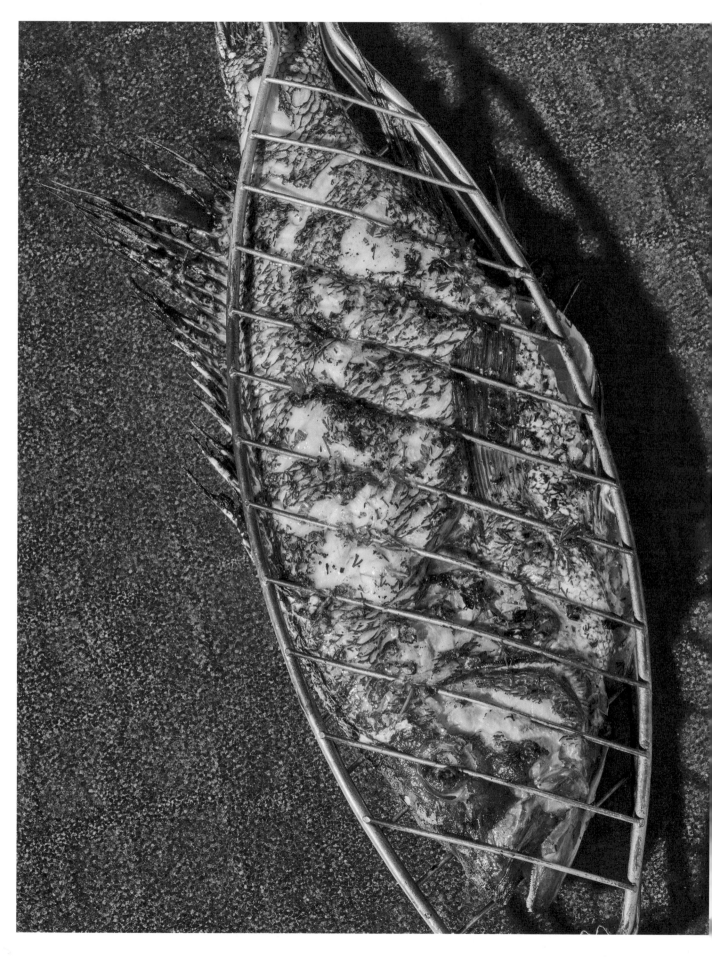

GRILLED WHOLE FISH WITH HERBS AND SPICES

Probably one of the quickest and easiest methods for cooking fish, grilling imparts a hearty, smoky flavor and keeps your kitchen free of fishy aroma. When grilling, I like to rub my fish with an herb oil to help combat natural carcinogenic by-products of high-heat fire cooking. The antioxidants in herbs and spices help protect your food from oxidative damage, which makes fats, in particular, inflammatory. Thwarting the damage with a dousing of herbs is an easy and flavorful remedy for food on the grill.

Makes 4 servings

---

2 cups [24 g] lightly packed soft herb leaves, such as parsley, cilantro, tarragon, mint, basil, or a combination

1 cup [240 ml] grapeseed oil

6 to 8 garlic cloves

Kosher salt (¾ tsp per 1 lb [455] of fish)

Freshly ground black pepper (¼ tsp per 1 lb [455 g] of fish)

1 whole large fish (4 to 5 lb [1.8 to 2.3 kg]) or 2 smaller fish (about 2 lb [908 g] each), cleaned, gutted, and scaled

1 lemon, sliced

Use a blender or food processor to pulse the herbs, oil, garlic, salt, and pepper until the herbs are finely chopped but the sauce is not totally homogenous, or finely chop by hand.

Set the fish in a dish large enough that it lies flat. Rub the marinade all over, stuff the cavity with the lemon slices, and pour any excess marinade evenly over the top of the fish. Cover and refrigerate for at least 1 hour, preferably overnight.

Before you're ready to cook the fish, bring it to room temperature for about 30 minutes while you get the grill ready. Clean and oil the grill grate well to prevent sticking. Heat the grill to medium in one part and a cooler temperature in another; if using charcoal, you can rake the coals to one side after they're ready, leaving a few on the other side for low-heat cooking. When the grill is hot, remove the fish from the marinade, shaking off any excess, and place it on the grill at a 45-degree angle to the grates with the back fin toward the warmer area, as it can handle more heat than the belly. (Alternatively, you can cook the fish in a grill basket to assist with flipping.) Allow the fish to cook without poking, prodding, or trying to move it for at least 5 minutes. Use a fish spatula to begin to carefully lift the belly area—it's ready to flip when it releases cleanly from the grates, so if it's still sticking, let it cook a bit longer. If you'd like to create a crosshatch pattern, rotate it 45 degrees and cook for a minute or two before flipping.

In order to gracefully flip the fish over, use a second spatula to guide the fish, raw-side down, with one spatula at the dorsal fin and one at the belly. Cook for at least 5 minutes on the second side. As soon as the second side releases, use a small knife to check for doneness at the thickest part; it should yield easily. If it's not quite there, move it to the cooler side of the grill and allow it to finish with ambient heat. When the fish is cooked all the way through, use both spatulas to carefully transfer it onto a platter. Serve warm.

FISH STEW WITH WINTER SQUASH AND GREENS

One of the most beloved dishes at Bar Tartine was an emerald fish stew brimming with greens, Hatch chiles, and gently poached fish. This riff is a collision between bouillabaisse and a Lebanese red lentil stew. The broth, moored by fish stock, fish sauce, and red lentils, is elegant without surrendering body, while the fish roulade adds a bit of finesse to the final dish. Take note of the technique, as it's a lovely and deceivingly simple way to elevate any fish dish.

Makes 4 servings

Fish Stew

1 small winter squash, preferably kabocha (about 1½ lb [680 g])

6 Tbsp [90 ml] extra-virgin olive oil

8 oz [230 g] stemmed shiitake mushrooms

1 yellow onion, thinly sliced

1 fennel bulb, thinly sliced

6 garlic cloves, thinly sliced

1 Tbsp kosher salt, plus more as needed

1 bunch lacinato kale, stemmed and chopped

2 Tbsp Anise Elixir (page 272) or anise-flavored liqueur

¼ tsp freshly ground black pepper, plus more as needed

Garlic Broth (recipe follows)

Four 4 oz [115 g] whitefish fillets, such as flounder or bass

½ cup [6 g] lightly packed parsley leaves, chopped, plus more for garnish

½ cup [6 g] lightly packed dill leaves, chopped, plus more for garnish

1 Tbsp fennel pollen or ground fennel seed

Smoked Paprika Oil (page 194)

Scallions for garnish

Fresh lemons for garnish

TO MAKE THE STEW: Preheat the oven to 350°F [180°C].

Peel the squash if necessary (there's no need if you're cooking kabocha or delicata, but butternut, for example, should be peeled). Halve, trim, and remove the seeds, then cut into roughly ½ in [1.25 cm] pieces. Toss to coat with 2 Tbsp of the oil, spread in a single layer in an ovenproof skillet or baking sheet, salt, and bake for 10 minutes. Meanwhile, halve or quarter any large shiitakes. After the squash has baked for 10 minutes, add the mushrooms and bake for another 10 minutes or so, until the squash is soft but not falling apart. Decrease the heat to 200°F [95°C], cover the pan, and keep it warm inside; the vegetables can be prepared and refrigerated up to 3 days ahead of time, then gently reheated, covered, in a 200°F [95°C] oven.

Meanwhile, in a wide-bottomed pot or a large skillet with tall sides, warm the remaining ¼ cup [60 ml] of oil over medium heat. Add the onion, fennel, garlic, and salt, and sauté until translucent and tender. Lower the heat to medium-low and add the kale and anise spirit (do this carefully to keep the alcohol from flaming up). Cover and cook until the kale is wilted and tender, 10 to 15 minutes. Stir in the pepper. Like the squash, this can be kept warm in a low oven if using immediately or made ahead and gently reheated the same way.

To make the fish roulades, fit a steamer inside the pot with the garlic broth, making sure the broth doesn't come high enough to seep inside (if need be, keep some of it warm in a separate pot). Cover and bring to a gentle simmer over medium heat.

Cut the fillets along the seam that runs down the middle so they break down into roughly 2 in [5 cm] wide strips. Scatter the parsley, dill, and fennel down the length of each strip and season lightly with salt and pepper. Roll each one like a spiral and secure with a piece of kitchen twine or a toothpick. Steam the fish, covered, until it's firm and cooked through, 6 to 10 minutes.

To serve, divide the warm vegetables among individual serving bowls and add two roulades to each. Ladle the broth into the bowls and garnish with the parsley, dill, pepper, paprika oil, scallions, and a squeeze of fresh lemon. Serve right away.

CONTINUED

Garlic Broth

1 lb [455 g] fish bones or 1 gal [3.8 L] seafood stock

4 garlic heads

2 yellow onions, quartered

1 fennel bulb, quartered

½ bay leaf

2 Tbsp tightly packed bonito flakes

½ cup [100 g] red lentils

½ cup [120 ml] white wine

½ tsp ground cumin

¼ tsp saffron threads

1 Tbsp fish sauce

TO MAKE THE BROTH: Add the fish bones to a stockpot and cover with 1 gal [3.8 L] of water, or, alternatively, add all the stock to the pot. Halve the garlic heads along their equator and add, along with the onion, fennel, and bay leaf. Bring to a simmer over high heat, then decrease the heat to medium and continue to cook until it's reduced by half, about 1 hour. Remove from the heat and add the bonito flakes while the stock is still steaming hot; allow to steep for 5 minutes.

Strain the broth, reserving two heads of garlic and discarding all the other solids. Add the broth and reserved garlic back to the pot with the lentils, wine, and cumin. Bring to a simmer over medium heat and cook until the lentils are tender, 6 to 10 minutes. Remove from the heat, crush the saffron with your fingers, and stir it into the broth, letting it bloom for 5 to 10 minutes.

Set a fine-mesh sieve over a large bowl. Working in batches, purée and strain the stock; to keep it smooth, don't press it too hard through the sieve. Add the fish sauce. Cover and keep warm over low heat until serving or refrigerate in an airtight container for up to 3 days.

SMOKED FISH AND POTATO HAND PIES

There's something deeply satisfying about a spread of whipped salt cod that can be slathered on virtually anything. Often referred to as brandade, this dish has origins all over the Mediterranean and into England. Salt cod is just that, salted fish, an Old World preservation technique for a perishable and (what was at the time) seasonal ingredient. I layer in extra flavor with smoked fish, spices, and herbs and then fold everything into little hand pies akin to Cornish fish pies, which became a New England staple in the late eighteenth century. These are smoky and creamy, fishy and salty, and can make a cold winter day feel sun-drenched. The filling also makes a lovely dip on its own: Spread it on Seeded Herb Crackers (page 232), Black Seeded Bread (page 242), Silver Dollar Corn Cakes (page 235), or any flatbread.

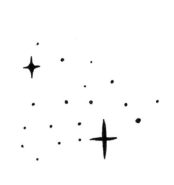

Makes 8 to 10 hand pies

Piecrust

¾ cup [170 g] cold unsalted butter

1¼ cups [175 g] rice flour

¼ cup plus 2 Tbsp [55 g] corn flour

⅔ cup [80 g] tapioca starch

2 tsp flaxseeds, finely ground

2 tsp kosher salt

1 tsp ground cayenne pepper

½ tsp xanthan gum

1 egg yolk

¾ cup [180 ml] ice-cold water

TO MAKE THE PIECRUST: Cut the butter into small cubes and refrigerate or briefly freeze to chill through.

Combine the rice flour, corn flour, tapioca, flaxseeds, salt, pepper, and xanthan gum in the bowl of a food processor or large mixing bowl. Scatter the butter evenly over the mix and drop in the egg yolk; pulse or work by hand until the pieces of butter range from lentil size to a little smaller than pea size. Pour in the water and mix again until just incorporated; the dough should be thick and well moistened, like a stiff cookie dough.

Shape the dough into a disk and wrap it tightly in plastic wrap. Refrigerate until firm and cool to the touch, at least 2 hours and preferably overnight.

CONTINUED

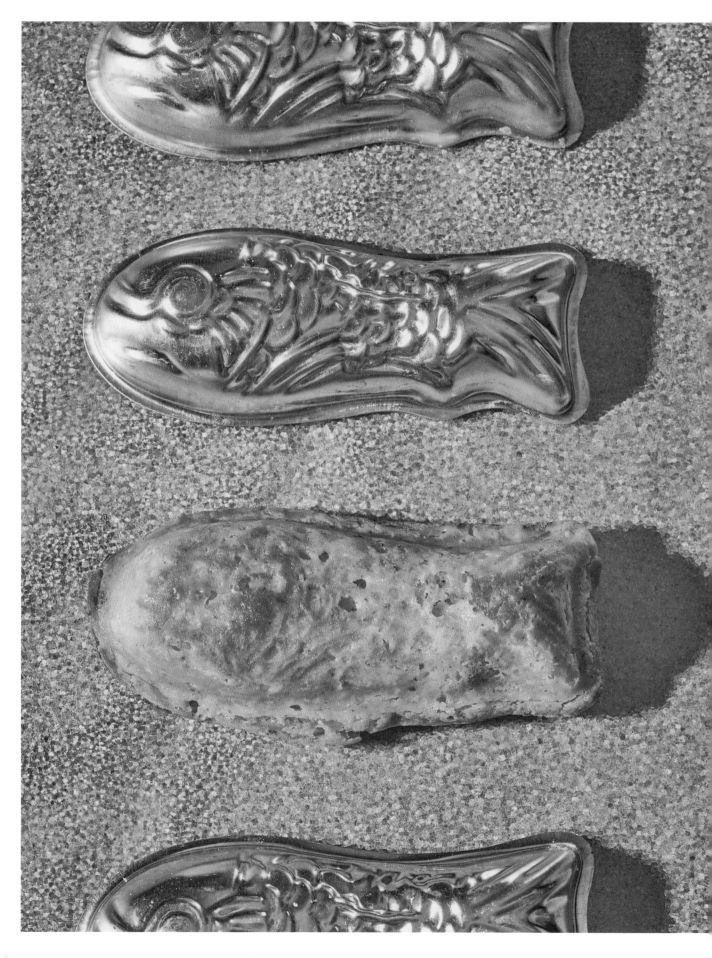

TO MAKE THE FILLING: To desalt the salt cod, rinse it well, then submerge it with plenty of water and cover overnight, preferably for 1 to 2 days, changing the water a few times throughout.

Place the rinsed salt cod in a small saucepan and cover with the milk. Bring to a gentle simmer over medium heat, then decrease the heat to medium-low and continue cooking until the fish flakes easily, 10 to 15 minutes for fresh fish and 20 to 25 minutes for salt cod. Remove the fish and reserve 3 Tbsp of the milk.

Meanwhile, cut the potatoes into 2 to 3 in [5 to 7.5 cm] chunks and add to a large saucepan full of well-salted water. Bring to a boil over high heat, then decrease the heat to medium and continue to cook until the potatoes are super tender, 20 to 30 minutes. Drain, return the potatoes to the pan, and cook over medium heat for 30 seconds or so, just to evaporate any excess moisture.

Turn the heat to low and add the reserved milk, along with the salt, garlic, celery seeds, paprika, black pepper, and cayenne. Use a fork to mash until smooth, then set aside to cool until the potatoes are warm but no longer hot.

Remove the pin bones from the cooked fish and the smoked whitefish and flake them both into a large bowl. Fold in the mashed potatoes, herbs, one of the eggs, and the lemon zest. Refrigerate in an airtight container for at least 2 hours or overnight.

TO ASSEMBLE THE HAND PIES: Line two baking sheets with parchment paper. Lightly flour a work surface and a rolling pin; beat the remaining egg with 1 Tbsp of water to make an egg wash.

Portion the dough into 1¾ to 2 oz [50 to 55 g] pieces and roll each piece into a disk about ⅛ in [4 mm] thick, dusting with more flour as needed to prevent sticking. Brush the egg wash along the border and drop 2 to 3 Tbsp of the filling in the center. (When in doubt, better to err on the side of less filling so it doesn't seep while baking.) Fold the dough over it to make a half-moon, gently press the edges to seal, and crimp with the tines of a fork. Use the tip of your knife to prick a hole in the top so steam can escape.

Repeat with the remaining dough and filling; as you finish, move the pies to the prepared baked sheets, leaving plenty of space between them. Refrigerate for about 1 hour or freeze for 10 to 20 minutes, until the dough is firm, which will help keep the butter from leaching out of the dough during baking.

Preheat the oven to 425°F [220°C]. Brush more egg wash all over the tops of the crusts and finish with a pinch of the sea salt. Bake, rotating the sheets after 10 minutes, until the crusts are crisp and deeply golden, 20 to 30 minutes. Serve warm; leftovers can be refrigerated in an airtight container for 3 days and gently reheated in a 200°F [93°C] oven.

KITCHEN NOTE:

This dough is fragile, so be patient and gentle. It will come together, but any store-bought dough, gluten free or otherwise, will also work brilliantly. I've given instructions for baking them in the half-moon shape traditional to Cornwall, but on the off chance you have fish-shaped molds like mine at your fingertips, you can press the crust into them instead for a bit of fun.

Filling

About ½ lb [230 g] salt cod or whitefish fillets, such as haddock, bass, or cod

2 cups [480 ml] whole milk

8 oz [225 g] Yukon gold potatoes, peeled

2 tsp kosher salt, plus more as needed

2 garlic cloves, grated

1 tsp celery seeds

¼ tsp sweet paprika

¼ tsp freshly ground black pepper

¼ tsp ground cayenne pepper

4 oz [115 g] smoked whitefish

½ cup [6 g] lightly packed herb leaves, such as dill, parsley, tarragon, or a combination, chopped

1 Tbsp lightly packed thyme leaves, chopped

2 eggs

Zest of 1 lemon

Flaky sea salt

Fundamental Cooking Methods: Meat Cookery

Whether you have a large cut of meat, a braising cut, or thin steaks, the size, type, and butchering of your meat all play a part in how it stands up to your cooking method of choice. Consider the thickness of the meat and its level of fat before cooking.

POACHED: Poaching chicken is quite simple: Submerge a whole chicken or chicken pieces in water or stock and simmer on the stovetop until the chicken is cooked through. The low temperature and moist-heat cooking method is gentle and prevents it from cooking too quickly, making it juicy and tender; plus, you're left with a lovely, full-bodied stock. The chicken is done when it is opaque through the middle and an instant-read thermometer in the thickest part of the meat registers 160°F [70°C].

ROASTED: Roasting is a cooking method that uses hot air from an open flame, oven, or other heat source to engulf the food in order to cook it evenly on all sides. Before the invention and widespread use of ovens, nearly all food was cooked over open flames in a hearth, making this one of the oldest known forms of cooking. Today, it's not solely a way of rendering meat edible; it's also a way to enhance flavor through caramelization and Maillard browning on the surface of the food. The goal in roasting is to retain as much moisture as possible in the process.

CONFIT: Confiting is the act of cooking meat submerged in fat. It was first used as a preservation technique: For meat in particular, this required the addition of salt. After being salted and confited, then sealed and stored in a cool, dark place, the meat could last for several months or even years.

MINCED/GROUND: Ground meat, called minced meat or mincemeat outside of North America, is a way of chopping meat either with a grinder or finely by hand. Grinding meat allows for inclusions to be made and flavorings to be combined evenly. It also helps render tough cuts more tender and usable for short-cooked preparations versus long braises.

GRILLED: Grilling means many things in many places, but for our purposes, we use the term to refer to cooking meat over dry, direct heat, most commonly fire. Grilling chars meat, creating a Maillard reaction that enhances the flavor of the finished product. Studies have shown that cooking meat at high temperatures can lead to the formation of carcinogens, but marinating meat with herbs may reduce the formation of these compounds (see page 197). Grilling is often presented as a healthy alternative to cooking with oils, although the fat and juices lost by grilling at too high heat can contribute to drier food. One can use direct or indirect heat from a grill to cook quickly or slowly, depending on the final desired outcome.

BRAISED: Braising meat is often a two-step process: It starts with searing (dry heat), with wet heat to follow, in the form of broth that slowly cooks the meat until it's fall-off-the-bone tender. Braising relies on heat, time, and moisture to break down the tough connective tissue that binds the muscle fibers together, making it an ideal way to cook tougher, more affordable cuts.

CHICKEN PÂTÉ WITH CREAMY SHALLOT-WATERCRESS SAUCE

I like to eat pâté in nearly any permutation: on its own, slipped inside a sandwich, or seared until golden. It's something that will last for days in your fridge, making it ideal to make ahead for hosting, though it never sticks around long enough for that at my house. In my experience, making pâté often feels to the home cook like an untouchable feat of culinary alchemy, but in truth, it's actually quite simple. Follow these steps, cook the chicken gently, and you're sure to have great success. For the sauce, I created a French fricassee doppelgänger of sorts. It's not traditional, but it has that same silkiness. It's an amped-up, creamy, onion gravy that feels more luxurious than a regular pan sauce, perfect for any meat or poultry dish. For a bit of an extra punch, add some smoked cheese or charred onions to the sauce.

Makes 4 to 6 servings

Chicken Pâté

1 Tbsp plus 2 tsp kosher salt, plus more for seasoning

1 Tbsp buckwheat groats

1 shallot

1 small carrot (about 1 oz [30 g])

1 celery stalk

3 button mushrooms

1 Tbsp unsalted butter or schmaltz

⅛ tsp freshly ground black pepper

⅛ tsp coriander seeds, ground

⅛ tsp fennel seeds, ground

1½ Tbsp sherry or sweet wine

1 Tbsp lightly packed parsley leaves, chopped

1 Tbsp lightly packed tarragon leaves, chopped

Zest of 1 lemon

7 oz [200 g] boneless chicken thighs (about 1 large) or ground chicken

1 oz [30 g] chicken liver

TO MAKE THE PÂTÉ: Fill a small saucepan with about 1 qt [960 ml] of water and 1 Tbsp of the salt; bring to a boil over high heat. Add the buckwheat and cook until tender but not mushy, 6 to 8 minutes. Drain.

Dice the shallot, carrot, celery, and mushrooms into very small (about ⅛ in [4 mm]) pieces. In a medium skillet over medium-low heat, melt the butter, then add the diced vegetables and the remaining 2 tsp salt and cook, stirring occasionally, until the vegetables are tender and beginning to brown, 15 minutes or so. Stir in the pepper, coriander, fennel, and buckwheat and toast for a minute or two, until fragrant; deglaze the pan with the sherry and allow it to reduce slightly. Remove from the heat and fold in the parsley, tarragon, and lemon zest, then transfer to an airtight container and refrigerate until completely chilled through.

Cut the chicken thighs into roughly 2 in [5 cm] pieces and spread them on a plate along with the chicken liver. (If you're using store-bought ground chicken, just chill the liver.) Refrigerate until very cold or freeze for about 15 minutes, until firm but not completely hard.

Fit a meat grinder with the medium attachment and grind the chicken and liver, or, if you're using store-bought ground chicken, mince the liver and combine it with the ground meat. Cover and refrigerate again for at least 15 minutes.

When you're ready to make the pâté, preheat your oven to 325°F [165°C]. Combine the ground chicken and cooked vegetables in a large bowl or in the bowl of a stand mixer. Using the stand mixer's paddle attachment or stirring vigorously with a wooden spoon, whip for 5 to 6 minutes, until the mixture is well incorporated and a little bit tacky.

CONTINUED

Cut a piece of parchment paper so it lines a small loaf pan (5½ by 3 in [14 by 7.5 cm]) or deep baking dish with several inches of overhang on all sides; this will help you compact the pâté before cooking and makes it easier to take it out of the pan when it's done.

Scrape the pâté into the pan, pressing it down into the corners. Lift the pan just a couple of inches off the counter and let it drop to expel any air bubbles; do this a couple of times. Fold the parchment over the top of the pâté like a gift, pressing the surface smooth and even, then wrap the pan tightly in foil.

Set the dish in a deeper pan and pour in enough hot tap water to come halfway up the sides. Bake until it feels very firm and registers 155°F to 160°F [68°C to 70°C] on an instant-read thermometer; check after 45 minutes and, if the temperature is not there yet, continue baking in 5-minute increments.

Allow the pâté to cool in the pan for 5 to 10 minutes before removing it, then cover or rewrap with foil. Refrigerate for at least 4 hours or until completely chilled before serving. The pâté can be made up to 3 days in advance.

Shallot-Watercress Sauce

4 tsp kosher salt, plus more as needed

¼ cup [45 g] buckwheat groats

3 Tbsp unsalted butter

1 lb [455 g] shallots, thinly sliced

1 celery stalk, thinly sliced

2 garlic cloves, minced

½ tsp coriander seeds, toasted and ground

¼ tsp freshly ground black pepper, plus more for serving

½ cup plus ⅔ cup [280 ml] Kombu Dashi (page 207) or vegetable stock

1 egg

¼ cup [60 g] drained ricotta or farmer's cheese

2 tsp sherry vinegar

8 oz [230 g] watercress or arugula, plus more for serving

Olive oil for serving

TO MAKE THE SAUCE: Fill a medium saucepan with lightly salted water and bring to a boil over high heat. Cook the buckwheat for 7 to 8 minutes, until it's tender but still has a slight bite; drain.

Meanwhile, in a medium pan, melt the butter over medium-low heat. Sauté the shallots, celery, garlic, and 2½ tsp of the salt until the shallots are silky with very little color, 10 to 15 minutes. Stir in the coriander and pepper and cook for another minute or two, until the spices are fragrant. Decrease the heat as low as it will go.

Warm ½ cup [120 ml] of the Kombu Dashi until steam rises from the surface (use a small saucepan or, if you don't have one small enough, heat it in a skillet and move it into a cup for easy pouring). Whisk the egg in a heatproof bowl and, whisking all the while, stream in the hot Kombu Dashi to temper the egg.

Pour this mixture into the pan with the cooked vegetables and cook over low heat, stirring constantly, for just a few minutes, until it thickens slightly. (Try not to let the egg scramble, but don't worry if you see tiny curds.) Remove from the heat and fold in the ricotta, vinegar, and cooked buckwheat. Cool for 5 to 10 minutes before puréeing in a blender until completely smooth. Cool to room temperature and serve right away or refrigerate in an airtight container for up to 3 days.

On the day you're serving the pâté, fill a large pot with lightly salted water and bring it to a rolling boil; separately, make an ice bath in a large bowl. Boil the watercress for just 15 seconds, until it becomes a darker green, then remove it with tongs or a slotted spoon and immediately plunge it into the ice bath to stop the cooking. Gather it in a clean dish towel and wring out as much excess water as you can. Finely chop the watercress, then transfer to a blender with the remaining ⅔ cup [160 ml] of the Kombu Dashi and the remaining 1½ tsp salt; purée until very smooth.

To serve, swirl the two sauces together on individual plates or on a large serving plate but not so much that they are completely uniform. Cut the chilled pâté into ¼ to ½ in [6 to 12 mm] slices and arrange them, overlapping, atop the sauce. Garnish with watercress, a splash of olive oil, and pepper.

CHICKEN WINGS IN GARLIC BUTTER

When I moved to New England, I was struck by the heirloom ingredients grown on the surrounding farms and orchards. California taught me about an unparalleled bounty, but here there is a deep sense of provenance. New England has a long history raising heritage chickens and I've been fortunate enough to try many. Some are gangly, gamey, and small; others are large, succulent, and gentler in flavor. But no matter the breed, one of my favorite parts is the chicken wing for the skin-to-meat ratio.

As I slinked into the rhythms of this region, I soon realized the extent of the French influence on the area, as French Canada is not far from here. Escargots à la Bourguignonne is a timeless garlic- and herb-doused dish, but here, chicken wings take the place of snails. I urge you to eat these wings straight from the bowl with butter cascading down your hands as part of the fun. And don't stop with the garlic sauce; some of my favorite alternatives are Harissa Vinaigrette (page 207) with seeds or Smoky Chimichurri (page 205).

Makes 4 to 6 servings

In a large bowl, whisk together the egg whites, baking soda, salt, black pepper, and cayenne, then add the lemon juice—you'll see it fizz up a bit as it interacts with the baking soda. Toss the wings in it to evenly coat, then spread in a single layer on a baking sheet or plates and refrigerate, uncovered, for at least 8 hours and preferably overnight.

Preheat the oven to 225°F [110°C]. Allow the wings to come to room temperature for 30 minutes before baking, then arrange them atop a wire rack on a baking sheet (if you don't have one, lightly grease the sheet with grapeseed oil before laying them directly on it). Cover loosely with foil and bake for 30 minutes.

Remove the foil and increase the temperature to 425°F [220°C]. Continue to bake for 15 to 25 minutes, or until the wings register 155°F to 160°F [68°C to 70°C] on an instant-read thermometer. Remove from the oven and heat the broiler.

Use a brush or spoon to lightly glaze the tops of the wings with a bit of the garlic butter. Place under the broiler for 3 to 5 minutes to help the skin crisp up and become a deeper golden shade.

Transfer the wings to a bowl and toss to coat with the remaining butter and the sesame seeds; season with flaky salt and pepper. Serve right away.

3 egg whites

1 Tbsp baking soda

1 Tbsp kosher salt

1 tsp freshly ground black pepper, plus more for serving

½ tsp ground cayenne pepper

2 tsp fresh lemon juice or apple cider vinegar

4 lb [1.8 kg] chicken wings

Garlic Butter (page 204)

¼ cup [35 g] black sesame seeds, toasted

2 Tbsp white sesame seeds, toasted

Flaky salt

BRINED WHOLE CHICKEN

During my student years I devoured Judy Rodgers's *The Zuni Cafe Cookbook*, its instructions guiding me through the movements but more importantly bestowing a sense of curiosity and confidence within me. While I'm on a never-ending quest to find the perfect roast chicken, this one is a welcome addition to any repertoire. Reach for pickle brine—a mix of multiple types will do just fine if you're low on quantity—to help tenderize and flavor the meat. Crank up the oven so that it's blistering hot, just like Judy's wood-fired pizza oven, and place the chicken in the pan, taking caution of the juice and fat that will bounce like sparklers. Once done, this chicken is beautifully tender with just a trace of flavor from the pickle jar.

Makes 4 to 6 servings

3½ to 4½ lb [1.6 to 2 kg] whole chicken

1 qt [960 ml] cold water, plus more as needed

1 cup [12 g] lightly packed dill leaves

½ yellow onion, quartered

2 garlic cloves

2 Tbsp kosher salt, plus more as needed

1 qt [960 ml] pickle brine from lacto-fermented vegetables (page 180) or store-bought salt-brined pickles

1 Tbsp unsalted butter

4 thyme or tarragon sprigs

Place the chicken in a container that will hold it snugly, such as a large bowl or pot.

In a blender, combine the water with the dill, onion, garlic, and salt. Combine the purée with the pickle brine and pour it over the chicken. If the chicken isn't completely submerged, add more salt brine, dissolving 1 Tbsp of salt per 1 pt [480 ml] of water. Cover and refrigerate for at least 8 hours and preferably for a full day.

Remove the chicken from the brine. Wipe it dry and refrigerate, uncovered, for at least 1 hour and preferably for another full day. The longer you let it dry, the crispier the skin will get as it cooks.

When you're ready to roast the chicken, wipe it dry once more and allow it to come to room temperature for about 30 minutes. Set an ovenproof pan or cast-iron skillet in the oven and preheat to 475°F [240°C].

Loosen the skin around the chicken breasts by gently easing your fingers underneath the flap by the collarbone, coaxing the skin gently away from the flesh to make a small pocket. Slice the butter and slip it under the skin along with the sprigs of thyme. Pull the oven rack partly out of the oven and place the chicken very carefully in the pan, breast-side up. Roast for 20 minutes, then reduce the heat to 250°F [120°C] and cook for another 25 to 30 minutes (figure around 10 minutes per 1 lb [455 g]), until the thigh registers 155°F to 160°F [68°C to 70°C] on an instant-read thermometer. Use a large spoon to baste the chicken with its fat every 10 minutes or so.

Carefully lift the chicken from the pan, allowing its juices to fall into the drippings, and let it rest for 10 minutes. Set the hot pan over medium heat and deglaze with a splash of water. Bring everything to a simmer and let it reduce slightly.

Cut the chicken into pieces; pour the pan sauce on top. Serve warm or at room temperature. Leftovers can be refrigerated in an airtight container for up to 3 days.

CHICKEN POTPIE WITH CREAMED FENNEL AND CAULIFLOWER

Chicken potpie is part of the Burns lexicon. Mom would always make them as individual parcels that smelled of butter and cream and filled the house with a warmth no matter the temperature outside. I didn't always love them growing up; I wasn't much of a piecrust person, so it wasn't until a bit later in life that I could fully appreciate their delicacy. My version is stippled with herbs, a nod to the herb gardens English settlers brought to this area, and calls on vegetables in lieu of dairy for that signature richness. Sautéed in butter and then simmered in broth, cauliflower and fennel become a lush, binding base while spices, herbs, and zest lend a little pep to all those rich, round notes.

Makes 6 individual pies or 1 large pie

Piecrust

1 cup plus 2 Tbsp [270 g] cold unsalted butter

1¾ cups [245 g] rice flour

⅔ cup [90 g] corn flour

1 cup [120 g] tapioca starch

1 Tbsp flaxseeds, finely ground

1 Tbsp kosher salt

1½ tsp ground cayenne pepper

¾ tsp xanthan gum

2 egg yolks

3 Tbsp lightly packed parsley leaves, chopped

1 cup [240 ml] ice-cold water

TO MAKE THE PIECRUST: Cut the butter into small cubes and refrigerate or briefly freeze to chill through.

Combine the rice flour, corn flour, tapioca, flaxseeds, salt, cayenne, and xanthan gum in the bowl of a food processor. Scatter the butter evenly over the mix and drop in the egg yolks and parsley; pulse until the pieces of butter range from lentil size to a little smaller than pea size. Pour in the water and pulse again until just incorporated; the dough should be thick and well moistened, like a stiff cookie dough.

Set aside one-third of the dough for the top crust. Shape it into a small disk and wrap it tightly in plastic; do the same with the remaining dough. Refrigerate until firm and cool to the touch, at least 2 hours and preferably overnight.

CONTINUED

Filling

½ head cauliflower (12 oz to 1 lb [340 to 455 g])

1 large carrot

2 celery stalks

2 Tbsp extra-virgin olive oil

4 tsp kosher salt, plus more for seasoning

12 oz [340 g] bone-in, skin-on chicken thighs (about 2)

½ tsp freshly ground black pepper, plus more for seasoning

2 Tbsp unsalted butter

1 small yellow onion, thinly sliced

½ fennel bulb, thinly sliced

2 garlic cloves, minced

½ tsp fennel pollen or ground fennel

½ tsp coriander seeds, ground

¼ tsp ground cayenne pepper

1 Tbsp rice flour, plus more for baking

½ cup [120 ml] chicken stock

3 scallions, thinly sliced

2 Tbsp lightly packed parsley leaves, chopped

2 Tbsp lightly packed dill leaves, chopped

1½ Tbsp minced chives

1½ tsp lightly packed thyme leaves, chopped

Zest of 1 lemon

1 egg

TO MAKE THE FILLING: Preheat the oven to 375°F [190°C]. Chop the cauliflower into small florets; add half to a large bowl and reserve the rest for later. Dice the carrot and celery into about ½ in [12 mm] pieces and toss them into the bowl; toss to coat with 1 Tbsp of the oil and 2 tsp of the salt.

Spread the vegetables in a square baking dish or ovenproof pan. Season the chicken thighs with a bit of salt and pepper and set then atop the vegetables, skin-side up. Bake until the chicken is cooked through (it should register 155°F to 160°F [68°C to 70°C] on an instant-read thermometer), 40 to 50 minutes.

Meanwhile, warm the butter and the remaining 1 Tbsp of oil over medium heat in a large skillet or saucepan. When the butter stops foaming, stir in the remaining cauliflower along with the onion, fennel, and the remaining 2 tsp of salt. Cook, stirring regularly, until the vegetables are soft and translucent, 8 to 10 minutes. Add the garlic, fennel pollen, coriander, black pepper, and cayenne and toast for a minute, or until fragrant, then stir in the rice flour until incorporated.

Pour the stock into the pan, bring to a gentle simmer, and reduce the heat to medium-low. Continue to cook until the vegetables are very soft and velvety, 15 to 20 minutes. Allow to cool for about 5 minutes before transferring to a blender; purée until very smooth, then fold in the scallions, parsley, dill, chives, thyme, and lemon zest.

Pull the chicken from the bones and roughly chop or shred by hand. Drain any excess liquid from the roasted vegetables. Fold the chicken and vegetables into the cauliflower purée and set aside at room temperature or refrigerate in an airtight container for up to 3 days.

TO MAKE THE PIES: Allow the filling to come to room temperature if you made it in advance. Flour a counter and rolling pin. Divide the larger disk of dough into six equal pieces (about 3½ oz [100 g] each) and, working with one at a time, lightly flour the top and roll into a circle ¼ in [6 mm] thick, flouring more as needed to prevent sticking.

Gently transfer each crust to a 5 in [12 cm] pie pan and, with a fork, prick holes over the bottom of the crust. Refrigerate or freeze for 15 to 30 minutes, until chilled through.

Preheat the oven to 425°F [220°C]. Press a square of parchment paper against the surface of each crust and fill with pie weights or a single layer of dried beans. Arrange the pies on a baking sheet and bake for 15 to 20 minutes, until the edges are golden and the crust is set. Carefully remove the weights and parchment and bake for another 3 to 5 minutes to let the bottom dry out a bit. Remove the crusts from the oven to cool completely and decrease the temperature to 400°F [200°C].

Add about ½ cup [140 g] of the filling to each pie. Divide the remaining disk of dough into six equal pieces (1¾ to 2 oz [50 to 60 g] each); once again, flour your surface, rolling pin, and dough, and roll each piece into a 6 in [15 cm] circle. Place atop the pies and use the tines of a fork to crimp the edges; this will help them meld to the bottom crust. Refrigerate or freeze for 10 to 15 minutes to cool through one last time to keep the butter from quickly melting in the oven.

Lightly beat the egg with 1 Tbsp of water and brush it over the tops of the crust. Use the tip of your knife to cut 4 small slits in the crust so steam can escape. Set the pies on a baking sheet and bake until the crust is nicely golden, 25 to 30 minutes. Serve warm or at room temperature.

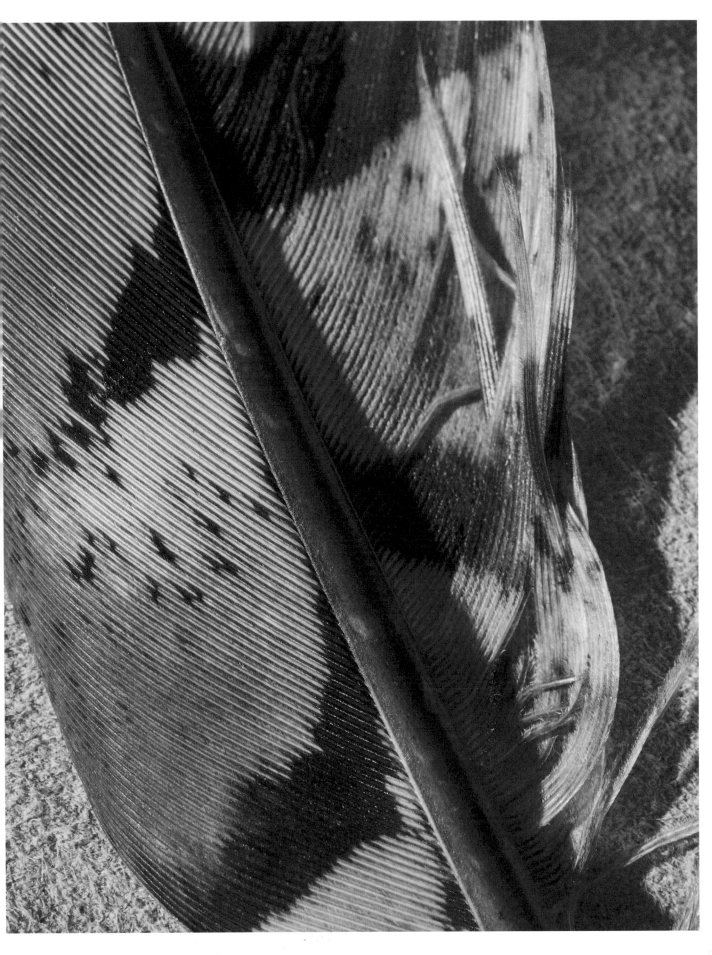

GRIBENES TERRINE

Crispy chicken skin is a textural wonderland. When I was a child, my mother would make chopped liver with an old-timey hand-cranked grinder that clamped onto the side of the countertop. Once secure, she'd reach for the sauté pan to crisp up gribenes (chicken skin) until fat pooled and the skins turned crackly. She'd cool them far from my reach, knowing that otherwise I would eat them all up. This is an ode to those crispy skins, paired here with a creamy gribiche-style sauce. Serve with a bitter green salad, one with enough bite to balance the richness. This also pairs well with the Shallot-Watercress Sauce (page 151).

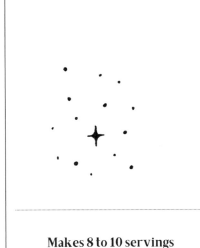

Makes 8 to 10 servings

Terrine

¼ cup plus 2 Tbsp [60 g] kosher salt

3 lb [1.3 kg] chicken skins

TO MAKE THE TERRINE: Combine 3 qt [3 L] of water with the salt in a large bowl. Submerge the skin and refrigerate overnight.

Drain and discard the water. Transfer the skins to a pot large enough to hold them all with room to spare. Cook over low heat until they are submerged in their own fat and tender enough to easily tear with your finger or a chopstick, 40 minutes to 1 hour. Drain, reserving fat if desired.

Preheat the oven to 250°F [120°C]. Line a small loaf pan (5½ by 3 in [14 by 7.5 cm]) with parchment paper, leaving 3 to 4 in [7.5 to 10 cm] of overhang on each side. When the skins are cool enough to touch, layer them in the pan, packing them in tightly. Fold in the sides of the parchment and cover tightly with foil. Place on another sheet pan or in a baking dish to catch any fat that may weep out. Bake for 1½ hours. Remove from the oven.

Fill a second loaf pan of the same size with pie weights or beans and place it on top, or press plastic against the surface of the terrine and weight it down with a heavy book or two. The goal is to apply even pressure so it compresses. Refrigerate, weighted, overnight or for up to 3 days.

CONTINUED

TO MAKE THE GRIBICHE: In a large pot, add the salt to 2 qt [2 L] of water and bring to a boil.

Set up an ice bath. When the water is boiling, carefully add the eggs and cook for 7 minutes. Drain and immediately plunge the eggs into the ice water to stop the cooking, then refrigerate them in their shells until completely cool.

Peel the eggs; set 2 aside for garnish. Chop the remaining 2 eggs and, in a medium mixing bowl, combine them with the aioli, herbs, ramps, anchovies, vinegar, mustard, lemon zest, and pepper. Season to taste.

An hour before serving, preheat the oven to 300°F [150°C]. Unmold the terrine; it should be dense and tightly layered. Cut it into four ½ in [1.25 cm] thick slices and freeze each slice for 30 minutes; this will help them stay intact while they're seared.

Set an ovenproof, nonstick or stainless steel pan over medium heat. Let it get hot but not smoking; test by splashing water on the surface, where it should skitter and evaporate. Add 1 Tbsp of the schmaltz. When it is melted, add the slices of terrine, taking care not to overcrowd the pan. Sear until crispy, 3 to 5 minutes per side. Add more schmaltz as needed, 1 Tbsp at a time. Transfer the pan to the oven so the slices warm through, 5 to 8 minutes.

To serve, spread the gribiche over a serving platter, then set slices of the terrine on top (for individual plates, use a large spoonful of gribiche per slice of terrine). Lightly toss the greens with a bit of olive oil and lemon juice, season with the coarse salt, then scatter over the top of the platter. Finish with a bit more coarse salt and freshly ground black pepper and serve immediately.

Gribiche

2 Tbsp plus 1 tsp [22.5 g] kosher salt

4 eggs

1 cup [240 g] Aioli (page 204) or mayonnaise with 2 cloves grated garlic

¼ cup [3 g] gently packed mixed chopped herbs, such as flat-leaf parsley, chervil, and/or tarragon

3 Tbsp chopped Lacto-Fermented Ramps (page 184) or capers

2 oil-packed anchovies, minced

1 tsp red wine vinegar

½ tsp Dijon mustard

Zest of 1 lemon

Freshly ground black pepper

2 Tbsp [30 g] schmaltz, plus more as needed

Bitter greens, watercress, olive oil, lemon juice, and coarse salt for garnish

MOM'S POT ROAST

I believe food that evokes nostalgia can be some of the most powerful. Sure, we can elevate a dish or give it a new twist, but it's the essence of the dish that can transport us to another time and place. This is one such dish for me. When I was growing up, my mom would make pot roast every year for my birthday. I can still see her in the kitchen gracefully peeling whole garlic cloves with perfectly manicured nails. With a paring knife, she'd pierce the flesh of the meat, creating secret pockets for the cloves to slip into, infusing the roast as it cooked with its mellow sweetness. I loved how the meat, bathing in a Cream of Onion soup mix, nearly melted in my mouth, but perhaps the real treat was the leftover sandwiches—we would layer soft white bread, the kind that sticks behind your teeth, with lots of margarine; smashed, broth-infused carrots; and slices of warm beef. Now, I prefer my vegetables more on the al dente side, so I add them about an hour before the beef is done, which also preserves their flavor and nutrition. Spices and Kombu Dashi (page 207) bolster the savoriness of my version, but the rusticity and soul are still the same.

Makes 6 to 8 servings

---

2 Tbsp coriander seeds, toasted

1 Tbsp black peppercorns

3 Tbsp dried oregano

2 Tbsp dried thyme

1 Tbsp dried mint

2 Tbsp kosher salt

2 Tbsp onion powder

1 Tbsp smoked paprika

1 Tbsp sweet paprika

4 to 5 lb [1.8 to 2.3 kg] beef chuck roast

6 garlic cloves, quartered

1 qt [960 ml] Kombu Dashi (page 207) or stock of your choice

1 lb [455 g] carrots, roughly chopped

1 lb [455 g] fingerling potatoes or chopped Yukon gold potatoes

12 shallots, peeled

Use a spice grinder to grind the coriander and peppercorns into a fine powder, then add the oregano, thyme, and mint and pulse a few more times until uniform. Stir in the salt, onion powder, smoked paprika, and sweet paprika by hand.

Pat the beef dry with paper towels. Using your hands, rub the herb and spice mix all over and into any crevices. Refrigerate, covered, in an ovenproof container or Dutch oven for at least 4 hours and preferably overnight.

Preheat the oven to 275°F [135°C]. Allow the beef to come to room temperature for 30 to 60 minutes before cooking. Leaving the beef (and any errant spices) in the same container, use a paring knife to cut twenty-four slits all over the beef and slip a quarter of a garlic clove into each slit. Pour in the stock.

Bake, covered, for 4 hours, or until the beef is easily pierced with a fork or knife but not yet fall-apart tender. Remove the lid and carefully add the carrots, potatoes, and whole shallots, then continue cooking, uncovered, until the vegetables are tender but not mushy, 30 to 45 minutes.

CONTINUED

To serve, carefully transfer the pot roast onto a serving platter and use a slotted spoon to follow suit with all of the vegetables. Skim away as much fat as you can get from what's left in the pan; you'll get more if you first pour it into a tall, transparent container. The juice that's left over is a luscious gravy that you can serve as is or reduce slightly in a saucepan before spooning it over the meat and vegetables. Leftovers store beautifully and even develop a little more dimension overnight. Rewarm gently before serving.

Seasonal Variations

WINTER

Substitute parsnip for the carrots or use in addition to the carrots in a 50:50 ratio. Add charred cabbage to the finished dish or serve on the side. Add Oil-Preserved Shallots (page 193).

AUTUMN

Substitute halved and roasted Brussels sprouts for the carrots or use in addition to the carrots in a 50:50 ratio. Add wilted kale or spinach to the finished dish.

SPRING

Substitute radishes for the carrots or use in addition to the carrots in a 50:50 ratio. Add asparagus or peas to the finished dish, cooking them at the last minute to keep them really fresh.

SUMMER

Substitute charred fennel for the carrots or use in addition to the carrots in a 50:50 ratio. Add roasted peppers, Vinegar-Pickled Squash Blossoms (page 189), or Oil-Preserved Tomatoes (page 193) to the finished dish.

BEEF SHORT RIB STEAKS

I accidentally stumbled upon this technique on a busy restaurant day, placing a steak into a dehydrator before grilling it off (as all the ovens were full with the evening's prep and at a higher temperature than I wanted). Cooking meat in a dehydrator (or at a very low temperature in your oven) mimics much of the same processes as sous vide. Now, this is usually my preferred method whenever I cook steaks, pork belly, or really any meats.

Makes 4 servings

Finely chop the herbs (by hand or in a food processor), then place in a small bowl. Stir in the oil and garlic by hand. Pat the short ribs dry and season them all over with the salt, then arrange them snugly in a container or zip-top bag and cover with the herb marinade. Refrigerate, covered, for 8 to 12 hours.

Preheat the oven as low as it will go (about 175°F [80°C]) or set a dehydrator to 125°F [52°C]. Arrange the rib steaks in a single layer, side by side, in a rectangular baking dish or ovenproof pan. Tightly cover with foil or a lid. Cook until the ribs are about 125°F [52°C] internally. This will take 4 to 6 hours in a dehydrator, so use an instant-read thermometer to check every 1 to 2 hours and flip the steaks when you do to ensure even cooking. In an oven, they'll cook quite a bit faster—around 1½ hours—so check after 1 hour and then every 15 minutes as the temperature gets close. Grill right away or refrigerate in an airtight container for up to 3 days.

If you made the ribs in advance, gently rewarm them, covered, in a low oven or in the dehydrator before grilling.

Preheat a grill to medium-high heat, leaving one area for low or indirect heat, or set a cast-iron skillet over a medium-high flame until a drop of water immediately sizzles and evaporates on contact. Grill the ribs without disturbing (do only one or two at a time if you're cooking on a stovetop) until they are deeply golden, 1 to 2 minutes per side. If the herbs appear to scorch, transfer the ribs to indirect heat on the grill or decrease the stove's heat slightly until the ribs finish cooking. Let them rest for 10 minutes, then serve warm. Leftovers can be gently rewarmed in a covered dish at your oven's lowest temperature.

1 cup [12 g] lightly packed herbs, such as parsley, cilantro, dill, marjoram, and/or tarragon

½ cup [120 ml] extra-virgin olive oil

4 garlic cloves, minced

4 lb [1.8 kg] short ribs, cut crosswise into 1 to 1¼ in [2.5 to 3 cm] steaks

1 Tbsp kosher salt

SLOW-COOKED PORK STEAK

Most people think of pork shoulder as a braising meat, but its marbling actually lends itself to so many other cooking methods. The idea here is to cut it into steaks that cook low and slow, to ensure none of the proteins seize. A final sear in a hot pan or on the grill gives the meat a nice bit of char and color. This method is pretty hands-off, but it does require a bit of time in the fridge for the seasonings to flavor the pork, so plan ahead.

Makes 4 servings

3 to 3½ lb [1.4 to 1.6 kg] boneless pork shoulder, cut into 1 to 1½ in [2.5 to 4 cm] steaks

½ cup [70 g] Dried Chimichurri Spice Blend (page 199)

Pat the steaks dry with paper towels and rub each one with 2 to 3 Tbsp of the chimichurri mix so they're generously and evenly coated. Place the steaks in a container or zip-top bag and refrigerate, covered, for 8 to 24 hours.

Preheat the oven as low as it will go (about 175°F [80°C]) or set a dehydrator to 135°F [57°C]. Place the steaks side by side in a rectangular baking dish or pan where they can lie flat and tightly cover with foil or a lid.

Cook until the pork's internal temperature is 135°F to 140°F [57°C to 60°C]. In a dehydrator, this will take 6 to 8 hours, and the steaks should be flipped every couple of hours to ensure the seasoning is evenly distributed. In an oven, this will happen much faster, 1 to 2 hours, so flip the steaks and check the internal temperature every 30 minutes, or more frequently as the temperature gets closer. Move on to searing right away or cover and refrigerate for up to 3 days.

Sear the steaks while they're warm—either right after cooking or after they've been very gently rewarmed in the dehydrator or a low oven. Preheat a grill over high heat or set a dry cast-iron skillet over a high flame until a drop of water sizzles and evaporates immediately upon contact. Grill the steaks without disturbing them (cook only one or two steaks at a time if you do this on the stovetop) until the spices caramelize into a fragrant, browned crust. Transfer to a cutting board to rest for 10 minutes. To serve, slice the steaks thinly against the grain. Refrigerate leftovers for up to 3 days and serve warm or at room temperature.

BRITISH-BERKSHIRE HOT POT

This is the first dish my partner, JP, made for me. It's a rare gift to have someone cook me a meal, and rarer still for them to take over my own kitchen. This is JP's favorite dish, a Lancashire classic hot pot. Hot pot, which is often thought of as the ceramic dish used to cook British casseroles, more likely refers to the hodge-podge of ingredients thrown into the vessel. Whatever the true history, it's an indisputable northern classic and a warming, honest, moreish meal. There's a silent language that happens with food, especially when someone offers you a dish that tastes of home. Perhaps there isn't a greater sign of adoration than nourishing the ones you love. Since that first day, we've made the dish our own—rutabagas and turnips go into the pot with potatoes and a quartet of spices; a savory pickled red cabbage balances it out on the plate. To me, it tastes of *our* home.

Makes 6 servings

Pickled Red Cabbage

1 small head red cabbage (about 1 lb [455 g])

1½ cups [360 ml] apple cider vinegar

½ cup [120 ml] water

¼ cup [85 g] honey

⅓ cup [55 g] kosher salt

¼ cup [60 ml] red wine

2 Tbsp yellow mustard seeds

2 tsp freshly ground black pepper

1 tsp coriander seeds, toasted and ground

6 bay leaves

TO MAKE THE CABBAGE: Peel away the cabbage's tough or wilted outer leaves. Halve and core it, then cut it into smaller wedges and slice them very thin (about ⅛ in [4 mm]) with a mandoline or knife. Pile it into a heatproof container (6½ cups [1.5 L]), pressing it down gently so it fits.

Combine the vinegar, water, honey, salt, wine, mustard seeds, pepper, coriander, and bay leaves in a small saucepan and bring to a simmer over medium heat, stirring occasionally to help everything dissolve. Decrease the heat slightly and continue to cook for another 10 minutes or so, giving the mustard seeds a chance to bloom in the heat. Immediately pour it over the cabbage and let cool to room temperature. Cover and refrigerate for up to 4 weeks. Remove the bay leaves before serving.

CONTINUED

Transfer the lamb to a cutting board and let it rest for 15 minutes. To carve it, slice the meat against the grain, perpendicular to the leg bone, then, with your knife hewing as close to the bone as you can, cut the slices away. Serve warm, with a bit of the rendered juices and oil spooned over the top if you'd like. Leftovers keep beautifully for a few days, during which time they can even deepen in flavor; gently reheat, covered, in a low oven or stack the cold slices in a sandwich.

LARDER

These days, preservation presents a tug-of-war between necessity and creativity. For most of history, food preservation was a means of survival. It ensured food availability throughout the leaner seasons. This is how preserved foods became the culinary bedrock of many of the world's cuisines.

In our modern time, with so many different varieties of produce available year-round, we cooks have the pleasure of preserving for creativity's sake. We preserve not only to produce a type of seasonless kitchen, but also to capture flavor and concentrate, layer, and experiment with flavors and textures that reveal themselves over time. From fresh to funky, the transformation of foods is exhilarating to experience, and over the past decade, fermentation fervor has taken hold. There's abundant information available from all over the globe, so we can adopt different techniques from different cultures, blending flavors and methods into something unique to this moment in time, and uniquely our own.

In this section, I share my basic preserving techniques. These are the methods used to create the pickles, ferments, powders, and more that lend contours to the food I cook. If you take away just one or two methods from this chapter, you'll always be able to easily create new, layered flavors. Experiment. Use these recipes and techniques as templates for your own flavor combinations.

Pickling

I use two basic pickling mediums: salt and vinegar. Foods preserved by salt brine are soured naturally by lactic acid fermentation, a process that converts sugars into lactic acid, producing flavorful, probiotic-rich raw pickles. It's important to note that salt levels are key: The right amount is high enough to prevent bad bacteria from forming but low enough to encourage good bacteria to grow.

Foods preserved by vinegar rely on acetic acid, which was created in a previous fermentation, and are considered a quick pickle. Both techniques result in delicious but very different end products.

The Basics

Just about any glass or ceramic container can be used as a pickling crock. Food-grade plastic vessels are good, too. Avoid metal containers, however, as they can react with the salt and acid. Most pickles can be refrigerated indefinitely, but textures and flavors will change slightly as the pickles age.

For lacto fermentation, I use a basic ratio of 3.5 percent salt by weight of the water for wet salting (see following). For dry salting (see following), I start with 2.5 percent salt by weight of whatever vegetables I'm pickling unless I'm fermenting a purée that's destined for paste; the flavors become so concentrated that it's best to err light on salt. Some vegetables need more salt after a bit of time in the fermenter; you'll have to taste them to know if more should be added. The vegetables should seem slightly salty at first. As time passes, that salinity will wane and the flavors will mature. I don't use a set ratio for vinegar brines. Each recipe is unique to the ingredient being processed.

Refrigerate vinegar pickles in airtight containers or pressure seal them according to the jars' manufacturer's specifications. Mold can develop on exposed vinegar pickles. When lacto fermenting, I use Ball jars or buckets with airlocks, which keep the oxygen out while allowing the carbon dioxide to escape. I also use ceramic crocks outfitted with a water-trough or airlock-lid system. Containers with airlocks are not necessary as long as the pickles are monitored closely for mold growth while souring. The less air space at the top of the pickle container the better, so use the smallest pickling vessel possible.

Lacto-fermented foods must be completely submerged in liquid to keep mold from forming, so a weight of some type is necessary. Some specialty crocks come with weights. Otherwise, select a plate that inverts snugly in your container and top it with a jar of water, a clean rock, or another weight of similar heft; a plastic bag filled with salted water will also do the job, and if the bag breaks, your brine won't be diluted. Once the weight is in place, secure the lid of your container to keep as much oxygen out as possible. Although it may look unpleasant, mold that forms on the surface of a brine is almost always harmless and can simply be skimmed away with a clean utensil. Molds develop primarily because of too much exposure to oxygen, a too-warm environment, or a brine that's not salty enough. Keeping food submerged in brine helps keep mold to a minimum and makes it easier to skim it off when it appears.

Once lacto fermentation gets under way, the brine will change from clear to cloudy, and natural yeasts will settle on the bottom of the vessel. This opacity shift indicates active fermentation. These changes are natural and are not cause for alarm.

As for extra brine left over from your ferments, drinking it is a wonderful way to get healthy probiotics into your body, but you can also use it to brine chicken (page 155) or add it back to new ferments, a technique called slopping, which imbues the brine with good bacteria from the onset.

Get creative with your seasonings: Purée onions, chiles, herbs, and garlic into your wet brines, or add sachets of whole spices or toasted ground spices to your mixes to change the flavors and spice things up a bit.

Wet Salting

Wet salting is a fermentation technique used to immerse food in a salt brine in order to preserve it. The right amount of salt encourages healthy lactic acid bacteria to colonize the brine and protects the vegetables from uncontrolled spoilage. This method is used for any vegetable that needs a brine poured over it, such as whole vegetables.

Basic Wet Salt Method

This works for any amount of dense vegetables or dense, underripe fruit, either whole or cut up, such as carrots, turnips, beets, winter squash, onions, green beans, Brussels sprouts, green tomatoes, small apples, underripe peaches, and whole baby cabbages.

Peel off any tough skins, such as on beets, winter squash, and onions, and trim the tops. Leave the vegetables whole or cut them into the desired finished shape. Place the vegetables in a nonreactive container and pour water to completely submerge them; as you do so, keep track of how much water you're adding since the amount of water will dictate the amount of salt (generally 3.5 percent salt by weight of the water for most vegetables, although cucumbers can handle 4 to 5 percent and the increased salt assists with keeping their texture crispy). With a long wooden spoon, stir kosher salt into the brine (or add the salt, cap the jar, and give it a hearty shake) until the salt is dissolved. Place a weight on top of the vegetables to keep them submerged in the brine. Seal the container, using a lid with an airlock if you have one. If you don't have an airlock, you'll just need to open the container every few days or so to release carbon dioxide buildup and check for mold. Place the container in a clean, low-light area with an ambient temperature of 60°F to 68°F [16°C to 20°C] until the pickles taste sour, about 3 weeks. Refrigerate indefinitely.

Dry Salting

Dry salting is a fermentation method where salt is added to dry shredded vegetables, like cabbage (sauerkraut) and carrots. Shredding exposes the cell walls, allowing the salt to draw out the naturally present water from within, which creates its own brine. Once some liquid has been coaxed out, the vegetables can be massaged, encouraging more liquid to release

until eventually they're completely submerged. Sometimes, a bit of wet brine has to be added to the ferment if the vegetables are too dry to produce a substantial brine. Wet brine also helps get the healthy bacteria colonizing your jars from the onset.

Basic Dry Salt Method

Peel, trim, chop, and weigh your vegetables; add 2.5 percent salt by weight and combine well. Massage liquid from the vegetables and pack them firmly in a small, nonreactive, and airtight container. Press down until they are beginning to let off their own juices. Weight them down and cap tightly. After a few hours, they should be submerged in their own juices. If not, add a bit of 3.5 percent salt brine. Place in a clean, low-light area with an ambient temperature of 60°F to 68°F [16°C to 20°C] and begin checking after 1 week; you may leave them to ferment this way for 2 months, turning the container over every couple of weeks to disperse the liquid evenly. The vegetables are done when they taste slightly soured. If you want to quicken the process, add a bit of brine from another ferment.

Lacto-Fermented Carrots

MAKES ABOUT 1 QT [960 ML]

1 lb [455 g] carrots

Kosher salt

Wash the carrots thoroughly to remove any dirt; if they're large, cut them into a size that can fit in your container. Place them in a nonreactive container, like a large jar or fermentation crock, and pour enough water to completely submerge them; as you do, keep track of how much water you add since this will dictate how much salt

you need. Based on the amount of water, measure 3.5 percent salt by weight.

Stir kosher salt into the jar using a long wooden spoon (or add it, cap the jar, and shake it well) until the salt is dissolved. Place a weight on top of the vegetables to keep them submerged in the brine. Seal the container, using a lid with an airlock if you have one; if you don't, open the container every few days to release carbon dioxide buildup and check for mold. Place the container in a clean, low-light area with an ambient temperature of 60°F to 68°F [16°C to 20°C] until the pickles taste sour, about 3 weeks. Refrigerate indefinitely.

Fermented Squash

MAKES ABOUT 1 QT [960 ML]

2 lb [910 g] winter squash, such as butternut, kabocha, hubbard, or fairytale

Kosher salt

Peel, halve, and deseed the squash; cut it into whatever size chunks you'd like. Place the squash in a nonreactive container, like a large jar or fermentation crock, and pour enough water to completely submerge it. As you do, keep track of how much water you add since this will dictate how much salt you need. Based on the amount of water, measure 3.5 percent salt by weight of water.

Stir in the salt with a long wooden spoon (or add it, cap the jar, and shake it well) until the salt is dissolved. Place a weight on top of the vegetables to keep them submerged in the brine. Seal the container, using a lid with an airlock if you have one; if you don't, open the container every few days to release carbon dioxide buildup and check for mold. Place the container in a clean, low-light area with an ambient temperature of 60°F to 68°F [16°C to 20°C] until the pickles taste sour, about 3 weeks. The pickles will keep in the fridge indefinitely.

Lacto-Fermented Dilly Green Beans

MAKES ABOUT 1 QT [960 ML]

1 lb [455 g] green beans, ends snipped

Kosher salt

Lots of dill

Place the beans in a nonreactive container, like a large jar or fermentation crock, and pour enough water to completely submerge them. As you go, keep track of how much water you add since this will dictate how much salt you need. Based on the amount of water, measure 3.5 percent salt by weight.

Stir in the salt and dill with a long wooden spoon (or add it, cap the jar, and shake it well) until the salt is dissolved. Place a weight on top of the vegetables to keep them submerged in the brine. Seal the container, using a lid with an airlock if you have one; if you don't, open the container every few days to release carbon dioxide buildup and check for mold. Place the container in a clean, low-light area with an ambient temperature of 60°F to 68°F [16°C to 20°C] until the pickles taste sour, about 3 weeks. The pickles will keep in the fridge indefinitely.

Lacto-Fermented Cucumbers

MAKES ABOUT 1 QT [960 ML]

1 lb [455 g] cucumbers, flower ends cut off

Kosher salt

Grape leaves or horseradish leaves (optional)

Place the cucumbers in a nonreactive container, like a large jar or fermentation crock, and pour enough water to completely submerge them. As you go, keep track of how much water you add since this will

dictate how much salt you need. Based on the amount of water, measure 3.5 percent salt by weight.

Stir in the salt with a long wooden spoon (or add it, cap the jar, and shake it well) until the salt is dissolved. Add in grape leaves, if using. Place a weight on top of the vegetables to keep them submerged in the brine. Seal the container, using a lid with an airlock if you have one; if you don't, open the container every few days to release carbon dioxide buildup and check for mold. Place the container in a clean, low-light area with an ambient temperature of 60°F to 68°F [16°C to 20°C] until the pickles taste sour, about 3 weeks. The pickles will keep in the fridge indefinitely.

Lacto-Fermented Beets

MAKES ABOUT 1 QT [960 ML]

2 lb [910 g] beets, peeled and greens removed

Kosher salt

Place the beets in a nonreactive container, like a large jar or fermentation crock, and pour enough water to completely submerge them. As you go, keep track of how much water you add since this will dictate how much salt you need. Based on the amount of water, measure 3.5 percent salt by weight.

Stir in the salt with a long wooden spoon (or add it, cap the jar, and shake it well) until the salt is dissolved. Place a weight on top of the vegetables to keep them submerged in the brine. Seal the container, using a lid with an airlock if you have one; if you don't, open the container every few days to release carbon dioxide buildup and check for mold. Place the container in a clean, low-light area with an ambient temperature of 60°F to 68°F [16°C to 20°C] until the pickles taste sour, about 3 weeks. The pickles will keep in the fridge indefinitely.

Lacto-Fermented Ramps

These alliums grow wild and represent the first sign of spring. They look like leggier, more delicate scallions with broad, flat greens. Their growing season is short and they're difficult to cultivate, but green onions are a year-round substitute.

MAKES ABOUT 1 QT [960 ML]

1 lb [455 g] ramps or green onions

Kosher salt

Trim any tufty bits from the ramp greens and clean away any dirt. Pack the ramps into a nonreactive container, like a large jar or fermentation crock, and pour enough water to completely submerge them. As you go, keep track of how much water you add since this will dictate how much salt you need. Based on the amount of water, measure 3.5 percent salt by weight.

Stir in the salt with a long wooden spoon (or add it, cap the jar, and shake it well) until the salt is dissolved. Place a weight on top of the vegetables to keep them submerged in the brine. Seal the container, using a lid with an airlock if you have one; if you don't, open the container every few days to release carbon dioxide buildup and check for mold. Place the container in a clean, low-light area with an ambient temperature of 60°F to 68°F [16°C to 20°C] until the pickles taste sour, about 3 weeks. Refrigerate for up to 1 year.

Lacto-Fermented Corn

MAKES ABOUT 1 QT [960 ML]

5 ears corn, husked

1 medium sweet bell pepper, finely diced

3 shallots, minced

1 serrano chile, grated

2 tsp sumac powder

1 tsp coriander seeds, toasted and ground

1 tsp fennel seeds, toasted and ground

Kosher salt

Cut the kernels from the corn and combine them with the bell pepper, shallots, serrano, sumac, coriander, and fennel in a bowl, gently massaging everything together to coax out some of the corn liquid. Weigh the mixture, and add 2.5 percent salt by weight to the vegetables. Pack the mixture into a nonreactive container, like a large jar or fermentation crock, pushing it down as you go to release more liquid, and place a weight on top to keep it submerged (don't worry if there's not much liquid to begin with; the vegetables will give up their inherent water in the first days of fermenting). Wipe the inside walls of the container clean, cover, and place in a clean, low-light area with an ambient temperature of 60°F to 68°F [16°C to 20°C] for 2 to 3 days. When the mix tastes gently sour but still has some of the corn and pepper sweetness, transfer to the refrigerator, where it will keep indefinitely. If you continue to ferment at room temperature, the sweetness will continue to sour, so taste as you go if you want to experiment with it at different stages.

Clam "Kimchi"

MAKES 1½ QT [600 G]

1½ lb [680 g] Napa cabbage

6 Tbsp [60 g] kosher salt

2½ lb [1.2 kg] clams (about 2 dozen), such as cherrystone or littleneck

1 Tbsp cornmeal

6 garlic cloves, minced

2 in [5 cm] piece fresh ginger, peeled and minced

3 Tbsp white miso

2 Tbsp fish sauce

½ cup [70 g] green bell pepper powder

1 to 2 fresh jalapeños, grated, or 3 Tbsp green chili flakes, such as Hatch, Padrón, or jalapeño

1 fennel bulb, cored and thinly sliced

8 scallions, sliced

Halve the cabbage lengthwise and remove the core, then cut it into 1 in [2.5 cm] sections.

In a large bowl, combine the salt with 1 qt [960 ml] of cold water and stir to dissolve. Submerge the cabbage in the brine and refrigerate for at least 6 hours or overnight, stirring occasionally.

Meanwhile, place the clams in a large bowl with the cornmeal, which helps remove sand and grit. Cover completely with water and let sit at room temperature for 1 hour, or refrigerate for longer. To steam the clams, bring 2 in [5 cm] of water to a simmer in a large saucepan or Dutch oven. Drain and rinse the clams, then steam, covered, until they start to open, 4 to 6 minutes. Pull them out as they finish cooking and remove the meat from the shells when they are cool enough to handle. Discard any clams that do not open. Roughly chop the clams and reserve.

Remove the cabbage from the water and give it a quick rinse with clean water. You don't need to rinse all the saltiness out, as it will give the kimchi flavor, but do squeeze as much water from the leaves as possible; you can do this with a vigorous shake or by running it through a salad spinner.

In a large bowl, combine the garlic, ginger, miso, and fish sauce. Stir in the green pepper powder and grated jalapeño. Add the cabbage, clams, fennel, and scallions, and mix very well to coat.

Divide the mixture between two 1 qt [960 ml] canning jars, pressing down firmly to remove any air bubbles. Press a layer of plastic wrap against the surface of the contents in each jar, then tightly seal. Leave

to ferment in a clean, low-light area with an ambient temperature of 60°F to 68°F [16°C to 20°C] for about 1 week, checking back every couple of days and gently pressing down on the plastic wrap to release any trapped carbon dioxide from the jar. The warmer and more humid it is, the faster the kimchi will ferment. Taste it as the days go on; follow what tastes good to you to determine when it's finished.

Don't worry about keeping the cooked clams at room temperature—the salt will keep them preserved as the kimchi ferments.

Transfer the kimchi to the bowl of a food processor (in batches, if necessary) and pulse a few times to give it a rough chop. Refrigerate in the original jars for up to 2 months.

Preserved Lemons

MAKES 1 QT [950 ML]

2½ lb [1.2 kg] lemons

½ cup [80 g] kosher salt

Juice 1½ lb [680 g] of the lemons, strain the juice through a fine-mesh sieve, and set the juice aside.

Trim the stems from the remaining 1 lb [455 g] of lemons, taking care not to cut into the flesh. Using a paring knife and starting at the stem end, cut each fruit into four wedges, cutting to, but not through, the base so each lemon stays intact. Hold each lemon over a bowl, gently pry the quarters apart from each other, and then press salt against all of the cut surfaces, capturing any salt that fails to adhere in the bowl. Continue with the remaining lemons.

Pack the salted lemons into a 1 qt [960 ml] canning jar. Pour in the reserved lemon juice to cover the fruit completely. Seal the jar and place in a clean, low-light area with

CONTINUED

an ambient temperature of 60°F to 68°F [16°C to 20°C] for 3 to 4 weeks, turning the jar upside down occasionally to prevent mold growth. Keep submerged. The lemons are ready when the peels look slightly translucent, but they're best if left to mature for 3 months before serving. Transfer the jar to the refrigerator, where the lemons will keep indefinitely.

"Capers"

Lots of little buds and seeds can be salted in the style of capers for a briny pop of flavor. It's a punchy way to preserve fresh herb seeds before they dry out. The flavors are quite different in each form.

Green elderberries, underripe green blueberries, pine buds, onion buds, and underripe grapes can all be made into "capers." You can also salt fresh seeds—some of my favorites are fennel, nasturtium, cumin, caraway, and dill. Just swap them out with the coriander seeds in the following recipe, keeping all weights the same.

If you can't find fresh herb seeds from a farmer or your own garden, you can still get some herbal, salty bites from dried seeds. The capers' flavor will be more subdued and they won't have the same little fresh pop, but they're still a nice addition to salads, dips, and anything else where you want a tiny burst of herbal brininess. Use any tender, dried seeds such as fennel, anise, caraway, dill, or cumin. Harder seeds like peppercorns should be avoided unless fresh.

Green Coriander Capers

MAKES 1 CUP [280 G]

3½ oz [100 g] green coriander berries
Kosher salt

Place the coriander berries in a nonreactive container and pour enough water to completely submerge them. As you go, keep track of how much water you add. Based on this amount, measure 3.5 percent salt by weight.

Seal the container tightly, and shake well. Place the container in a clean, low-light area with an ambient temperature of 60°F to 68°F [16°C to 20°C] for 5 weeks. Give the berries a taste; they're done when they taste slightly sour. These will keep in the refrigerator indefinitely.

Dry Fennel Seed Capers

MAKES 1 CUP [280 G]

½ cup [40 g] dried fennel seeds
Kosher salt

Place the seeds in a nonreactive container and pour enough water to completely submerge them. As you go, keep track of how much water you add. Based on this amount, measure 3.5 percent salt by weight. In a small saucepan over low heat, combine the fennel seeds with 1 cup [240 ml] water; bring to a simmer over medium heat and let simmer until tender, about 5 minutes. Transfer the whole mix to a small, nonreactive jar, seal tightly, and leave to ferment in a clean, low-light area with an ambient temperature of 60°F to 68°F [16°C to 20°C] for at least 3 weeks. The seeds are done when they taste lightly soured but still clearly of fennel. These will keep in the refrigerator indefinitely.

Fermented Condiments

Sweet-Sour-Spicy Pepper Paste

MAKES 1½ CUPS [360 G]

7 lb [3.2 kg] sweet red bell and/or hot peppers, stemmed and seeded
Kosher salt

I use a 3:1 bell-to-hot pepper ratio. Use a blender to purée the peppers; weigh the purée and stir in 1.5 percent of its weight in kosher salt. Transfer to a nonreactive container or an airlocking jar, wiping down the inside walls so they're as clean as possible, and press a piece of plastic wrap directly against the surface of the mixture to dispel as much air as possible and prevent mold growth. Cover with a tight-fitting lid and place in a clean, low-light area with an ambient temperature of 60°F to 68°F [16°C to 20°C] for 1 week, checking back every couple of days and gently pressing the back of a spoon against the plastic wrap to release any trapped carbon dioxide from the jar. (If you notice any small, white mold spores, use a clean spoon to carefully remove them; they're harmless.) After 1 week, the paste should taste gently sour, but if you think it needs more time, continue to ferment and check on it daily.

Pour the paste into a nonreactive shallow pan, such as a glass baking dish, so the paste is no more than 2 in [5 cm] deep; you may need to use two pans. Place in a dehydrator set at 125°F [52°C], stirring every 4 to 6 hours, or partially cover and let dry in an oven set to the lowest possible temperature (the offset lid allows moisture to escape without drying the paste too quickly), stirring every 30 minutes.

The paste is ready when it's thick and concentrated; depending on your drying method and the thickness of the paste's layer in the dish, this can take anywhere from 12 to 16 hours in a dehydrator or 3 hours in an oven. Transfer to a nonreactive container and refrigerate for up to 1 year.

Harissa

MAKES ABOUT 3 CUPS [720 G]

1½ tsp coriander seeds

1 tsp caraway seeds

1 tsp fennel seeds

1 tsp black peppercorns

½ tsp cumin seeds

2½ Tbsp ground cayenne pepper or hot paprika

1 Tbsp sweet paprika

1 cup [240 ml] extra-virgin olive oil

1 cup [12 g] lightly packed fresh parsley leaves

½ cup [6 g] lightly packed fresh dill leaves

½ cup [6 g] lightly packed fresh marjoram leaves

½ cup [6 g] lightly packed fresh mint leaves

¼ cup [35 g] white onion or shallot, coarsely chopped

12 garlic cloves

2 Tbsp chopped Preserved Lemon (page 185)

1 Tbsp plus 1 tsp lemon juice

1½ cups [360 g] Sweet-Sour-Spicy Pepper Paste (page 186)

2 Tbsp sherry vinegar

2 Tbsp dried mint, ground

2 tsp tomato paste

2 tsp honey

1½ tsp kosher salt

1 tsp red wine vinegar

1 tsp sumac powder

1 tsp urfa biber

In a spice grinder, combine the coriander, caraway, fennel, peppercorns, and cumin; grind to a fine powder, then combine with the cayenne pepper and sweet paprika. Gently warm half of the oil in a medium saucepan over low heat. Add the spices and cook, swirling occasionally, until very fragrant, 10 minutes.

In a blender, combine the other half of the oil with the fresh herbs, onion, garlic, preserved lemon, and lemon juice. Purée until smooth. Add this mixture to your saucepan, set over medium-low heat, and whisk in the pepper paste, sherry vinegar, ground dried mint, tomato paste, honey, salt, red wine vinegar, sumac, and urfa biber. Cook, stirring frequently to prevent scorching, until it's very thick, with most of the water cooked out, about 20 minutes. Transfer to a blender and purée until perfectly smooth and emulsified. Refrigerate in an airtight container for up to 1 year.

Preserved Lemon Paste
Harissa

MAKES 1 PT [480 G]

1 qt [425 g] Preserved Lemons (page 185), strained and brine reserved, lightly packed, seeds removed

½ cup [120 ml] brine

½ cup [120 ml] fresh lemon juice

Using a blender, purée the lemons with the brine and fresh lemon juice until completely smooth. Pour the mixture into a nonreactive shallow pan, such as a glass baking dish, so that the paste is no more than 2 in [5 cm] deep. Place in a dehydrator set at 125°F [52°C], stirring every 4 to 6 hours, or partially cover and let dry in an oven set to the lowest possible temperature (the offset lid allows moisture to escape without drying the paste too quickly), stirring every 30 minutes.

You'll know it's done when it's thick like tomato paste; depending on your drying method and the thickness of the paste's layer in the dish, this can take anywhere from 3 to 8 hours. Use a blender to purée it once more, until perfectly smooth and emulsified, and refrigerate in an airtight container indefinitely.

Infused Vinegars and Vinegar Pickles

Infusing vinegars is a surefire way to preserve flavors of a season in something you can use year-round while providing yourself and others with nourishment.

Vinegar itself has been used for thousands of years to deodorize, disinfect, and preserve food, as well as for medicinal formulas. It is said that before the invention of high-proof alcohols, many medicines were made using just water, wine, and vinegar. Herbal vinegars can provide us with a myriad of vitamins, minerals, and trace elements, and make nutrients like calcium more readily available to the body. Add in the power of medicinal herbs and spices and you up the nutritional content even more.

Any vinegar can be infused; start by making your own or buying high-quality vinegars as a base. When using store-bought vinegar for infusing, rice vinegar has a neutral flavor and mild acidity that I find ideal for this type of project.

Base Recipe

Put your cleaned herbs, vegetables, or fruit into a sterilized glass jar and fill it with the vinegar of your choice. Close tightly and set aside to infuse for at least 2 weeks, preferably up to 6 weeks. Taste the vinegar as time progresses to track the flavor as it develops.

Once your vinegar is as aromatic as you'd like it to be, strain the vinegar through a fine-mesh sieve or cheese-cloth and discard any sediment or debris. For a doubly potent infusion, repeat this process with fresh aromatics. You can safely store the infused vinegar in sealed containers indefinitely, no refrigeration required; just make sure you use non-corrosive lids (plastic or cork), or, if using metal bands, place plastic wrap over the neck before capping the jar to prevent rusting.

Currant Vinegar

MAKES 1 QT [960 ML]

2 cups [280 g] smashed red currants

1 qt [960 ml] rice vinegar or champagne vinegar

In a 1 qt [960 ml] jar, combine the currants and vinegar. Cover and let stand at an ambient temperature of 60°F to 68°F [16°C to 20°C] until the vinegar has taken on the flavor of the fruit, about 3 weeks. Strain through a fine-mesh sieve, transfer to an airtight container, and store at room temperature indefinitely.

Queen Anne's Lace Vinegar

In North America, the most common wild carrot is the taproot of a plant known as Queen Anne's lace. Numerous Native American tribes gathered these wild carrots and stored them for winter use. Their leaves have an aroma of parsley when crushed between your fingers and their flowers have a sweet, gentle waft of carrot at the end. Here, we infuse the lovely flowers in vinegar so they can impart it with their carrot-like aroma. Be aware that there is a similar flowering plant, wild hemlock, that is poisonous and can be mistaken for Queen Anne's lace—so just be sure you know what you're picking when you're out in the field. Most Queen Anne's lace has a reddish-purple dot in the center of its blossom head, but take a look at photos before you begin your hunt.

MAKES 1 QT [960 ML]

1 qt [960 ml] rice vinegar

10 to 12 Queen Anne's lace clusters

In a 1 qt [960 ml] jar, combine the vinegar and flowers. Cover and let stand at an ambient temperature of 60°F to 68°F [16°C to 20°C] until the vinegar has taken on the flavor of the plant, about 3 weeks. Strain through a fine-mesh sieve, transfer to an airtight container, and store at room temperature indefinitely.

Vinegar-Pickled Squash Blossoms

MAKES ½ CUP [120 ML]

½ cup [120 ml] rice vinegar

2 tsp honey

2 tsp salt

12 squash blossoms

Combine the vinegar, honey, and salt in a container; stir until the honey is fully dissolved. Remove the stamens from inside the blossoms and submerge the flowers in the liquid. Leave to pickle at an ambient temperature of 60°F to 68°F [16°C to 20°C] for about 4 hours or refrigerate for up to 1 week.

Vinegar-Pickled Red Carrots

MAKES 2 CUPS [480 G]

8 oz [230 g] carrots, preferably red

1 qt [960 ml] rice vinegar

Use a vegetable peeler or mandoline to shave the carrots in long ribbons. Twirl the ribbons into a jar, protecting them from breaking, and cover with the vinegar. Let stand at an ambient temperature of 60°F to 68°F [16°C to 20°C] until the vinegar has taken on the flavor and color of the carrots, about 3 weeks. Store in the refrigerator indefinitely to keep the pickled carrots crisp.

Vinegar-Pickled Daylilies

MAKES 1 CUP [240 ML]

In peak summer, daylilies are so abundant that you'd think they were showing off. Pick their unopened green buds and tight, unopened flower heads right up until they're nearly open. This is a base recipe, so feel free to add aromatics of your liking; I like a little heat in mine, so I'll often add a pinch of red pepper flakes or a couple slices of fresh green chiles.

1 cup [240 ml] rice vinegar

4 tsp honey

4 tsp kosher salt

20 tight daylily flower heads and/or green daylily buds

Combine the vinegar, honey, and salt in a nonreactive container and stir until the honey is fully dissolved. Submerge the buds and flowers in the liquid and leave to pickle at an ambient temperature of 60°F to 68°F [16°C to 20°C] for about 4 hours, or refrigerate for up to 1 week.

Vinegar-Pickled Red Onions

MAKES ½ CUP [120 G]

½ cup [120 ml] rice vinegar

2 tsp honey

2 tsp kosher salt

1 tsp caraway seeds, toasted and finely ground

½ red onion, thinly sliced

Combine the vinegar, honey, salt, and caraway seeds in a small saucepan and bring to a simmer over medium heat. Add the onion and bring the liquid back up to a simmer for 1 to 2 minutes, just long enough to remove any raw bite from the onion. Remove from the heat and cool to room temperature before eating or refrigerating; they will keep in an airtight container in the refrigerator for 1 month.

Vinegar-Pickled Blueberries

MAKES 3 CUPS [420 G]

2 cups [280 g] fresh blueberries, preferably small, wild, and slightly underripe

1 cup [240 ml] raw apple cider vinegar

2 Tbsp Maple Sugar (page 203)

1 tsp kosher salt

Pick over the blueberries for any mushy or unripe berries; discard those. Place the nice ones into a jar, preferably one that's small enough that it will be nearly full.

In a small saucepan, combine the vinegar, sugar, and salt and bring to a boil over medium heat. Let the mixture cool for 5 minutes, then pour over the blueberries. Wipe the rim clean and cap the jar. Kept this way, the blueberries will last a year or more in the refrigerator.

Oil Preserving

Oil preserving is a delicious alternative to lacto fermenting or vinegar pickling. Olive oil is a simple, tasty way to both marinate and preserve nature's bounty, extending summer's crop for a few seasons of enjoyment.

All of these variations include vegetables that are cooked before going into a marinade of oil, vinegar, and salt; each of these components keeps unhealthy bacteria at bay. Experiment with adding fresh herbs, and garlic to the oil for an extra layer of flavor; just note that it's best to remove the aromatics after a week of infusion or they may become too pungent. Refrigerate in a jar or sealed container, ensuring the vegetables are fully covered with the marinade.

Base Recipe

Choose your cooking technique (roast, grill, or steam) and your vegetable (those that follow are just a starting point; also try zucchini, bell peppers, mushrooms, sliced onions, whole garlic cloves, beets, turnips, green beans, artichoke hearts, heirloom beans, and so forth). Cook them as you would for eating and season generously with salt and pepper; add a bit more than you'd typically use, as you'll be offsetting the flavor with oil and vinegar.

Place the cooked vegetables in a jar and add flavorings—fresh herbs, whole cloves of raw or roasted garlic, lemon zest, preserved lemon, red pepper flakes, and/or hot chiles. Add oil and vinegar in a 2:1 ratio until the jar is full. After a week, remove any raw herbs or garlic, cover, and refrigerate for up to 4 months.

Oil-Preserved Eggplant

MAKES 1 LB [455 G]

1 lb [455 g] medium Japanese eggplants

1 cup [240 ml] dry white wine

⅓ cup [80 ml] raw white wine vinegar

1 Tbsp kosher salt

1 garlic clove, thinly sliced

¼ tsp red pepper flakes

1 oregano sprig

Extra-virgin olive oil

Set a metal grate directly over a gas burner, heat a grill, or use a broiler. Grill the eggplants over a medium-high flame, turning regularly, so that the skin blisters and blackens in some areas but the eggplants stay relatively firm.

When the eggplants are cool enough to handle, peel away as much skin as you can (don't worry about making it perfect) and trim the stems. Place the eggplants on a grate or wire rack positioned over a bowl to catch the juices; set a baking sheet on top of the eggplants and weight it down with some cans or a heavy book. This will expel excess liquid without crushing the eggplants. Let stand at room temperature for 2 to 4 hours or refrigerate overnight.

Gently pack the eggplant into a heatproof container with about 2 cups [480 ml] capacity. In a small saucepan, combine the wine, vinegar, salt, garlic, red pepper flakes, and oregano. Bring to a boil over high heat, then immediately pour it over the eggplant so the eggplant is completely submerged. Allow to marinate for at least 2 hours or overnight.

Gently drain the eggplant and pack it into the same container. Cover completely with olive oil (you may need to do this in increments since the oil can take some time to settle). Refrigerate for up to 3 months.

Oil-Preserved Hot Peppers

MAKES 2 CUPS [480 ML]

8 oz [230 g] fresh Calabrian chiles

Kosher salt

Freshly ground black pepper

Extra-virgin olive oil

Raw red wine vinegar

For small peppers: Use a paring knife to stem the peppers and make a small incision where the stem was, exposing the inside of the pepper. Set a metal grate directly over a gas burner on medium-high heat, heat a grill to medium-high, or heat your broiler with a rack 4 in [10 cm] below the heating element. Gently char the peppers until they just start to lose their rigidity and collapse a bit. Remove from the heat, season generously with salt and pepper, transfer to a glass jar, and cover completely in a 2:1 solution of oil and vinegar. Cover and refrigerate for up to 4 months

For large peppers: Set a metal grate directly over a gas burner on medium heat, heat a grill to medium, or heat your broiler with a rack 8 in [20 cm] below the heating element. Roast the peppers, rotating as needed, until the skins are bubbly and blackened in places, being sure not to overcook them to mush. Set aside to cool. Remove the stems and gently wipe away any charred, papery skin; don't obsess about removing all of it unless it seems very tough. Try to leave peppers as whole as possible—this gives you more freedom to decide how to cut them from dish to dish—and season them generously with salt and pepper. Transfer to a glass jar and cover completely in a 2:1 solution of oil and vinegar (add ¼ cup [60 ml] oil for every 2 Tbsp vinegar incrementally until the peppers are fully submerged). Cover and refrigerate for up to 4 months.

Oil-Preserved Tomatoes

MAKES 1 QT [960 ML]

1 lb [455 g] cherry tomatoes

Kosher salt

Freshly ground black pepper

Extra-virgin olive oil

Raw red wine vinegar

Set an oven rack about 4 in [10 cm] below the heating element and heat the broiler; alternatively, use your oven's convection setting at 450°F [232°C]. Place the tomatoes in a small baking dish or pan where they can fit in a single layer and roast until they're beginning to burst and are lightly charred in places, 5 to 8 minutes under the broiler, or 15 to 20 minutes in the convection oven. Season generously with salt and pepper and transfer to a glass jar; cover completely in a 2:1 solution of oil and vinegar (add ¼ cup [60 ml] oil for every 2 Tbsp vinegar incrementally until the peppers are fully submerged). Cover and refrigerate for up to 4 months.

Oil-Preserved Shallots

MAKES 1 QT [960 ML]

1 lb [455 g] shallots

Grapeseed oil or extra-virgin olive oil

Kosher salt

Freshly ground black pepper

Raw red wine vinegar

Preheat the oven to 325°F [165°C].

Peel the shallots, leaving their root ends intact, and place them in an ovenproof pot or large saucepan. Submerge the shallots completely in oil, then cover the pot with a lid or tightly wrap it with foil.

Bake until the shallots are completely tender, 1 to 1½ hours. Use a slotted spoon to gently fish the shallots out of the pot;

reserve the oil. When the shallots are cool enough to handle, trim away the root ends and peel away any tough outer layers.

Season the shallots generously with salt and pepper and transfer to a glass jar; cover completely in a 2:1 solution of oil and vinegar. Cover and refrigerate for up to 4 months.

Infused Oils

Oil infusing is a technique where ingredients are added to neutral oils to impart them with flavors.

Cold infusing is best for delicate ingredients like herbs or flowers that can lose quality with long exposure to heat. These are often quickly blanched and shocked in water to set their color, but not long enough to degrade the integrity of the ingredient. Herb oils offer an extra bit of herbaceous flavor in liquid form, their vibrant color bringing the oil to life.

Some ingredients release their aroma into oil best when gently heated. Peppers only truly show their full potential when cooked in oil or fat. Chili oil made from dried peppers is so flavorful that it is almost more of a sauce than a garnish. Be careful that the temperature is not too high, as this can compromise the flavor and color of the oil. The ideal temperature to infuse the ingredients into the oil in these recipes is 175°F [80°C]. If you are concerned that even at the lowest setting the heat is too high, slip a heat diffuser under the pan.

Herb Oil

MAKES 2 CUPS [480 ML]

3 bunches (6 cups [72 g]) fresh herbs, such as flat-leaf parsley, cilantro, chives, basil, tarragon, carrot tops, marjoram, or dill, large stems removed

2 cups [480 ml] grapeseed oil or other light-flavored oil

Chill a blender beaker in the freezer for at least 15 minutes. Line a fine-mesh sieve with cheesecloth and set it over a medium bowl. Prepare an ice bath.

Bring a large pot of water to a boil, add the herbs, and boil for 10 seconds; using tongs or a slotted spoon, immediately transfer the herbs to the ice bath to preserve their bright green color. When cool, wring them dry and chop coarsely. Add to the chilled blender beaker with the oil and blend on high speed just until the oil turns bright green. Pour the oil into the prepared sieve and immediately refrigerate the whole setup to keep it as fresh as possible while it slowly strains; you can squeeze the last bit from the cheesecloth. Discard any solids and transfer the oil to an opaque container, which will help keep your oil nice and bright. Refrigerate for up to 3 weeks.

Tomato Leaf Oil

MAKES 2 CUPS [480 ML]

3 cups [36 g] lightly packed tomato leaves
1 cup [240 ml] extra-virgin olive oil
1 cup [240 ml] grapeseed oil

Chill a blender beaker in the freezer for at least 15 minutes. Line a fine-mesh sieve with cheesecloth and set it over a medium bowl. Prepare an ice bath.

Bring a large pot of water to a boil, add the tomato leaves, and boil for 30 seconds; using tongs or a slotted spoon, immediately transfer the leaves to the ice bath to preserve their bright green color. When cool, wring them dry and chop coarsely. Add to the chilled blender beaker with the oils and blend on high speed just until the oil turns bright green. Pour the oil into the prepared sieve and immediately refrigerate the whole setup to keep it as fresh as possible while it slowly strains; you can squeeze the last bit from the cheesecloth. Discard any solids and transfer the oil to an opaque container, which will help keep your oil nice and bright. Refrigerate for up to 3 weeks.

Sumac Oil

MAKES ¼ CUP [60 ML]

¼ cup [60 ml] extra-virgin olive oil
2 Tbsp sumac powder
½ tsp kosher salt

In a small pot over low heat, gently warm the oil until it's shimmering. Remove from the heat, add the sumac and salt, and allow to cool to room temperature. Transfer to a sealed container and store at room temperature or in the refrigerator for up to 3 months.

Fennel Oil

MAKES ¼ CUP [60 ML]

¼ cup [60 ml] extra-virgin olive oil
2 Tbsp fennel seeds, toasted and ground
¼ tsp kosher salt

In a small pot over low heat, gently warm the oil until it's shimmering. Remove from the heat, add the ground fennel and salt, and allow to cool to room temperature. Transfer to a sealed container and store at room temperature or in the refrigerator for up to 3 months.

Tarragon Chili Oil

MAKES 1 CUP [240 ML]

1 cup [240 ml] grapeseed oil
3 Tbsp red pepper flakes
3 star anise pods
2 tsp coriander seeds
1 in [2.5 cm] piece cinnamon bark
Leaves from 1 thyme sprig
4 garlic cloves, grated or minced
½ in [12 mm] piece fresh ginger, peeled and grated or minced
¼ cup [3 g] lightly packed fresh tarragon leaves, chopped

In a small pot over low heat, gently warm the oil until it's shimmering. Add the red pepper flakes, star anise pods, coriander, cinnamon, and thyme leaves. Remove from the heat and stir the garlic and ginger into the oil; set aside to infuse at room temperature for at least 3 hours or overnight.

Line a fine-mesh sieve with cheesecloth and set over a medium bowl. In a blender, purée the infused oil with the tarragon until very smooth. Pour the oil into the

prepared sieve and allow it to strain slowly; you can use the cheesecloth to squeeze out the last drops at the end. Discard any solids and transfer the oil to a sealed, opaque container. Refrigerate for up to 3 weeks.

Smoked Paprika Oil

MAKES 1 CUP [240 ML]

1 cup [240 ml] extra-virgin olive oil
¼ cup [35 g] smoked paprika
1 tsp kosher salt

In a small pot over low heat, gently warm the oil until it's shimmering. Remove from the heat and add the paprika and salt; set aside to infuse for at least 3 hours or overnight.

Line a fine-mesh sieve with cheesecloth and set over a medium bowl. Pour the oil into it and set aside to strain slowly; you can use the cheesecloth to squeeze out any last drops at the end. Discard the solids and refrigerate in a sealed, opaque container for up to 3 months.

Drying

Dehydration is more than just a method for preserving food. Extracting the bulk of the water from fruits, vegetables, meats, and fish concentrates flavors and changes textures. It's one of my most important tools for building flavor.

Drying flowers and seeds captures their aromas, making it possible to utilize their individual characteristics in teas, sodas, pastries, and spice mixes. Lavender, yarrow, citrus blossoms, elderflower, coriander, calendula, geranium, and rose are some of my favorites. Try making your own herbal tea mixes; there are many possible combinations. Seeds are easy to dry for your spice shelf or salt, as in the "Capers" section (page 186). Dried herbs can act as a substitute for fresh herbs in many recipes. Use one-third the amount of dried herbs when substituting for fresh.

Drying in a Dehydrator

If you want to get into drying your own food in a bigger, more systemized way, a dehydrator is a good addition to your culinary arsenal. It maximizes airflow exposure and yields consistent results. Experiment with drying all kinds of herbs, seeds, and even blossoms that you forage or grow. The general rule is if the thing that the blossom is going to turn into is edible, then the blossom itself is edible.

For fresh, stemmed, leafy herbs such as basil, celery leaf, chervil, cilantro, dill, lemon balm, marjoram, oregano, mint, parsley, and tarragon:

Dehydrate at 95°F [35°C] until brittle to the touch but still brightly colored, 6 to 8 hours.

For heartier herbs such as fir tips, lemon verbena, rosemary, bay leaf, sage, eucalyptus, and thyme: Dehydrate at 95°F [35°C] until brittle to the touch but still brightly colored, 8 to 12 hours.

For flowers such as fennel, cilantro (coriander), elderflower, chamomile, calendula, lavender, and hops: Pluck the flower heads, discarding the stems or putting them to another use. Dehydrate at 95°F [35°C] until brittle to the touch but still brightly colored, 2 to 6 hours.

For seeds such as celery, coriander (cilantro), dill, fenugreek, and fennel: Remove the seeds from the flower stems. Dehydrate at 120°F [48°C] for 12 to 24 hours, until dry all the way through. Check by cracking a couple of them open.

Oven-Drying

Dried foods have been around far longer than any gadget, so there's no need to invest in special equipment for many of the projects in this section. A gas oven warmed only by its pilot light is an excellent tool for drying food.

Air-Drying

Hanging food to dry in a cool, ventilated area is one of the easiest ways to preserve certain ingredients. Indoor or outdoor drying can work. Take into account both density and water content when choosing foods to hang-dry. Herbs and peppers are excellent choices, but tomatoes would likely spoil. I like to tie the stems of herb bunches together with twine and hang them to dry.

Herbs and flowers should dry quickly, within 24 hours. Seeds may take another 8 to 12 hours. After the leaves, flowers, or seeds are dry, shake or pick them from the stem and store in a sealed container. Plants dried in this manner will keep for up to 6 months.

Sun-Drying

Drying foods in the sun requires a few specific conditions. Warm days that reach 75°F to 85°F [24°C to 29°C] with relative humidity below 60 percent are perfect; air movement is helpful too. Arrange produce on a rack to allow air to circulate. A screen propped atop two cinder blocks works well. Cover the food with cheesecloth or another screen to keep flies and other insects out. Turn the produce at least once a day, and bring it indoors at night if necessary to protect it from moisture. Taste a little each day to decide when the process is complete.

Storing Dried Foods

Opaque containers and cool, dark cupboards are ideal for storing dried foods. It is important to keep the food away from light, which can cause both colors and flavors to fade. Generally, dried spices retain aroma and color for at least 6 months at room temperature, or longer if frozen. Use your judgment; if the aroma or color fades, start a new batch. Keep your spices whole until you are ready to use them, since the flavors will be brightest this way.

Toasting Dry Spices

Spices are most fragrant just after toasting, so toast in small batches as needed. Preheat the oven to 325°F [165°C], spread the whole spices in an even layer on a sheet pan, and toast just until fragrant, 7 to 10 minutes. Alternatively, warm a dry pan over medium-high heat, add the spice to the pan, and toast, tossing occasionally as it heats, just until fragrant. Timing will depend on the spice; most will take 5 to 7 minutes. Allow to cool completely before grinding.

Grinding Dried Ingredients into Flakes and Powders

Use a spice grinder or mortar and pestle to pulverize dried ingredients. If possible, freeze the grinder bowl for at least 15 minutes to keep foods from overheating, which can deplete essential oils. If you're making a fine powder, sift and regrind any larger pieces for a uniform texture.

Spice Blends

The Maillard reaction is responsible for caramelization of proteins, rendering them toasty and savory. Though it's wildly delicious, it makes food—especially meat—less digestible, destroys nutrients, and produces carcinogens. It may be that the other benefits of cooking food massively outweigh these detriments, and so we have evolved to prefer browned food. But there are ways to combat some of the negative effects of charring meat by adding lots of herbs and spices

to its exterior. Spices to note for their strong antioxidant properties include those from the mint family, such as basil, mint, hyssop, rosemary, sage, savory, marjoram, oregano, and thyme. Marinades made with vinegar or lemon change meat's acidity to help prevent other harmful by-products of high heat from sticking to the surface of your meat. It's said that you don't even need to marinate your meat very long because it only takes a few minutes to get the full cancer-preventing effect. Longer marination will just add more flavor.

Spiced Seed Mix

MAKES ABOUT 1½ CUPS [240 G]

Be sure to toast the seeds and spices separately, as they brown at different rates. I make this in big batches to always have on hand for poached eggs, rice, or avocado toast.

2 sheets (about ¼ oz [5 g]) nori

1½ Tbsp dulse flakes, finely ground

1½ tsp dried thyme leaves, finely ground

1½ tsp dried dill leaves, finely ground

1½ tsp dried marjoram leaves, finely ground

1½ tsp dried mint leaves, finely ground

1½ tsp coriander seeds, toasted and finely ground

1 tsp fennel seeds, toasted and finely ground

½ tsp cumin seeds, toasted and finely ground

½ tsp caraway seeds, toasted and finely ground

¼ cup [35 g] pumpkin seeds, toasted and chopped

¼ cup [35 g] sunflower seeds, toasted

¼ cup [35 g] unhulled sesame seeds, toasted

2 Tbsp black sesame seeds, toasted

1 Tbsp sweet paprika

1 Tbsp sumac powder

1½ tsp citrus powder (see Drying section, page 196), such as lemon, orange, or black lime

1½ tsp onion powder

1½ tsp green chili powder

1 tsp kosher salt

½ tsp garlic powder

Preheat the oven to 325°F [165°C] and set a wire rack over a baking sheet. Toast the nori for 15 to 20 minutes, until very dry and brittle. Cool completely, then crumble enough to fit into the grinder and pulse into a powder with the dulse flakes, dried thyme, dill, marjoram, and mint.

Combine the coriander, fennel, cumin, and caraway seeds; grind to a fine powder.

In a medium bowl, toss the pumpkin, sunflower, and sesame seeds with all of the powdered spices and herbs, along with the remaining ingredients. Store in an airtight container for up to 1 month.

Pumpkin Spice Mix

MAKES ABOUT ½ CUP [80 G]

⅓ cup [45 g] pumpkin seeds, toasted

1 Tbsp coriander seeds, toasted

1 tsp cumin seeds, toasted

2 Tbsp black sesame seeds, toasted

2 tsp sumac powder

½ tsp ground turmeric

½ tsp kosher salt

½ tsp freshly ground black pepper

¼ tsp ground cayenne pepper

Combine half the pumpkin seeds with the coriander and cumin; finely grind with a spice grinder or mortar and pestle. Chop the remaining pumpkin seeds coarsley and combine with the ground spices, black sesame seeds, sumac, turmeric, salt, black pepper, and cayenne. Store in an airtight container at room temperature for up to 1 month.

Hibiscus-Za'atar Spice Blend

MAKES ½ CUP [85 G]

1½ Tbsp white sesame seeds, toasted

1 Tbsp black sesame seeds, toasted

1 Tbsp dried hibiscus, finely ground, or sumac powder

1 Tbsp dried thyme or 2 Tbsp lightly packed thyme leaves, minced

½ tsp dried marjoram or oregano or 1½ tsp lightly packed marjoram or oregano leaves

½ tsp kosher salt

¼ tsp coriander seeds, ground

¼ tsp aniseeds, ground

⅛ tsp freshly ground black pepper

Combine all the ingredients in a small bowl. Store in an airtight container at room temperature for up to 3 months.

Chutney-esque Spice Blend

MAKES ½ CUP [85 G]

3 Tbsp onion powder

3 Tbsp sumac powder

2 Tbsp garlic powder

2 Tbsp sweet paprika

1 Tbsp anise or fennel seeds, toasted and ground

1 Tbsp coriander seeds, toasted and ground

1 Tbsp dried dill, powdered

1 Tbsp dried mint, powdered

2 tsp black peppercorns, ground

2 tsp kosher salt

1 tsp ground cayenne pepper

½ tsp dried celery seeds, toasted and ground

Combine all the ingredients in a small bowl. Store in an airtight container at room temperature for up to 2 months.

Lamb Spice Blend

MAKES ABOUT 1 CUP [165 G]

¼ cup [35 g] coriander seeds, toasted and ground

¼ cup [35 g] fennel seeds, toasted and ground

3 Tbsp kosher salt

3 Tbsp sweet paprika

1 Tbsp cumin seeds, toasted and ground

1 Tbsp ground ginger

1 Tbsp ground cayenne pepper

2 tsp black peppercorns, toasted and ground

1½ tsp yellow mustard seeds, toasted and ground

Combine all the ingredients in a small bowl. Store in an airtight container at room temperature for up to 2 months.

Dried Chimichurri Spice Blend

MAKES ABOUT 1 CUP [165 G]

3 Tbsp dried marjoram or oregano, ground

3 Tbsp dried dill, ground

3 Tbsp kosher salt

2 Tbsp dried thyme, ground

1 Tbsp smoked paprika

1 Tbsp sweet paprika

1 Tbsp onion powder or scallion powder

1 tsp lemon powder or orange powder (see Drying section, page 196)

1 Tbsp dried mint, ground

1 Tbsp black peppercorns, ground

1 Tbsp coriander seeds, toasted and ground

2 tsp garlic powder

1 to 2 tsp red pepper flakes

1 tsp fennel seeds, toasted and ground

½ tsp cumin seeds, toasted and ground

Combine all the ingredients in a small bowl. Store in an airtight container for up to 1 month. Use as a dry rub or, to make a marinade, combine ¼ cup [35 g] of the mix with 1 cup [240 ml] of oil and ¼ cup [60 ml] of red wine vinegar. Ideally, let it steep for a couple hours or overnight before adding protein. Marinade will keep refrigerated for 1 month or longer.

Five-Spice Blend

MAKES ABOUT ¼ CUP [35 G]

2 star anise pods, toasted and ground

2 Tbsp fennel seeds, toasted and ground

2 Tbsp caraway seeds, toasted and ground

2 Tbsp peppercorns, toasted and ground

2 Tbsp ground dried Persian lime (limu omani) or sumac powder

Combine all the ingredients in a small bowl. Store in an airtight container at room temperature for up to 1 month.

Dried Summer Vegetables

MAKES ABOUT 2 CUPS [320 G]

2 cups [320 g] cherry tomatoes

2 sweet peppers, such as bullhorn, piquillo, or bell

2 small zucchini or summer squash

1 medium eggplant

1 ear corn, husked

Kosher salt

Halve the tomatoes. Halve the peppers lengthwise, scrape out the seeds and membranes, and slice lengthwise. Quarter the squash lengthwise. Cut the eggplant into planks about ½ in [12 mm] thick. Cut the kernels from the corn.

Arrange the vegetables on multiple baking sheets or dehydrator trays so they stay separate, with plenty of space between them, and season very lightly with kosher salt. Dehydrate at 115°F [46°C] or bake at the lowest temperature your oven will go until all the moisture has been pulled out; if you're using the oven, you may need to flip the larger vegetables halfway through cooking. Check each vegetable for doneness—it should be dry and very light—and remove

as they finish. Cool to room temperature; store in airtight containers for months.

Infused Salts

Infused salts are a great way to preserve flavors in a seasoning for salting meat and fish before cooking or dusting over vegetables and dips as a finishing touch. The options are endless, really. Infused salts can be stored indefinitely at room temperature in an airtight container. I recommend using a flaky sea salt, such as Jacobsen kosher salt, Maldon salt, or fleur de sel, for all of these recipes.

- For onion salt: Combine onion powder and salt in a 2:1 ratio by weight.

- For garlic salt: Combine garlic powder and salt in a 2:1 ratio by weight.

- For pickled vegetable salt: Combine pickled vegetable powder and salt in a 2:5 ratio by weight. Some vegetables won't need the addition of any salt as they will have concentrated flavors from drying. Taste the powder alone first and decide for yourself.

Fresh Rose Salt

3 oz [100 g] fresh rose petals or ¼ oz [7 g] dried rose petals

½ cup [80 g] flaky salt

Pound the rose petals into a paste or use a blender to purée them with water to cover until smooth. Combine the rose purée and salt and dry in the dehydrator at 110°F [43°C] or in your oven at the lowest possible setting until all moisture is removed. Break

up large pieces and pound in a mortar and pestle or grind in a spice grinder to a fine powder.

Nasturtium Salt

3½ oz [100 g] nasturtium flowers or greens, or ¼ oz [7 g] dried nasturtium flowers or greens

1¾ oz [50 g] flaky salt

If using fresh flowers or greens, dry them in a dehydrator at 110°F [435°C] or in your oven at the lowest possible setting until bone dry. Pulse dried flowers/greens in a spice grinder until fine, then combine with the salt.

Herby Salt

3½ oz [100 g] fresh herbs or ¼ oz [10 g] dried herbs

1¾ oz [50 g] flaky salt

If using fresh herbs, dry them in a dehydrator at 110°F [43°C] or in your oven at the lowest possible setting until bone dry. Pulse dried herbs in a spice grinder until fine, then combine with the salt.

Concentrated Juices and Syrups

100% Fruit Syrup

Use any juicy fruit, such as pears, cherries, or peaches

Clean and prepare the fruit for juicing or puréeing; pit as needed. Run it through a juicer or purée it in a blender and strain through a fine-mesh sieve.

Pour the juice into a nonreactive pan so it makes a shallow layer; use multiple pans if necessary. Dehydrate the juice at 125°F [52°C], stirring every 6 to 8 hours, to break

CONTINUED

up any skin that forms on the top. If you don't have a dehydrator, cover with the lid slightly offset to allow moisture to escape and bake at your oven's lowest temperature, stirring every hour.

When the juice is as thick as maple syrup, transfer it to a jar and press a piece of plastic wrap or parchment paper onto the surface of the paste to help prevent it from oxidizing. Close the jar and refrigerate for up to 1 year; if any mold appears on the top, simply scrape it off and reseal.

Infused Fruit Syrup

MAKES ABOUT 2 CUPS [480 ML]

2 cups [about 280 g] fruit, fresh or frozen

¾ cup [255 g] honey or maple syrup

⅓ cup [80 ml] lemon juice or water

Clean and prepare the fruit for puréeing; pit as needed. Purée in a food processor or blender. In a medium saucepan over medium-low heat, bring the honey to a gentle simmer with the lemon juice. Add the fruit purée and simmer until the mixture is about as thick as warm maple syrup. Alternatively, set up a dehydrator to 115°F [46°C] or heat your oven as low as it will go.

Purée the mixture until super smooth and strain through a fine-mesh sieve, to achieve a liquidy smooth syrup.

Infused Herb Syrup

MAKES ABOUT 2 CUPS [480 ML]

1¼ cups [300 ml] fresh fruit or vegetable juice or water

½ cup [170 g] honey

8 oz [230 g] herbs, large stems removed

Gently warm the juice with the honey until the honey is dissolved. Refrigerate to cool completely. Use a blender to purée the herbs with the syrup. Line a fine-mesh sieve with cheesecloth and add the purée. Refrigerate overnight to slowly strain, then bottle.

Saffron Syrup

MAKES ABOUT ¼ CUP [60 ML]

¼ cup [60 ml] fresh lemon juice

3 saffron threads

2 tsp honey

Allow the lemon juice to come to room temperature. Break the saffron threads into small pieces by hand and let them bloom in the lemon juice for at least 20 minutes. Stir in the honey until incorporated.

Honey-Lemon Syrup

MAKES ABOUT 1 CUP [240 ML]

2 Tbsp honey

1 Tbsp fresh lemon juice

1 Tbsp Preserved Lemon Paste Harissa (page 187)

1 Tbsp rose water

1½ tsp extra-virgin olive oil

Pinch of kosher salt

Stir everything together in a small saucepan over medium heat for a few minutes so that it reduces slightly. Transfer to an airtight container and refrigerate for up to 2 weeks.

Sumac-Honey Infused Syrup

Native Americans frequently collected and used wild sumac for both food and medicine. Its bark, leaves, and fruit can be utilized for different purposes, but here, I opt for the dried, powdered berries, high in antioxidants and vitamin C, to infuse honey with their tart, ever-so-slightly funky aroma. Among sumac's

wide range of health-boosting properties, its antiaging, antifungal, antioxidant, anti-inflammatory, and antimicrobial effects are most touted. Raw honey also has many antibacterial and antimicrobial properties, so combining these two ingredients makes quite the health tonic. Use this infusion whenever you'd like a little sour with your sweet.

MAKES 1 CUP [340 G]

¼ cup [30 g] sumac powder

1 cup [340 g] honey

Put the sumac in a clean, heatproof jar that has a tight-sealing lid. In a small saucepan, warm the honey over medium-low heat until just pourable. Pour over the sumac and stir to combine. Leave at room temperature to infuse for at least 3 days, then transfer to an airtight container and refrigerate for up to 1 year.

Honeyed Pine Cones

I collect the pine buds when they're the size of two pine nuts put together and really young and tender.

MAKES 2 CUPS [240 G]

1 cup [120 g] baby pine cones

2½ cups [850 g] honey

Rinse any debris from the pine cones and place them in a large heatproof jar.

Gently warm the honey in a saucepan. When it's just warm to the touch, pour it over the pine cones. Cover and set aside at room temperature for at least 1 month before using; you can use the infused honey as is or finely chop the pine cones and use them as a delicate garnish.

Sugar Substitutes

HONEY

Honey can be substituted for sugar in many recipes. Here are a few rules of thumb to help you achieve good texture and sweetness in your baked goods.

For every 1 cup [200 g] of sugar, substitute ½ to ⅔ cup [170 to 230 g] of honey. For every 1 cup [340 g] of honey you're using, subtract ¼ cup [60 ml] of other liquids from the recipe.

Honey Sugar

Spread a thin layer of honey (at least 2 cups [680 g] on a parchment-lined baking sheet. Dehydrate at 120°F [50°C] for about 24 hours, or until the honey is dry to the touch. Cool the baking sheet in a place with no humidity, like a turned-off dehydrator, after which you can break the dry honey into shards or grind it to a powder using a food processor, spice grinder, or mortar and pestle. Store the honey sugar in an airtight container with desiccator packets, if you have them; it will keep indefinitely.

MAPLE

Because of its high sugar content, maple can be substituted for sugar in many recipes. When substituting, use 1½ cups [510 g] pure maple syrup for each 1 cup [200 g] of granulated sugar, and add ¼ tsp of baking soda for each 1 cup [340 g] maple syrup used. When maple syrup is substituted for all the sugar in a recipe, reduce the amount of liquid used in the rest of the recipe by half. If maple syrup is substituted for half the sugar, reduce liquid amounts by one-fourth.

Maple Sugar

Pour the maple syrup into a high-sided, heavy-bottomed saucepan over medium-high heat. (It will bubble up quite a bit as it heats, so err on the larger side.) Clip a candy thermometer or deep-fry thermometer to the side of your pot. Reduce the syrup by half and allow it to reach the hard ball stage at 257°F to 262°F [125°C to 128°C] (this means that when you drop a small spoonful into cold water, it should form a firm ball), about 20 minutes. As the syrup cooks down, watch it carefully so it doesn't boil over. If it creeps close to the top of the saucepan, stir it with a long wooden spoon. As it continues to reduce, you may need to reduce the heat to keep the syrup from scorching. You may also need to tip the pan toward the end to fully immerse the bulb of your thermometer in the syrup so you get an accurate temperature reading.

Once the syrup reaches the right temperature range, remove it from the heat and, with a wooden spoon, stir vigorously until the syrup becomes granulated, similar in look and feel to light brown sugar, about 5 minutes.

Sift the maple sugar through a fine-mesh sieve to remove the larger clumps and then break up those larger clumps in your food processor or with a mortar and pestle until they become granulated. Mix this back in with the rest of the maple sugar. Store in an airtight container and keep sealed with desiccator packets, if you have them. It will keep indefinitely.

Maple Cream

Use light-colored grades of syrup for the best results. Fill a large heatproof bowl with ice cubes. Heat the syrup as you did for the sugar, but this time, bring it only to 234°F to 236°F [112°C to 113°C]. Remove from the heat and immediately set the pan inside the ice bath, rapidly bringing the temperature to 70°F [21°C] or below (50°F [10°C] is preferable). Stir the stiffened, cooled syrup with a wooden spoon and watch it become a thick, pale, creamy consistency, almost like condensed milk. Transfer the maple cream into storage jars or containers while it's still pourable and store them in the refrigerator indefinitely.

Sauces and Other Condiments

Fresh Ricotta

MAKES 3 CUPS [720 G]

2 qt [2 L] whole milk

1 cup [240 ml] heavy cream

1 Tbsp fresh lemon juice

1 tsp kosher salt

Set up a triple layer of cheesecloth in a sieve set over a tall container.

Combine the milk, cream, lemon juice, and salt in a pot and bring to a gentle simmer over medium-low heat. Leave it on the heat for 1 to 2 minutes after you start to see it curdle; a longer time on the heat will render larger curds for a drier ricotta. Transfer the mixture to the cheesecloth and let it drain for several hours at room temperature. If you're not using it right away, refrigerate in an airtight container for up to 2 days.

Aioli

MAKES ABOUT ⅔ CUP [160 ML]

1 egg yolk

2 garlic cloves

1 Tbsp fresh lemon juice

¼ tsp kosher salt

⅓ cup [80 ml] extra-virgin olive oil

⅓ cup [80 ml] grapeseed oil

Freshly ground black pepper

Place the egg yolk in a bowl and allow it to come to room temperature. Use a Microplane to grate the garlic into the bowl and add the lemon juice and salt; whisk to incorporate.

In a separate bowl, combine the olive oil and grapeseed oil. Whisk the yolk mixture vigorously while you slowly and gradually drip the oil into it, taking care that each addition is fully incorporated before you add more so the emulsion doesn't break. As the mixture thickens and becomes opaque, you can add the oil a bit more quickly, in a thin stream, still whisking constantly. Season with pepper and set aside or refrigerate in an airtight container until ready to use.

Herby Yogurt

MAKES ABOUT ¾ CUP [180 ML]

¾ cup [180 g] strained full-fat Greek yogurt

2 Tbsp extra-virgin olive oil

1 Tbsp lightly packed dill leaves, chopped

1 Tbsp lightly packed parsley leaves, chopped

Zest of 1 lemon

½ tsp coriander seeds, toasted and ground

½ tsp fennel seeds, toasted and ground

½ tsp kosher salt

¼ tsp freshly ground black pepper

⅛ tsp rose water

In a small bowl, combine the yogurt and oil, then add the dill, parsley, lemon zest, coriander, fennel, salt, pepper, and rose water. Stir all the ingredients together up to 1 day in advance.

Buttermilk Dressing

MAKES ⅔ CUP [160 ML]

3 oz [85 g] summer squash, peeled and cut into ½ to 1 in [1.2 to 2.5 cm] pieces

2 Tbsp plus ½ tsp extra-virgin olive oil

¼ tsp kosher salt

½ cup [120 ml] buttermilk

½ garlic clove, grated

Zest of ½ lemon

¼ serrano chile, grated

2 Tbsp lightly packed dill leaves, finely chopped

Freshly ground black pepper

Set an oven rack 2 to 3 in [5 to 7.5 cm] beneath the heating element and preheat the oven to 375°F [190°C]. Toss the squash with ½ tsp of the oil and ¼ tsp of the salt. Roast until tender, 15 to 20 minutes, then finish under the broiler for a couple of minutes until lightly browned. Set aside to cool.

In a blender, purée the squash with the remaining 2 Tbsp of oil, the remaining ½ tsp of salt, the buttermilk, garlic, lemon zest, and serrano until very smooth. Stir in the dill by hand and season with pepper. Refrigerate in an airtight container until you're ready to serve, up to 3 days.

Garlic Butter

MAKES ABOUT 1 CUP [240 ML]

1 cup [225 g] unsalted butter

2 large shallots, minced

4 tsp kosher salt

1 Tbsp dry white wine

1 tsp freshly ground black pepper

12 garlic cloves, grated

½ in [12 mm] piece fresh ginger, grated, or ¼ tsp ground ginger

Zest of 1 lemon

2 Tbsp rice flour

½ cup [6 g] loosely packed parsley leaves, finely chopped

2 Tbsp loosely packed tarragon leaves, finely chopped

Melt 2 Tbsp of the butter in a large skillet over medium heat. Add the shallots and salt and sauté for a few minutes, until the shallots are tender and translucent. Add the wine, pepper, garlic, ginger, and lemon zest and cook until the garlic is fragrant, about 2 minutes more, then stir in the rice flour and cook for a minute or two to eliminate its raw flavor. Transfer to a bowl and refrigerate until completely chilled through. Meanwhile, allow the remaining butter to soften at room temperature.

Use a stand mixer fitted with the paddle attachment or an electric mixer to cream the butter with the cooked shallots, parsley, and tarragon. Keep at room temperature to serve right away or refrigerate in an airtight container for up to 3 days; soften at room temperature before serving.

Smoky Chimichurri

MAKES ABOUT 1 CUP [240 ML]

1 recipe Smoked Paprika Oil (page 194)

2 garlic cloves, grated

1 shallot, minced

½ serrano chile, grated

½ cup [6 g] lightly packed cilantro leaves, finely chopped

¼ cup [3 g] lightly packed parsley leaves, finely chopped

2 Tbsp lightly packed dill leaves, finely chopped

2 Tbsp sherry vinegar

4 tsp fresh lemon juice

1 Tbsp lightly packed marjoram leaves, finely chopped

1 tsp kosher salt

½ tsp lightly packed thyme leaves, finely chopped

⅛ tsp freshly ground black pepper

In a medium bowl, combine all the ingredients. Use right away or refrigerate in an airtight container for up to 1 day.

Parsley Sauce

MAKES ½ CUP [120 ML]

1 bunch flat-leaf parsley, plus more for garnish

½ cup [120 ml] Kombu Dashi (page 207), vegetable stock, or water

1 tsp coriander seeds, toasted and ground

1 tsp caraway seeds, toasted and ground

½ tsp kosher salt

Chill a blender beaker in the freezer for at least 15 minutes. Add the parsley, Kombu Dashi, coriander, caraway, and salt; purée until smooth. Transfer to a small bowl and keep very cold until ready to use; this will keep the color vibrant.

Ramp Salsa Verde

MAKES 1 CUP [240 ML]

2 oz [55 g] Lacto-Fermented Ramps (page 184) or pickled onions, plus brine

2 oz [55 g] fresh ramps

¾ cup [180 ml] extra-virgin olive oil

¾ cup [9 g] lightly packed parsley leaves, chopped

2 Tbsp fresh lemon juice

2 Tbsp lightly packed dill leaves, chopped

1 Tbsp lightly packed marjoram leaves, chopped

2 tsp lightly packed thyme leaves, chopped

¾ tsp kosher salt

½ tsp freshly ground black pepper

½ tsp red pepper flakes

2 oil-packed anchovy fillets, minced

1 garlic clove, minced

Zest of 1 lemon

Squeeze the fermented ramps to eliminate any excess liquid. Mince the fermented and fresh ramps (both whites and greens) and combine them with the oil, parsley, lemon juice, dill, marjoram, thyme, salt, pepper, red pepper flakes, anchovies, garlic, lemon zest, and about 1 Tbsp of the pickle brine. Refrigerate in an airtight container until you're ready to serve, up to 5 days.

Tomato Leaf Pesto

Use this where you'd use classic basil pesto: add to pasta; smother roast veggies; sauce a frittata; or spoon over roast chicken, pork, or beef.

MAKES ¾ CUP [180 ML]

1 cup [12 g] lightly packed parsley leaves

¾ cup [12 g] lightly packed tomato leaves or baby spinach

2 Tbsp lightly packed marjoram leaves

½ cup [120 ml] extra-virgin olive oil

2 Tbsp grapeseed oil or Tomato Leaf Oil (page 194)

2 Tbsp fresh lemon juice

1 tsp kosher salt

⅛ tsp freshly ground black pepper

3 Oil-Preserved Tomatoes (page 193) or oil-packed sun-dried tomatoes, drained and chopped

1 garlic clove, grated

¼ cup [30 g] walnuts, toasted

On the day you plan to serve the dip, combine the parsley, tomato leaves, and marjoram in a food processor and pulse until finely chopped. Add the olive oil, grapeseed oil, lemon juice, salt, pepper, tomatoes, and garlic and process until the oil turns a light shade of green. Hand chop the walnuts coarsely. Add the walnuts and pulse once or twice, just until incorporated.

Hibiscus-Za'atar Pesto

MAKES ABOUT ½ CUP [120 ML]

4 garlic cloves, grated

2 tsp fresh lemon juice

⅓ cup [80 ml] extra-virgin olive oil

¼ cup [6 g] lightly packed cilantro leaves, minced

1 recipe Hibiscus-Za'atar Spice Blend (page 199)

½ serrano chile, stemmed and minced

In a small bowl, combine the garlic and lemon juice; stir to combine and let it sit for 5 minutes so the garlic's flavor can mellow.

Separately, combine the oil, cilantro, spice blend, and serrano. Stir in the garlic-lemon mixture. Use right away or refrigerate in an airtight container for up to 1 day.

Pumpkin Seed and Cilantro Sauce

MAKES 1 CUP [240 ML]

8 garlic cloves, chopped

⅓ cup [80 ml] extra-virgin olive oil

2 scallions, white and light green parts only

¼ serrano pepper

3 Tbsp fresh lime juice

1 Tbsp pumpkin seed oil

¾ cup [105 g] pumpkin seeds, toasted

1 tsp kosher salt

⅓ cup [4 g] lightly packed cilantro leaves, finely chopped

Combine the garlic and oil in a small saucepan. Cook over low heat until the garlic is soft and easily smashes against the sides of the pan, about 15 minutes; keep an eye on it since you don't want it to brown. Allow to cool completely.

Set a metal grate directly over a gas burner or heat a grill to medium-high. Cook the scallions and serrano directly over the flame so they blister but don't wilt. Keep all the charred black bits—they have a lot of flavor. When the vegetables are cool enough to handle, coarsely chop.

Add the garlic and oil mixture, lime juice, pumpkin seed oil, and 2 Tbsp of water to a blender, followed by the chopped scallions and serrano, pumpkin seeds, and salt. Blend until combined, then add the cilantro and continue to purée until very smooth. Refrigerate in an airtight container for up to 3 days.

Green Onion–Citrus Sauce

MAKES 1 CUP [240 ML]

2 dried árbol chiles, stemmed

8 scallions

1 large orange or 2 small oranges

½ cup [120 ml] untoasted sesame oil

4 garlic cloves, minced or finely grated

2 Tbsp unhulled white sesame seeds, toasted

2 Tbsp black sesame seeds, toasted

2 Tbsp Lacto-Fermented Ramps (page 184), greens and bulbs, chopped

2 Tbsp rice vinegar

2 Tbsp fish sauce

Freshly ground black pepper

Place the chiles on a slotted spoon or mesh spider and toast directly over a medium-high flame until mostly black (this should take only a few seconds), or char them under the broiler. When they are cool enough to handle, grind them in a spice grinder or mortar and pestle and set aside.

Thinly slice the scallions and reserve the greens. Zest the orange for the sauce.

In a small pot over medium heat, warm the oil until it begins to dance. Add the scallion whites and garlic and cook, stirring occasionally, until tender, about 6 minutes. Add the orange zest, white sesame seeds, black sesame seeds, and ground chile; stir to combine.

Turn off the heat and allow the sauce to cool to room temperature. Stir in the scallion greens, ramps, vinegar, and fish sauce, and season with pepper. Use right away or refrigerate in an airtight container for up to 1 day.

Sorrel-Anchovy Vinaigrette

MAKES 1 CUP [240 ML]

2 cups [40 g] lightly packed sorrel leaves

½ cup plus 1 Tbsp [135 ml] extra-virgin olive oil

¼ cup [3 g] lightly packed dill leaves

¼ cup [60 ml] fresh lemon juice

1½ tsp honey

½ tsp kosher salt

¼ tsp freshly ground black pepper

6 oil-packed anchovy fillets

1 garlic clove

Combine the sorrel, oil, dill, lemon juice, honey, salt, pepper, anchovies, and garlic in a blender and purée until very smooth.

Harissa Vinaigrette

MAKES ABOUT 3 CUPS [720 G]

1½ tsp coriander seeds

1 tsp caraway seeds

1 tsp fennel seeds

1 tsp black peppercorns

½ tsp cumin seeds

2½ Tbsp ground cayenne pepper or hot paprika, or more to taste

1 Tbsp sweet paprika

1 cup [240 ml] extra-virgin olive oil

1 cup [12 g] lightly packed parsley leaves

½ cup [6 g] lightly packed dill leaves

½ cup [6 g] lightly packed marjoram leaves

½ cup [6 g] lightly packed mint leaves

½ Preserved Lemon (page 185), seeds removed

1 Tbsp plus 1 tsp lemon juice

¼ cup (about 2 oz [60 g]) white onion or shallot, coarsely chopped

12 garlic cloves (about 1 oz [30 g])

1½ cups [360 g] Sweet-Sour-Spicy Pepper Paste (page 186)

2 Tbsp sherry vinegar

2 Tbsp dried mint, ground

2 tsp tomato paste

2 tsp honey

1½ tsp kosher salt

1 tsp red wine vinegar

1 tsp sumac powder

In a spice grinder, combine the coriander, caraway, fennel, peppercorns, and cumin; grind to a fine powder, then combine with the cayenne and sweet paprika.

Gently warm ½ cup [120 ml] of the oil in a medium saucepan over low heat. Add all the ground spices and cook, stirring frequently, until very fragrant, 10 minutes.

In a blender, combine the remaining ½ cup [120 ml] of oil with the fresh herbs, preserved lemon, lemon juice, onion, and garlic; purée until smooth. Add this mixture to the saucepan with the spices and oil, increase the heat to medium-low, and whisk in the pepper paste, sherry vinegar, dried mint, tomato paste, honey, salt, red wine vinegar, and sumac powder. Cook, stirring frequently to prevent scorching, until the sauce is very thick, with most of the water cooked out. Purée once more until it's perfectly smooth and emulsified and refrigerate in an airtight container for up to 2 weeks.

Lemon-Dill Vinaigrette

MAKES ABOUT 1 CUP [120 ML]

½ cup [120 ml] fresh lemon juice

¼ cup [60 ml] extra-virgin olive oil, plus more for charring

¼ cup [3 g] lightly packed dill leaves

1½ tsp honey

½ tsp kosher salt, plus more as needed

2 garlic cloves, chopped

¼ serrano chile, chopped

In a blender, purée the lemon juice, oil, dill, honey, salt, garlic, and serrano. Store, refrigerated, in an airtight container for up to 2 weeks.

Kombu Dashi

MAKES 3½ QT [3 L]

4 sheets dried kombu, each 3 by 6 in [7.5 by 15 cm]

4 qt [3.8 L] soft or filtered water

Trim small slits into the kombu with a pair of scissors to help it release its flavor. In a large pot, combine the kombu and water and let soak until the kombu starts to soften, about 2 hours.

Place the pot over medium heat and bring to a gentle simmer (ideally 140°F to 160°F [60°C to 71°C]), making sure the water never boils. Cook gently until the broth develops a mild sea-like aroma and noticeable but delicate salinity and flavor, about 1 hour. At this point, the kombu should be tender enough to pierce easily with a chopstick.

Strain the dashi through a fine-mesh sieve, discarding the solids. If not using immediately, let the dashi cool at room temperature until lukewarm, about 30 minutes. Cover and refrigerate for up to 2 days or freeze for up to 3 months.

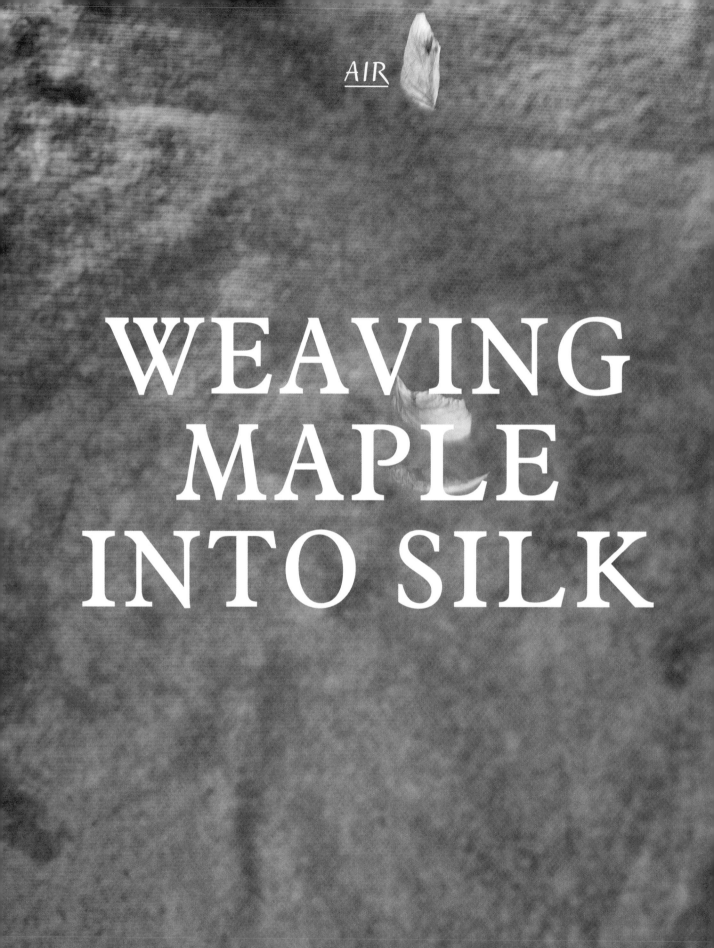

WEAVING MAPLE INTO SILK

CHAPTER 5

Air in the spiritual realm

East, the direction of the sunrise, represents the element of air and the power of the mind. Air is movement manifested; it's the four winds, a message bearer, a mental clarifier, and a space holder. Imagination, inspiration, truth, sound, and smell are all carried upon the winds, which offer change and growth as they travel through us, across us, and behind us. It is through air that we transform thoughts into spoken word and dreams into vivid realities. If we can visualize our reality, then we can manifest it. Air is connected to our souls and allows us lightness, levity, and actualization. In nature, air forms wind, the atmosphere, and breath. At times, something may be so beautiful or mesmerizing that it actually takes our breath away. But air can never be captured or tamed.

Air in the physical realm

Though we cannot tame air or hold it in our hands, we can harness its powers.

It was in the early autumn of 1999, while I was hiking solo through the Himalayas to summit Gokyo Ri, where I first felt what it's like to fight for air. The air was thinner than I had ever known, the altitude higher than I had ever been, but by the light of the moon, I began my ascent to the top of that peak to watch the sunrise at 17,575 feet [5,375 m]. First, I had to jump from rock to rock along the edge of the lake, lit only by my headlamp as I found my way to the trail, and then the 2,000-foot [610 m] climb began. With each step and breath, I made my way closer to the top.

At 10,000 feet [3,048 m], the atmosphere is only 50 percent of that found at sea level, and our lungs must expand to keep up with our racing hearts. The feeling of taking air deep within the lungs is the essence of being alive, and being on top of a mountain is truly the essence of being free. These moments give way to the honor that air deserves. Air is our first nourishment from the womb and the last gasp before we float away.

From air bubbles expanding and lifting doughs and batters, to invisible air pockets created from creaming butter with sugar, to the rich umber glaze of convection, air is indispensable in the baking world. The oven's dry heat helps cakes rise and breads form crackly crusts. This chapter showcases baking and pastries as a form of culinary wizardry, with an emphasis on harnessing natural sweeteners—from roasting fruits into rich pastes to dehydrating parsnips into a sugar-like powder. I also share a few small bites that you can always have on hand as a way to start a meal, for *mignardises* platters, or for when friends and neighbors drop by for a cup of tea. I have included a few starchy snacks, such as crackers and breads, for the indispensable way they round out a meal.

CHOCOLATE AND FIR TIP COOKIES

This cookie was created during a brainstorming session with one of the most magnificent women I know, Erin Merrigan. Erin is regal, strong, and one of the most humble humans I've had the pleasure of sharing time and space with. As the head baker of my North Adams kitchen, Erin worked with me to create a cookie to herald the opening of Tourists, a boutique hotel in Western Massachusetts. Drawing on the Tollhouse cookie history Erin had learned in school, we hoped to link our cookie to something historical, but all we found was the town where the cookies were created, tiny, foresty Whitman, Massachusetts. Dreaming of the forests I left behind in Northern California and the foraged sweet fir tips I used to cook with, my mind wandered to the young spruce tips I had recently picked in my new surroundings. I folded the flavors I dreamed of from both coasts into a cookie.

Makes about 1 dozen cookies

Line two baking sheets with parchment paper. Freeze the fir tips until brittle, at least 2 hours. Pulse into a fine powder using a spice grinder.

Sift the flours, salt, baking powder, and baking soda into a medium bowl and set aside.

Using a stand mixer fitted with the paddle attachment on medium speed, or a whisk in a large bowl, cream the sugar and butter until very light, about 5 minutes. Add the egg, mix well, then add the fir tips.

Reduce the mixer speed to low, gradually fold in the flour mixture, and mix until just combined, 5 to 10 seconds. Stir in the chocolate chips.

Scoop the dough into 2½ oz [70 g] balls; space them 2 in [5 cm] apart on the baking sheets and flatten them gently using the heel of your hand. Cover the sheets with plastic wrap and refrigerate for at least 24 hours or up to 72 hours.

To bake the cookies, preheat the oven to 300°F [150°C] and allow the cookies to sit at room temperature for 15 minutes. Just before baking, top each one with a pinch of flaky salt. Bake for 12 to 15 minutes, rotating halfway through, until the edges are golden brown and the tops just barely set. Cool completely, and store in an airtight container at room temperature for up to 3 days.

¼ cup [10 g] fresh fir or spruce tips

1¼ cups [200 g] Cup4Cup flour

⅓ cup [45 g] buckwheat flour

1 tsp kosher salt

1 tsp baking powder

½ tsp baking soda

¾ cup plus 2 Tbsp [240 g] Maple Sugar (page 203)

½ cup plus 2 Tbsp [140 g] unsalted butter, softened

1 large egg

1½ cups [270 g] dark chocolate chips

Flaky salt

PUMPKIN SEED AND BUCKWHEAT COOKIES

This is a simple French shortbread (*sable*) recipe, given a twist with the inclusion of buckwheat flour and ground pumpkin seeds. While the cookies are tempting in their own right, I like to think they allude to early human life when hunter-gatherers subsisted predominantly on grasses and seeds. Pairing buckwheat, a gluten-free pseudo-cereal, with pumpkin and flax lends an earthy quality to an otherwise straightforward treat. And just like a classic sable, the dough is tender, meaning the final texture lands somewhere between melt-in-your-mouth and barely crumbly. While I adore this pairing, the fun of these cookies is that they're completely riffable. Try them with any number of flours (gluten free or otherwise), seeds, or nuts.

Makes about 18 cookies

Cut the butter into ½ in [12 mm] cubes and chill until very cold.

In a food processor, pulse the pumpkin seeds a few times until they're finely chopped. Add the buckwheat flour, maple sugar, ground flaxseeds, ginger, salt, and orange zest. Pulse to combine, then dot the butter evenly over the mix and keep pulsing just until the dough holds together but is still crumbly. Add the egg yolk and pulse a couple more times to incorporate.

Scrape the dough onto a sheet of parchment paper and roll it into a roughly 1½ in [4 cm] thick log. Refrigerate until fully chilled or tightly wrap and freeze for up to 2 weeks.

Preheat the oven to 350°F [180°C] and line a baking sheet with parchment paper. Cut the dough into ½ in [12 mm] slices and bake until set but still slightly soft, 15 to 20 minutes. Cool completely before eating.

½ cup [110 g] unsalted butter

½ cup [80 g] pumpkin seeds, toasted

1 cup [120 g] buckwheat flour

⅓ cup [55 g] Maple Sugar (page 203)

1 Tbsp flaxseeds, coarsely ground

1 tsp ground ginger

½ tsp kosher salt

Zest of 1 orange

1 egg yolk

STUFFED COOKIES WITH PRESERVED FRUIT

There's something magical about a stuffed cookie. Although a tad fiddly to make, they're fun to eat, like unwrapping a gift with a surprise inside. This one's dough is buttery and crumbling, of the shortbread ilk, while its filling is a great way to utilize preserved fruit pastes from summer's glut. I especially enjoy eating them on cold, dreary mornings with a cup of hot tea, their fruity underbellies reminding me of warmer months.

I soak my oats prior to preparing the jam in order to increase their digestibility and make their nutrients more bioavailable. Oats, like all grains, contain phytic acid, which can inhibit the proper absorption of minerals like zinc and iron. By soaking and draining off the liquid, you eliminate some of the acid and make the jam more nutrient-dense.

Makes about 18 cookies

TO MAKE THE COOKIES: Preheat the oven to 325°F [165°C]. Spread the oats in a single layer on a baking sheet and toast until very fragrant, 15 to 20 minutes. Allow to cool, then use a food processor or, preferably, a spice grinder to mill the oats into a fine powder. Separately, cut the butter into ½ in [12 mm] cubes and chill until very cold.

In a food processor, combine the oat flour, almond flour, maple sugar, flaxseeds, citrus powder, salt, and lemon zest. Dot the butter evenly over the mixture and pulse until the dough holds together in a crumbly mass. Add the yolks and pulse a couple more times to incorporate. Press the dough into an airtight container and refrigerate until very cold.

To assemble the cookies, preheat the oven to 350°F [180°C]. Line a baking sheet with parchment paper. Portion the dough into mounds about the size of an apricot (about 1½ oz [40 g]) and shape each one so it resembles a beehive, tapered at the top.

Use your fingers to make a deep, narrow indentation in the dough, keeping the sides tall, and fill each cookie with about 1 tsp of the jam. Pinch the indentation closed (wet your fingertips to help seal) and smooth the sides and top into a ball.

Space the cookies about 2 in [5 cm] apart on the prepared baking sheet and bake until set but still slightly soft, 25 to 30 minutes. Cool completely before eating. Cookies can be stored in an airtight container for up to 3 days, though they're best eaten the day they're made.

Thumbprint Cookies

1 cup plus 6 Tbsp [240 g] old-fashioned rolled oats or 2 cups [240 g] toasted oat flour

1 cup [225 g] unsalted butter

1⅓ cups [160 g] almond flour

⅔ cup [110 g] Maple Sugar (page 203)

2 Tbsp flaxseeds, coarsely ground

2 tsp citrus powder (see Drying section, page 196)

1 tsp kosher salt

Zest of 2 lemons

2 egg yolks

1 cup [240 g] Fruit and Oat Jam (recipe follows) or jam of your choice

TO MAKE THE JAM: In a small bowl, combine the oats and lemon juice with ½ cup [120 ml] of water. Cover and let stand at room temperature for 12 to 24 hours.

Drain the oats and rinse them well. In a small saucepan, combine the oats with the milk and salt. Bring to a simmer over medium-high heat, then lower the heat to medium-low and stir frequently until the oatmeal is very thick and the bottom of the pan stays dry when you scrape it. Stir in the fruit paste and honey and set aside to cool completely. Refrigerate in an airtight container for up to 3 days before using.

Fruit and Oat Jam

Makes 1 cup [240 g]

¼ cup [25 g] old-fashioned rolled oats

1 tsp fresh lemon juice, apple cider vinegar, or whey

¼ cup [60 ml] whole milk

½ tsp kosher salt

½ cup [140 g] fruit paste

1½ tsp honey

BLACKINTON TEA COOKIES

I was after a Welsh breakfast cake when I began experimenting with this antique recipe, an homage to the large Welsh community in Blackinton, a historic district within North Adams, Massachusetts. As I tinkered with old recipes, I wanted something reminiscent of thick oatmeal cookies rather than a classic scone's texture, so here's my modern take on an old delicacy. The cookies pair beautifully with tea but are equally wonderful on long hikes, their freshness lasting much longer than you'd expect. While sauerkraut might seem like a strange addition to a sweet, it lends a bit of moisture, a whole bunch of texture, and a savoriness that balances the sweet. However, if kraut in cookies feels too curious, shredded unsweetened coconut will do just fine in its place.

Makes 18 to 24 cookies

Preheat the oven to 350°F [180°C]. For drop cookies, line two baking sheets with parchment paper or silicone baking mats; for rounder, more uniform cookies, lightly grease the wells of 2 muffin tins.

Combine the oats, rice flour, oat flour, maple sugar, hazelnut flour, and flaxseeds in a large mixing bowl; set aside.

In a colander, rinse the sauerkraut thoroughly to eliminate its briny flavor. Use a clean dish towel or a few layers of cheesecloth to wring it dry, then finely chop. Dice the fruit and combine with the sauerkraut.

In a saucepan over medium-low heat, melt the butter with the honey and lemon zest. When the honey has thinned out and melded with the butter, add the baking soda and whisk continuously until the mixture is frothy. Add this to the dry ingredients in two additions, stirring between each one, then fold in the chopped sauerkraut and dried fruit.

Divide the dough into roughly 1½ oz [40 g] balls, either dropped onto the prepared baking sheets or pressed into the muffin tins. Bake until the tops are set but still soft, 20 to 25 minutes; rotate the sheets or tins halfway through. If using muffin tins, allow to cool completely before popping out of the molds. Store in an airtight container at room temperature for up to 1 week.

1½ cups [150 g] old-fashioned rolled oats, toasted

¾ cup [100 g] rice flour

½ cup [50 g] oat flour

½ cup [85 g] Maple Sugar (page 203)

⅓ cup [30 g] hazelnut flour or almond flour

⅓ cup [50 g] flaxseeds, coarsely ground

¾ cup [90 g] drained sauerkraut or finely shredded unsweetened coconut

⅔ cup [100 g] dried tart fruit, such as apricots or cherries

¾ cup [165 g] unsalted butter

2 Tbsp [40 g] honey

Zest of 2 lemons

1 tsp baking soda

MAPLE AND CARDAMOM CANDIES

There's a moment in late winter when its icy clutch begins to soften, heralding the thaw of spring. As the weather hints at warmer days, it's as though the natural world heaves a collective exhale, and we're reassured that time does indeed march toward light evenings, the return of rhubarb and flower-laden salads. It's at this moment, when one season begins to give way to the next, that maple tapping abounds. I'm a creature of habit and I slip on my running shoes in the peak of summer's humid heat or winter's deepest frost. I remember trail running during my first winter in New England and seeing groves of maple trees fastened with buckets to collect the sap. It seemed as though every tree had an appendage. Maple, quite literally, is New England's liquid gold. Cardamom gives these candies a floral, citrusy hit, but feel free to experiment with other warm spices.

**Makes about sixteen
2 in [5 cm] candies**

Vegetable oil for cooking

2 cups [480 ml] pure maple syrup

1 Tbsp unsalted butter

1 tsp finely ground cardamom, plus more for garnish

Place silicone candy molds on a small rimmed baking sheet, or line a square baking dish with parchment paper.

Brush oil along the sides of a medium, high-sided saucepan (the syrup foams up as it heats; the oil helps minimize this) and clip a candy thermometer to the side so its bulb hovers just above the bottom of the pan. Add the syrup and butter.

Cook the syrup over medium heat, without stirring, until it reaches 240°F [116°C]; it should form a soft ball when you drop a small spoonful into cold water. This can take a while—up to 30 minutes on some burners—but resist the urge to crank the heat. Remove from the heat and allow the temperature to come down to 190°F [88°C] on its own.

Making big, folding strokes with your spatula, stir in the cardamom. The mixture will (fairly quickly) start to change color and texture—it should look opaque and may feel like you are scraping sugar off the bottom of the pan. At this point, spoon or pour it into the molds or prepared dish, working quickly so it doesn't crystallize. It can be helpful to do this with a partner—one person pours and another levels off each mold—and an offset spatula smooths the tops of the candies quickly.

Dust the tops of the candies with more ground cardamom. Tightly cover and leave to set at room temperature for 1 to 2 hours before popping the candies out of the molds or cutting into squares. Store in an airtight container for up to 1 month.

MAPLE HALVA

Visually, blocks of halva always remind me of Earth's glacial striations, their flavors streaked throughout as if telling tales of times past. Halva is a traditional sesame confection from the Middle East and one of my favorite treats from childhood. For the unfamiliar, it has a somewhat quirky texture, shattering between your fingers before it softens on your tongue, its flaky shards quickly melting away into memories and longing. This version uses maple as the sweetener. I always wanted to make halva without refined sugars but found honey too overpowering for the subtle flavor of the sesame. Other nut/seed butters work well too, but sesame is classic and nostalgic for me.

Makes 20 small pieces

Brush oil along the sides of a medium, high-sided saucepan (the syrup foams up as it heats; the oil helps minimize this) and clip a candy thermometer to the side so its bulb hovers just above the bottom of the pan. Separately, place the tahini in a large heatproof bowl. Line a small plate or baking sheet with parchment and set a 4 to 5 in [10 to 12 cm] mold or small loaf pan (5½ by 3 in [14 by 7½ cm]) on top.

Pour the syrup into the saucepan and warm it over medium heat, ensuring that the thermometer is fully submerged in the syrup as it simmers, until it reaches 248°F [120°C]. When you drop a small spoonful into cold water, it should form a firm ball. Be patient—the temperature may take a while to warm up but it can quickly jump.

Immediately pour the syrup over the tahini and begin to fold them together with a spatula or wooden spoon, making wide strokes to combine as the mixture sets up (it will thicken quickly). Spoon it into the prepared mold, scatter sesame seeds and flaky salt over the top, and cover. Allow to rest at cool room temperature for 24 to 36 hours, then cut it into small bites. Store in an airtight container to keep humidity at bay; desiccator packets make this easy but aren't necessary.

Vegetable oil for cooking

½ cup plus 2 tsp [150 g] tahini

½ cup plus 2 Tbsp [200 ml] maple syrup

Black sesame seeds and flaky sea salt for garnish

DATE AND PRESERVED LEMON BALLS

In Jewish culture and lore, dates are a symbol of grace and elegance. Many other cultures believe in the magic of dates in aiding fertility and fostering love and connection. To me, the date is a reminder of food's sacred side. The act of preparing, cooking, and eating food is, if you let it be, a meditative moment. Your kitchen can be a place of powerful magic. For me, these little truffle-like bites, packed with salt, acid, and caramel notes, signify the different layers of life—tart, sweet, crunchy, and luscious.

Makes 36 to 48 balls

¾ cup [165 g] unsalted butter

1¼ cups [225 g] pitted Medjool dates

3 Tbsp lemon juice

1 Tbsp tahini

½ tsp kosher salt

¼ cup [70 g] Preserved Lemon Paste Harissa (page 187) or store-bought marmalade

Black and/or white sesame seeds, toasted, for rolling

Preheat the oven to 200°F [95°C]. In a small, ovenproof saucepan, combine half of the butter with the dates, lemon juice, tahini, and salt (don't worry about stirring them together).

Cover the saucepan and place it in the oven, allowing time for the butter to completely melt and soften the dates, 45 minutes to 1 hour. Cool the mixture to room temperature.

To finish the date balls, allow the remaining butter to soften. Use a food processor to purée the date mix, softened butter, and preserved lemon paste until everything is completely smooth and emulsified. Refrigerate, covered, until completely chilled before rolling the balls.

Combine the sesame seeds in a bowl. Use a small scoop or spoon to portion the dough into balls (roughly 2 tsp each) and roll to coat in the sesame seeds. Refrigerate the balls, covered, for up to 3 weeks.

HONEY MARZIPAN

As a little kid, I would join my mother on her shopping trips to Bloomingdale's in Chicago for one reason only: the Italian candy shop at the entrance. If I was well-behaved while trying on new clothes, I'd be rewarded with two carefully painted, jeweled marzipan treats.

Here, honey replaces refined sugar, lending a strong but unique twist on the original sweet. The texture is a bit looser than the standard sugar ones, but they mold nicely just the same; refrigerate the marzipan if you want it to retain its shape for long periods of time. Have fun with the base: add flavors and colors according to your whims. Try rose water, orange blossom water, freshly ground cardamom, or lavender.

Makes 24 to 36 bite-size pieces

½ cup [170 g] honey

2 cups [240 g] nut meal, such as almond, pistachio, or hazelnut

1 egg white

½ tsp almond extract

¼ tsp salt

Additional flavors (optional)

Clip a candy thermometer to the side of a small saucepan and set up an ice bath in a bowl large enough to hold the bowl of your stand mixer. Set the bowl of the stand mixer in the ice bath. Add the honey to the saucepan and bring it to 240°F [115°C] over medium heat. Immediately remove the thermometer and pour the honey into the prepared bowl, returning it to the mixer. Fit the mixer with the paddle attachment and beat the honey for 5 minutes. It will thicken and set up as it cools. Work in the nut meal, egg white, almond extract, salt, and any additional flavors, if using. Beat for 5 minutes more. It should feel stiff and a bit tacky.

Fill a large saucepan with 2 in [5 cm] of water and bring to a simmer. Set the bowl of marzipan on top to form a double boiler. The mixture will be too thick to stir, but use a spatula to break it up and move it around so it warms through.

Return the bowl to the stand mixer and beat on medium-low speed until the bowl feels cool to the touch and the mixture is thick, chewy, and smooth, 15 to 20 minutes, scraping down the sides every 5 minutes. Mold into bite-size pieces and store, refrigerated, in an airtight container for up to 2 weeks or freeze for up to 2 months.

Seasonal Variations

WINTER
Add dried turmeric or dried mace.

SPRING
Add dried hibiscus or dried rose.

AUTUMN
Add dried sage or dried lavender.

SUMMER
Add dried lemon, anise hyssop, or dried orange blossom.

PASTILLES

When I hear "pastille," I immediately picture treats from my childhood, little round white tins with jewel-like candies inside. They were always brightly colored and wildly aromatic. To me, they were a sweet treat, but in truth, they were formulated after medicinal balls meant to act as a curative or remedy for treating a myriad of ailments. Candies to soothe the throat date back to 100 BC, when the Egyptians would fold herbs and spices into honey for herbal remedies. The ones I recall eating were a far cry from these ancient lozenges, so here I channel the pastilles of the past, with a myriad of flavors and colors to choose from.

Mixtures for Health

Digestion: ginger, lemon, mugwort, fennel

Calming: lemon balm, mint, chamomile, valerian, lavender

Antibacterial: marjoram, oregano, bee balm, cranberry, honeysuckle

Sore throat: cinnamon, spruce, elderberry, licorice root, sage

Coughs: thyme, horehound, hyssop, white pine, yarrow, marshmallow root

Stomachache: ginger, lemon, peppermint, fennel, holy basil, mint

Inflammation: clove, pine, ginger, turmeric, black pepper, tarragon

Ingredients by Color

Red: sweet paprika, rose, cayenne, saffron, sumac, bee balm

Orange: marigold, bee pollen, orange peel

Yellow: turmeric, fennel pollen, chamomile, mustard, lemon peel

Green: mint, lemon balm, lemon verbena, parsley, nettle, algae

Blue: bachelor buttons, blue pea flowers, dried blueberry

Purple: hibiscus, violet, lavender, anise, hyssop flowers

Makes about 10 lozenges

Base Recipe

2 to 3 Tbsp powdered herbs, flowers, roots, bark, and/or leaves, plus 2 Tbsp more for rolling

2 Tbsp honey, preferably raw

Oil for rolling

Preheat a dehydrator or the oven to its lowest setting, approximately 95°F [35°C]. Line a baking sheet with parchment paper.

Place the powder in a small bowl and gradually pour in the honey so as not to thin the candies too much; add just enough to make a thick, consistent paste, like a sticky pie dough. Work the mixture with a mortar and pestle, a wooden spoon, or your hands until it is well combined.

Roll the mixture out into a long, uniform cylinder about the thickness of your pinkie finger. Cut the roll every ¼ in [6 mm] or so, depending on how large you want the lozenges to be. I make mine about the size of a blueberry. Alternatively, just pinch little pieces from the cylinder. Roll each piece into a small ball or oval. (Coating your hands first with olive oil or coconut oil keeps the mixture from sticking to your fingers.) Once formed, roll each ball in more of the spices to create a lovely color coating that keeps the lozenges from sticking together.

Place on the prepared baking sheet and let them dry in the oven for 2 to 3 hours. Drying completely without an oven or a dehydrator may take up to 2 days uncovered at room temperature.

Store in a glass jar with a tight-fitting lid for up to 3 months.

ICE POPS

Ice pops—and the inevitable juice they send dripping down my elbow, onto my dress and sandals—scream summer. These frozen pops have an uncanny way of bringing me back to my five-year-old self, tromping up to the snack bar window and staring at the rainbow display of Mr. Freeze pops. My sister would pick me up so I could choose my flavor, which was usually green, my favorite color regardless of the taste. Then, I'd squeeze, slurp, and push the ice pop up its plastic tubing, sucking with all my might to rescue the last dribbles of syrup from the bottom of the wrapper.

These days, I make ice pops for their cooling effects and whimsical flavor pairings. They're a blank canvas, really. Think of your favorite fruit smoothie and freeze it. Turn ice pops into icy stirrers for a summer cocktail. Be a kid again and let the ice pop dribble down your hands—it's all part of the fun.

Flavors I love:

- Red: strawberry–poppy seed, watermelon–lime–black sesame, raspberry-rose

- Orange: apricot-almond, tangerine-carrot

- Yellow: peaches and cream, ginger-peach, lemonade–lemon verbena

- Green: cucumber-mint-lemon-yogurt, lemon balm–white grape, green apple–anise

- Blue/Purple: blackberry-lilac, blueberry-tarragon, bronze fennel–anise hyssop

- Black: cocoa-cinnamon, black sesame–date

- White: rice-cinnamon, kefir–berry crunch

Makes 4 to 6 small ice pops

---

2 cups [280 g] fresh or frozen fruit, puréed until smooth

¼ cup [60 ml] liquid, such as juice, coconut milk, or nut milk

2 Tbsp [40 g] honey

Splash of lemon or lime juice

Pinch of salt

Seasonings of your choice, such as minced fresh herbs, ground cardamom or cinnamon, seeds scraped from a vanilla bean, or citrus powder (see Drying section, page 196)

Ice pop molds or paper cups and sticks

Mix all the ingredients together in a bowl or purée them in a blender. Strain if desired. Pour the mixture into ice pop molds and let freeze for at least 6 hours, or preferably overnight; if using paper cups, freeze halfway before inserting the ice pop sticks to help keep the sticks upright.

To remove the ice pops, carefully run the molds under warm water for 20 seconds. Keep them frozen in their molds until they're ready to eat, or pop them out and store in freezer-safe resealable plastic bags.

Apply the above method to any of the suggested fruity combinations.

CONTINUED

Watermelon–Black Sesame

These are fun because the sesame seeds stay at the bottom, making the pop look like a watermelon slice. After freezing, you can add a green layer on top for a rind-like effect.

MAKES 4 TO 6 ICE POPS

1 lb [455 g] watermelon, rind and seeds removed

¼ cup [60 ml] lime juice

1 Tbsp honey

1½ Tbsp coconut oil

Ice pop molds or sticks

Strawberry and Cream

When I was a child, my mother used to make dessert bowls full of strawberries, raw sugar, and sour cream that we'd eat on the deck at night with the fireflies. This is my ode to those summer evenings. Leave seeds in the mix for added texture.

MAKES 4 TO 6 ICE POPS

8 oz [230 g] strawberries, hulled and halved

½ cup [120 ml] buttermilk or nut milk

½ cup [120 g] plain Greek yogurt

¼ cup [8 g] honey

Pinch of salt

Ice pop molds or sticks

Apricot-Almond

Apricot pits have a little nugget inside of them, the noyaux, which tastes just like bitter almond. Here, the two are combined to bring out the flavors from flesh to seed.

MAKES 4 TO 6 ICE POPS

8 oz [230 g] ripe apricots, pitted and halved

½ cup [120 ml] fennel juice

1½ Tbsp honey

2 Tbsp lemon juice

2 tsp Apricot Pit Extract (page 280) or almond extract

Ice pop molds or sticks

Ginger Peach

The ginger packs a spicy kick and the sweet peach cools it down.

MAKES 4 TO 6 ICE POPS

1 lb [455 g] ripe peaches, pitted and diced

½ cup [120 g] plain Greek yogurt

½ cup [120 ml] peach nectar

½ oz [15 g] piece fresh ginger, thinly sliced

3 Tbsp [60 g] honey

2 Tbsp lemon juice

Pinch of salt

Ice pop molds or sticks

Black Sesame–Date

Black sesame seeds are chock full of vitamin E, omega 6, and calcium.

MAKES 4 TO 6 ICE POPS

1½ cups [210 g] black sesame seeds, soaked overnight in water and drained

1½ cups [360 ml] nondairy milk, such as rice, coconut, almond, or macadamia

1 Tbsp honey

1 tsp orange blossom or rose water (optional) or 1 tsp dried orange blossom

3 dates, pitted and roughly chopped

Pinch of salt

Ice pop molds or sticks

Green Apple

Tart and ultra-green in flavor, and packed with nutrients.

MAKES 4 TO 6 ICE POPS

3½ cups [40 g] lightly packed fresh spinach

1 small cucumber [120 g], chopped

½ cup [7 g] fresh lemon balm or mint

½ cup [120 ml] apple juice

½ cup [120 g] applesauce

Ice pop molds or sticks

Blueberry Kefir

A health tonic with blueberries for anti-oxidant powers and dairy kefir.

MAKES 4 TO 6 ICE POPS

1⅔ cups [230 g] blueberries

½ cup [120 ml] dairy kefir

2 Tbsp honey

1 Tbsp lemon juice

1 tsp ground cardamom

Ice pop molds or sticks

Grape-Rose

An homage to the grape.

MAKES 4 TO 6 ICE POPS

1 cup [240 ml] purple grape juice

2 Tbsp extra-virgin olive oil

1½ Tbsp honey

1 Tbsp balsamic vinegar or saba

2 tsp rose water

Ice pop molds or sticks

FRUIT LEATHERS

Fruit roll-ups are a playful food memory from my childhood. I loved anything chewy, gently tart, but mostly just good, silly fun. Fruit leather was and still is all of these things to me.

Although we think of the snack as a modern-day packaged food, it is really an Old World preservation technique. Prior to Silpats and fancy dehydrators, people would spread cooked and puréed fruit onto wet muslin before drying it under the sun. Once fully dry, it was often cut into strips and stored in glass jars to last throughout the year. This recipe is a wonderful way to get sugar-free snacks into the house and to preserve flavors for times with less sun and more chill in the air.

Makes six 3 in [7.5 cm] strips

1 lb [455 g] ripe fruit

Herbs, spices, or other desired seasonings (optional)

Preheat the oven to the lowest temperature it will go (about 175°F [80°C]) or set a dehydrator to 120°F [50°C]. Line a rimmed baking sheet or dehydrator rack with a nonstick silicone liner or wax paper.

Prepare the fruit as needed: Peel and core fruits such as apples and pears, remove pits from stone fruits, hull strawberries, and so forth. Use a blender to purée the fruit (along with any other seasonings) until it's as smooth as possible. Pour the fruit over the prepared baking sheet and use an offset spatula to spread it evenly into a roughly ⅛ in [4 mm] thick layer; take care that it's not spread *too* thinly or it will be hard to peel off the sheet.

Bake until the mixture is completely dry to the touch. Timing will depend on how you're making it (ovens will "cook" the fruit and take less time) and on how juicy the fruit is, so check after about 4 hours but be prepared to wait longer. When the leather is done, allow it to cool completely.

Starting on one end, gently peel the leather off of the silicone or parchment. You can store it as a single sheet or, for individual servings, cut it into long sections 3 to 6 in [7.5 to 15 cm] wide. Set each piece over a sheet of parchment and roll it up like a scroll, tie it with twine to secure it, and store at room temperature in an airtight container or zip-top bag for up to 3 months.

KITCHEN NOTE:

While 1 lb [455 g] of fresh fruit is listed, the exact quantity is extremely flexible. The important part is to spread the pulp very thinly before dehydrating.

CONTINUED

Flavors for Spring

Rhubarb and lilac

Sorrel and lemon balm

Green strawberry and orange blossom

Apricot and Apricot Pit Extract (page 280) or almond extract

Flavors for Summer

Strawberry and fennel: Purée and strain.

Blueberry and juniper: Purée and strain.

Raspberry and mint: Purée and strain.

Plum and charred eggplant: Use in a 3:1 ratio. (Char the Japanese eggplant over an open flame till it splits. Purée the eggplant with steamed plums. Pass the mixture through a strainer to get rid of the seeds.)

Cherry and rose geranium

Peaches and chamomile

Flavor for Autumn

Hachiya persimmon: Use when very soft and balloon-like.

Salt-roasted pears (page 263) and spruce powder

Apples and tarragon

Roasted sweet potato and clove

Flavors for Winter

Winter squash and burnt lemon

Fire-charred and roasted quince

Date and burnt lemon

Roasted carrot and cardamom

Roasted red beets and orange or orange blossom

SEEDED HERB CRACKERS

Seeds have long been important forms of nourishment. Not only do the pebble-like kernels give an earthiness to dishes, but they're also packed with loads of nutrients. Pumpkin seeds, for example, have antiparasitic benefits and are a good source of iron, while black sesame seeds are high in calcium, antioxidants, zinc, vitamin E, iron, and vitamin B. Flax seeds have a good amount of protein, fiber, and lots of omega-3 fatty acids, while poppy seeds are high in minerals like manganese, phosphorus, magnesium, calcium, and iron. It's fair to say that these nubby, flourless crackers are chockablock with nutrients, and I often find myself eating them by the handful. Try them with dips and spreads, serve them with a cheese plate, or eat as an on-the-go snack.

Makes 10 to 12 dozen crackers

In an electric spice grinder or mortar and pestle, grind half of the flaxseeds to a coarse powder. Pour them into a large bowl and add the remaining flaxseeds, sunflower seeds, chia seeds, black sesame seeds, white sesame seeds, pumpkin seeds, and poppy seeds; stir well to combine. Set aside.

In a blender, combine the brine, onion, garlic, dill, parsley, cilantro, and salt and purée until completely smooth. Transfer to a small saucepan and gently warm over low heat until just steaming, then pour the mixture over the seeds. Cover the bowl with plastic wrap and set it aside at room temperature for at least 2 hours or up to overnight.

Once the flax and chia seeds have gelled, creating a strong, gooey structure, set a dehydrator to 115°F [46°C]; if you're using an oven instead, set it to the lowest possible temperature. Line two dehydrator racks or baking sheets with nonstick silicone liners or wax paper, then use an offset spatula or the back of a spoon to spread the seed mixture over the sheets in a thin, even layer, about ⅛ in [4 mm] thick. (Dipping your spatula in water first can help it glide over the mixture more smoothly.) Use your spatula to score neat lines in the batter, making 2 by 1 in [5 by 2.5 cm] crackers; or, if you prefer, leave them unscored and crack them into rustic shards when they're done baking.

CONTINUED

¾ cup [120 g] whole flaxseeds

⅓ cup [45 g] sunflower seeds

¼ cup [45 g] chia seeds

¼ cup [35 g] black sesame seeds

¼ cup [35 g] unhulled white sesame seeds

3 Tbsp pumpkin seeds

1 Tbsp poppy seeds

1 cup [240 ml] brine from salt-brined vegetables (page 180), mushroom broth, or vegetable stock

¼ large yellow onion

2 garlic cloves

¼ cup [3 g] lightly packed dill leaves

¼ cup [3 g] lightly packed parsley leaves

¼ cup [3 g] lightly packed cilantro leaves

1 tsp kosher salt

Transfer the cracker mixture to the dehydrator and let it dry for 8 hours; after 4 hours, turn the whole piece over and remove the silicone or wax paper. If using the oven, it will take about half the time, so check it after 2 hours.

When the crackers are fully brittle, break them along your pre-scored lines or into rustic 2 to 3 in [5 to 7.5 cm] shards. Serve right away or store at room temperature in an airtight container; they'll keep for up to 2 weeks. If they get hydrated at all, just re-crisp them in a low oven, leaving to cool again before eating.

Seasonal Variations

To be puréed in with the brine

WINTER

Winter savory, with a similar aroma to thyme, does well during the coldest months, as does rosemary. In a pinch, use some of your favorite dried herbs and add 2 Tbsp more of the brine to compensate for the liquid in the fresh herbs.

AUTUMN

As the nights get cooler, heartier herbs will marry well with the seasonal shift. Substitute thyme, sage, hyssop, and chervil in place of the herbs listed in the recipe.

SPRING

Chives and ramps are two of the first herbs of spring; substitute them for the onion.

SUMMER

It's an herb wonderland in summer, so take your pick—basil, marjoram, dill, cilantro, parsley, wild fennel, or whatever you have on hand or fresh from the garden can be used in place of the herbs listed in the recipe.

SILVER DOLLAR CORN CAKES

Farinata, which in Italian means "made of flour," is an unleavened pancake or flatbread with a soft center and crispy shell, traditionally made from chickpea flour. One popular history dates its origins back to ancient Rome, where soldiers would prepare the simple batter and cook it on their round, metal shields in the hot sun as a quick and economical snack before battle. My version swaps chickpea flour for cornmeal since it's such a culinary staple of New England. Be sure to let the batter rest for a couple of hours since it helps hydrate the cornmeal, keeping it from baking up dense and heavy. Folding in seasonal bounty or topping the finished pancakes with whatever you have on hand turns the snack into a meal.

Makes about 18 silver-dollar-size cakes or one 10 to 12 in [25 to 30 cm] cake

1 cup plus 2 Tbsp [140 g] corn flour or fine cornmeal

1 cup plus 2 Tbsp [270 ml] lukewarm water or Kombu Dashi (page 207)

3 Tbsp [30 g] gluten-free flour mix (such as Cup4Cup or Bob's Red Mill 1-to-1)

1 egg

2 Tbsp extra-virgin olive oil, plus more for brushing

1 tsp kosher salt

If your corn flour is medium or coarse, first pulse it in a blender to make the texture finer and soft like sand. In a blender, purée all the ingredients into a smooth, uniform batter.

Allow the batter to sit and hydrate for 2 hours at room temperature or cover and refrigerate overnight or for up to 2 days. Mix very well right before using.

When you're ready to bake, preheat the oven to 400°F [200°C]. Set a large cast-iron skillet or silver dollar pancake pan over medium-high heat until it's very hot but not smoking. Brush the bottom of the skillet (or each well of the silver dollar pan) with a thin layer of olive oil; once the oil is shimmering, pour in the batter.

Cook over medium-high heat until bubbles appear all along the cakes' edges. Transfer the pan to the oven and bake until the cakes' tops are set and dry, 6 to 8 minutes for silver dollar pancakes and 10 to 12 minutes for one larger pancake.

Loosen the cakes around the edges and transfer to a plate or cutting board. If you're making silver dollar pancakes, continue with the remaining batter; if you made one larger cake, cut it into triangles or rectangles. Serve warm or at room temperature.

CONTINUED

Seasonal Variations

WINTER

Fold in 1 cup [60 g] of charred chopped cabbage or caramelized onions.

SPRING

Fold in 1 cup [40 g] of chopped wild ramps or chives.

AUTUMN

Fold in 1 cup [80 g] of roasted and chopped wild mushrooms and herbs.

SUMMER

Fold in 1 cup [80 g] of charred or fresh corn kernels, grated summer squash, or roasted sweet peppers.

RIVER STONE FLATBREAD

Rivers and streams that cut across the New England countryside made an extensive network of paths for indigenous peoples traversing the land. Early New England colonists used these vast thoroughfares, which extended as far west as the Rocky Mountains, to explore the new land. This flatbread is baked in a style that echoes these labyrinthine waterways. It's inspired by a Persian flatbread called *sangak*, which means "little stone"; it's traditionally baked atop a bed of river pebbles, which absorb the oven's dry heat much like a wood-fired oven would. You'll need 16 to 20 smooth river stones (check a craft store if you aren't river-bound), but if you can't find any, go without. You'll still get tender, crispy-edged flatbreads, albeit without the eye-catching divots. This (gluten-free) dough is a bit wet and loose, so be patient while you work with it. Once baked, it will be dimpled and golden, and is best eaten warm.

Makes 4 flatbreads

Preheat the oven to 350°F [180°C] (use the convection setting, if you have it). Line two baking sheets with parchment paper. Rub the stones with oil and place them on the prepared sheet pans, placing 4 or 5 stones in an oval to be covered by each flatbread mound. Place the pans in the oven.

In a small bowl, combine the chia seeds and ½ cup [120 ml] of warm water. Set aside to hydrate.

In large bowl, combine the tapioca, brown rice, white rice, potato, almond, and buckwheat flours with the sesame seeds and salt. In a separate bowl, combine ¾ cup [180 ml] warm water with the maple sugar and yeast. Mix well and set aside until foamy, about 10 minutes.

Make a well in the center of the dry ingredients and pour in the chia seeds, 2 Tbsp of oil, and the yeast mixture. Mix well to combine until all flour is incorporated. The dough should be a bit sticky but not wet. Cover and set aside in a warm place to rest for 20 minutes.

Dust a surface generously with tapioca flour. Divide the dough into four equal-size pieces and dust them with tapioca flour as well. Oil your hands and pat the dough into flat pieces about ¼ in [6 mm] thick. Brush or rub the tops with more oil; dust with sesame seeds and flaky salt. Carefully remove the sheet pans from the oven. Use a bench scraper or spatula to lift and drape each piece of dough over a mound of rocks. Bake until the edges are light brown, 8 to 12 minutes. Increase the heat and broil until darker brown on top, 1 to 2 minutes.

Allow the bread to cool until you can handle it. Gently pry the bread from the rocks. Serve warm; leftovers can be stored in an airtight container or zip-top bag for up to 1 day, and gently toasted in a low oven to reheat.

16 to 20 river stones (about 2 to 3 in [5 to 7.5 cm])

2 Tbsp olive oil for coating

2 Tbsp chia seeds

1⅓ cup [160 g] tapioca flour, plus more for dusting

¾ cup plus 2 Tbsp [125 g] brown rice flour

¾ cup [105 g] white rice flour

½ cup [90 g] potato flour

⅓ cup [40 g] almond flour

⅓ cup [45 g] buckwheat flour

2 Tbsp sesame seeds, plus more for garnish

4 tsp kosher salt

2 Tbsp Maple Sugar (page 203)

2 tsp instant yeast

Sesame seeds and flaky salt for garnish

LIGHT AS A FEATHER BROWN BREAD

"Brown bread is as old as our country," James Beard wrote in *American Cookery* (1972). It's true. It's one of those colonial-era foods that has stood the test of time. Traditionally, brown bread, or what is sometimes referred to as thirded bread, was made from an even ratio of cornmeal, wheat flour, and rye, though during the American Revolution, when wheat flour was a luxury, cornmeal and rye became the dominant ingredients. Sweetened with molasses and sometimes raisins, the loaves were steamed in a hot water bath over an open fire, a technique colonists supposedly adopted from older styles of regional corn puddings. This version pays tribute but diverges quite a bit—it's almost like a brown bread brioche.

Makes two 28 oz [795 g] can-size loaves or one 9 by 5 in [23 by 12 cm] loaf

¼ cup [105 g] buckwheat flour

¼ cup plus 2 Tbsp [50 g] oat flour

1 tsp caraway seeds, toasted and ground

2 Tbsp Maple Sugar (page 203)

1½ tsp instant yeast

⅔ cup [150 g] unsalted butter, melted, plus more for the bowl and pan

2 Tbsp honey

3 eggs

3 egg yolks

2⅔ cups [375 g] Cup4Cup Multipurpose Flour

1 Tbsp kosher salt

1 tsp dried dill

Combine the buckwheat and oat flours and spread them in an even layer on a sheet pan. Toast for 15 minutes, stirring every 5 minutes or so, until fragrant. Cool.

In a medium bowl, combine 1 cup [240 ml] of very warm water with the maple sugar and yeast. Whisk in the butter, honey, eggs, and 2 of the yolks, stirring well to combine.

In a large bowl, preferably the bowl of your stand mixer fitted with a dough hook, combine the flours with the caraway, salt, and dill. Gradually add the egg mixture and mix on medium speed (or by hand, starting with a wooden spoon and then kneading) for 5 minutes, scraping down the sides of the bowl periodically; the dough should look wet and feel thick and sticky.

Butter a clean mixing bowl and add the dough. Cover the bowl with plastic wrap and set it aside in a warm spot to rise for about 1 hour. Every 20 minutes or so, use a spatula or bowl scraper to gently pull the dough over itself to deflate it a bit. After this first rise, refrigerate the dough for 2 hours.

Preheat the oven to 350°F [180°C]. Grease, or line with parchment paper, two 28 oz [795 ml] cans or one 9 by 5 in [23 by 12 cm] loaf pan. Scrape the dough into the prepared baking pans. Make an egg wash by combining the remaining yolk with a splash of water and brush it over the top of the loaves. Set aside in a warm spot to proof for 45 minutes, until there's no longer a chill to the dough and it springs back when you touch it.

Bake for 30 to 40 minutes (55 to 65 minutes if using a loaf pan), or until the center reaches 190°F [88°C].

Cool the bread in the pan for 10 to 15 minutes, then loosen it and invert onto a plate. Cool completely, preferably on a baking rack, before slicing. Serve at room temperature or toast the slices; leftovers can be kept in an airtight container for up to 2 days.

BLACK SEEDED BREAD

For someone who doesn't eat a lot of bread, I'm always in search of new vehicles for scooping, mainly butter, but really any dip. I love how poppy seeds and black sesame seeds, nutrient powerhouses, stipple this loaf a dark complexion, but any seeds or nuts will do. Keep the eggs, liquid, and flax constant, but play with all the other inclusions, even sweet or savory spices. My favorite way to eat a slice is simple: slightly warmed with butter and flaky salt. Any of the dips in this book—Parsnip Skordalia (page 81), Green Tahini Sauce (page 72), or Herby Smashed Sardine Dip (page 61)—would be equally lovely. The other brilliance of this bread? It lasts a long time—a week, if not more, but it never sticks around long enough for me to truly test it.

Makes 1 loaf

Preheat the oven to 200°F [95°C]. Line a 9 by 5 in [23 by 12 cm] loaf pan with parchment paper, leaving 2 to 3 in [5 to 7.5 cm] of overhang from the sides.

Add the eggs, oil, and tahini to a large bowl and whisk to combine. Separately, with a spice grinder or mortar and pestle, grind ½ cup [80 g] of the flaxseeds into a fine meal. Add the ground flaxseeds and the remaining ½ cup whole flaxseeds, the black sesame seeds, white sesame seeds, poppy seeds, and salt to the bowl and stir until everything is incorporated. Set aside for 30 minutes to allow the flaxseeds time to hydrate.

Scrape the batter into the prepared loaf pan and bake until the top is firmly set, 2 to 2½ hours; if you have an instant-read thermometer, the temperature should read at least 165°F [74°C] at the center of the loaf. Allow to cool in the pan for 5 minutes, then use the overhanging parchment to lift the loaf from the pan. Cool completely at room temperature, preferably on a cooling rack. Serve right away or refrigerate, wrapped in a clean cloth, in an airtight container for up to 1 week.

6 eggs

3 Tbsp grapeseed or extra-virgin olive oil

1 Tbsp tahini

1 cup [160 g] whole flaxseeds

1 cup [140 g] black sesame seeds

½ cup [70 g] white sesame seeds

½ cup [70 g] poppy seeds

1 Tbsp kosher salt

APPLE ROSE CAKE WITH CHERRIES, RICOTTA, AND PISTACHIOS

One day, while harvesting apples, I began to imagine what it must have been like in my little mill town centuries earlier, when Italian and Lebanese people were living next to each other for perhaps the first time on American soil. What would the melding of their cuisines taste and look like, and what stories would it tell of the new land they called home? It got me thinking about a dessert that united the Mediterranean with the Middle East and America, something imaginary but also quite plausible.

This cake has its roots in the beloved *torta di mele*, a classic honey cake originally from Venice but enjoyed throughout Italy. Grated, diced, and dried apples lend moisture, texture, and, of course, a distinct taste of autumn, while rose and sumac tether it to the Middle East.

Makes 8 to 12 servings

Apple Cake

1½ lb [680 g] tart apples, such as Gravenstein, Granny Smith, or Pink Lady (about 4), cored

⅔ cup [40 g] diced dried apples

Zest of 2 lemons

2 Tbsp rose water

2 Tbsp lemon juice

1 cup [150 g] Cup4Cup flour mix, plus more for the pan

⅓ cup plus 1 Tbsp [50 g] corn flour

¾ cup plus 2 Tbsp [110 g] ground pistachios

2 Tbsp dried rose petals, ground

2 tsp baking powder

½ tsp baking soda

1½ tsp kosher salt

6 eggs, separated

1 cup plus 2 Tbsp [255 g] unsalted butter, at room temperature, plus more for the pan

¼ cup [40 g] Maple Sugar (page 203)

½ cup [120 ml] extra-virgin olive oil

⅓ cup plus 1 Tbsp [95 g] Fresh Ricotta (page 204), drained

TO MAKE THE CAKE: Preheat the oven to 375°F [190°C]. Put a baking sheet on the center rack to heat up. Butter and flour the bottom and sides of a 9 in [23 cm] springform pan.

Grate all but one of the apples and combine them with the dried apples, lemon zest, rose water, and lemon juice in a small bowl; set aside.

Combine the gluten-free flour, corn flour, pistachios, rose petals, baking powder, baking soda, and salt in a medium bowl; set aside.

In a large bowl, using a handheld mixer, or in the bowl of a stand mixer fitted with the whisk, begin whipping the egg whites on low speed, gradually increasing the speed over 5 minutes or until they hold stiff peaks. Reserve the whites in a separate bowl.

In a clean bowl, add the butter; if you're using a stand mixer, switch to the paddle attachment. Whip the butter until it's smooth and airy, about the consistency of mayonnaise. Add the maple sugar and beat for 2 minutes. Add the egg yolks, starting on low speed and gradually turning to high; whip until the butter-egg mixture is homogenized and a buttercup shade of yellow. Add the oil and ricotta, followed by the grated and dried apples. Add half the flour mixture, mix on medium-low speed just until incorporated, then add the rest of the flour and mix until there are no visible dry streaks. Gently but thoroughly fold in a third of the egg whites by hand, being careful not to deflate them but making sure they are fully incorporated,

CONTINUED

then gradually add the rest. Pour the batter into the prepared pan and smooth the top.

Cut the remaining apple into very thin half-moons, either by hand or using a mandoline. Starting around the border of the pan and working your way in concentrically, arrange the apple slices so they're overlapping slightly, like petals on a flower. When you get to the middle, take one last slice of apple, gently roll it into a loose spiral, and stick it in the center.

Set the cake directly atop the heated baking sheet and bake for 50 minutes or until the cake is set but still a bit wobbly at the very center and the apples are a deep golden brown. Turn the oven off and leave the pan inside for 15 minutes; the center will continue to set.

While the cake is baking, make the compote and ricotta.

TO MAKE THE COMPOTE: Combine the dried cherries, honey, juice, rose petals, and salt in a large saucepan over medium heat; bring to a simmer. Cook for 5 to 10 minutes, until the cherries are tender. Add the pitted cherries and cook, stirring occasionally, for another 10 minutes, just until the liquid has reduced to a syrup and the fruit is plump and jammy. Cool the compote to room temperature or store it in an airtight container in the refrigerator until you're ready to serve.

TO MAKE THE SUMAC RICOTTA: Use a food processor, stand mixer, or whisk to whip together the ricotta, honey, oil, lemon juice, sumac, and salt until smooth and light. Use right away or refrigerate in an airtight container for up to 2 days.

To serve, top each serving of cake with the sumac ricotta, cherry compote, and chopped pistachios. The leftover cake can be tightly wrapped or covered and stored at room temperature for 5 days, and freezes well for up to 1 month. Thaw frozen cake in the refrigerator overnight and gently rewarm before serving.

KITCHEN NOTE:

Since I can't eat gluten, I've experimented with all kinds of gluten-free substitutes, from the flours of other grains to store-bought mixes. Typically, I am equal opportunity, preferring anything that tastes flavorful, feels nourishing, and creates the same good texture as its wheat counterpart; with this cake, though, I've found Cup4Cup is the only way to create the moist, tender crumb I'm after while also giving the cake its integrity. It's worth seeking out.

Cherry Compote

1⅔ cups [230 g] dried sour cherries

1 cup [340 g] honey

1 cup [240 ml] cherry juice

2 Tbsp dried rose petals

1 tsp kosher salt

1½ lb [680 g] cherries, pitted

Sumac Ricotta

2 cups [480 g] Fresh Ricotta (page 204), drained

¼ cup [60 ml] honey

3 Tbsp extra-virgin olive oil

1 Tbsp lemon juice

½ tsp sumac powder

Pinch of kosher salt

Coarsely chopped pistachios for serving

Seasonal Variations

These suggestions are substitutes for the fresh grated apples.
Keep the dried apples consistent since they are always
available and add a nice toothsome texture.

WINTER

Unlikely as it might seem, parsnips' sweet, nutty aroma plays well in desserts such as cakes and ice creams. This time, reach for hazelnuts instead of pistachios, their deeply rich flavor works well with the toasty notes of the root. Grate 1 lb [455 g] of peeled parsnips for the cake batter and shave the rest into very thin, about ⅛ in [4 mm] rounds on a mandoline, layering them in a concentric circle just like the original recipe.

SPRING

The sharpness of rhubarb is a lovely foil to the sweeter notes of apple, honey, and ricotta. Use ¾ lb [340 g] thinly sliced rhubarb in place of the grated apples and another ½ lb [230 g] thinly sliced rhubarb to decorate the top, either in a ring form or placed at random.

AUTUMN

Bulbous autumn beets, which have been maturing under the ground for quite some time, are packed with an earthy sweetness. For a blush-toned cake, opt for red beets, which happen to also boost your daily dose of antioxidants. Grate 1 lb [455 g] of peeled beets for the cake batter and shave the rest into very thin rounds on a mandoline, layering them in a concentric circle just like the original recipe.

SUMMER

Summer fennel is very tender with a sweet anise aroma that adds a licorice-like note to the cake. Cut the fennel bulbs in half and remove the core. Shave 1¼ lb [570 g] very thinly on a mandoline or slice as thinly as possible with a sharp knife, releasing the petals from one another as you go. Use ¾ lb [340 g] in the cake batter; the rest can be used to decorate the top.

MAPLE "GRAHAM" TARTS

My mother always said, "There's more than one way to skin a cat," and the adage runs through my head every time I peel a peach. Placing the fuzzy fruit above an open flame may feel daunting, but the singe releases the skin, starts to caramelize the outer flesh, and imparts a hint of smoke.

You may notice that there isn't any graham flour in the "graham" crust. I wanted something gluten-free but with all the nutty notes of the nineteenth-century-health-food-turned-favorite-childhood-snack. Originally, graham flour kept its bran and germ, making it a whole grain, so flaxseeds do the trick here. Fashion into little individual servings, or feel free to press the crust into a standard tart pan, following the same method for blind-baking and filling while increasing the cook time as necessary. Enjoy a slice with a glass of Peach Leaf Wine (page 279).

Makes 6 to 8 tartlets or one 9 to 10 in [22.5 to 25 cm] tart

"Graham" Cracker Crust

⅔ cup [90 g] rice flour

¼ cup plus 2 Tbsp [55 g] buckwheat flour

¼ cup [30 g] almond flour

3 Tbsp [30 g] flaxseeds, coarsely ground

½ tsp kosher salt

¼ tsp baking soda

½ cup [120 g] unsalted butter, at room temperature

½ cup [80 g] Maple Sugar (page 203)

Zest of 2 lemons

2 egg yolks

2 Tbsp whole milk

TO MAKE THE CRUST: Combine the rice flour, buckwheat flour, almond flour, flaxseeds, salt, and baking soda in a medium bowl; set aside.

In a large bowl or in the bowl of a stand mixer fitted with the paddle attachment, cream the butter, sugar, and lemon zest. When the mixture is incorporated and airy, beat in the yolks and milk. Add the flour mixture and mix just until combined.

The dough will be somewhat sticky and soft. Scrape it onto a sheet of plastic wrap, which you can use to help shape the mixture into a flat disk, and chill for at least 1 hour or up to 3 days.

CONTINUED

Poppy Seed Frangipane

Makes 2 cups [500 g]

1 cup [140 g] almonds, toasted

⅓ cup [45 g] rice flour

½ tsp baking powder

½ tsp kosher salt

6 Tbsp Maple Sugar (page 203)

¼ cup [60 g] unsalted butter, at room temperature

3 eggs

½ tsp Peach Pit Extract (page 280, optional)

¼ cup [40 g] diced dried peaches

2 Tbsp poppy seeds

TO MAKE THE FRANGIPANE: In a food processor or spice grinder, pulse the almonds until they are very finely chopped—you want them essentially minced but not quite a coarse meal.

Combine the flour, baking powder, and salt in a small bowl; set aside.

In a large bowl or in the bowl of a stand mixer fitted with the whisk attachment, cream the maple sugar and butter on medium-high speed until light and fluffy, about 3 minutes. Add the flour mixture, eggs, and peach extract and continue to mix for a few more minutes, until very light. (Don't worry if it looks broken; that's normal.)

Fold in the dried peaches, poppy seeds, and chopped almonds by hand and refrigerate until well chilled. This will keep in an airtight container in the refrigerator for up to 3 days.

Seasonal Variations

Any dried fruit compote can work in many seasons.

WINTER

Substitute pears or apples for the peaches.

SPRING

Substitute rhubarb or apricots for the peaches.

AUTUMN

Substitute Fuyu persimmons for the peaches.

SUMMER

Substitute figs, plums, or blueberries and mint or cherries and lavender for the peaches.

TO MAKE THE CHARRED PEACHES: Heat a grill to high heat or set a metal grate directly over a gas burner. Set the peaches on the grate and char all over, turning occasionally until their skin is completely blackened and ashy. Remove from the heat.

When the peaches are cool enough to handle, peel and discard their papery black skins. (Some lingering black specks are fine.) Halve the peaches (reserve the pits to use for Peach Pit Extract, page 280) and thinly slice the fruit; let stand at room temperature or refrigerate in an airtight container for up to 2 days until you're ready to use.

TO MAKE THE TART: Preheat the oven to 350°F [180°C]. Butter the sides of eight 4 in [10 cm] ring molds or use six to eight tartlet pans. Divide the dough evenly into one ball per tartlet; work with one at a time, keeping the rest refrigerated until you're ready to use it. Use the pads of your fingers to press each ball into a thin, even layer inside the ring mold and all the way up the sides. If it breaks or tears, use a small pinch of dough to patch it back together. Repeat with all the tartlets and refrigerate for another 30 minutes or so, until the crusts are firm to the touch.

Press parchment paper over the surface of each tartlet and weight it down with pie weights or a layer of dried beans. Blind-bake the crust for 20 to 30 minutes, until it is somewhat dry and firm. Gently remove the parchment and weights and bake for another 15 to 20 minutes, until the bottom is completely set. Allow to cool completely at room temperature.

To assemble the tart, divide the frangipane evenly among the crusts once they've cooled completely. Top with the sliced peaches, brush the saffron syrup over the top, and bake for 15 to 20 minutes, until the frangipane has puffed up and is no longer wet to the touch. Brush the syrup over the peaches again and cool completely before serving.

Charred Peaches

2 or 3 peaches

¼ cup [60 ml] Saffron Syrup (page 202)

CARROT CAKE WITH WALNUT FROSTING

I'm not a huge fan of cake, but any dessert that packs in equal amounts of vegetables to flour is a win in my book. This version is a riff on a classic carrot cake, homey and familiar, but with enough adaptations to keep it intriguing. I turned to the trench cakes of World War I, in which vinegar and baking soda replaced eggs for leavening—think of those volcano projects from elementary science class. Wartime rations often led to culinary creativity, and eggless cakes held up when mailed to loved ones on the front lines. Swapping out commonplace ingredients can be a challenge, and there were many flops, albeit delicious ones, while testing this cake. Playing in the kitchen and making mistakes is part of the fun of cooking. Purple carrots are packed with anthocyanins, so if you can get ahold of some, use them here—but any old carrot will work.

Makes 8 servings

Red Carrot Cake

¾ cup [180 ml] grapeseed oil, plus more for the pan

3¼ cups [455 g] Cup4Cup Multipurpose Flour, plus more for the pan

¾ cup [90 g] walnut or almond flour

1 cup [160 g] Maple Sugar (page 203)

2 tsp kosher salt

2 tsp baking soda

3 Tbsp brine from Vinegar-Pickled Red Carrots (page 189) or apple cider vinegar

1¼ cups [300 ml] walnut milk

3 to 5 carrots (about 10½ oz [300 g]), grated

Zest of 3 oranges

Walnut Frosting (recipe follows, optional)

Walnuts, toasted, for garnish

Queen Anne's lace for garnish

Apricot-Saffron Compote (recipe follows)

TO MAKE THE CAKE: Preheat the oven to 350°F [180°C]. Grease and flour two 9 in [22.5 cm] cake pans.

Combine flours, maple sugar, salt, and baking soda in a large bowl.

Use a spoon to make two wells; pour the oil into one and the brine into the other (it will fizz).

Pour the milk over and stir to combine. Fold in the carrots and zest by hand.

Divide the batter among the prepared pans and bake, rotating every 30 minutes or so, until a tester comes out clean, about 1½ hours. Allow to cool completely before removing from the pans.

Serve the cake on its own or with walnut frosting, sprinkled with toasted walnuts and Queen Anne's lace. Serve each slice with a scoop of compote. This cake keeps, tightly covered, for up to 3 days.

CONTINUED

Walnut Frosting

Makes 2 cups [510 g]

2 cups [240 g] walnuts, toasted

½ small Japanese sweet potato (about 4 oz [115 g])

½ cup [120 ml] unsweetened nut milk

3 Tbsp honey

½ tsp kosher salt

Zest of 2 oranges

2 Tbsp extra-virgin olive oil

TO MAKE THE FROSTING: Soak the walnuts in water for at least 4 hours or overnight. Drain and discard the liquid.

Preheat the oven to 375°F [190°C]. Use a fork to prick a few holes in the sweet potato to allow the steam to escape. Roast until it feels tender and mashable, 40 to 50 minutes. Cool at room temperature and peel away the papery skin.

In a blender, purée the nuts, nut milk, honey, salt, and orange zest; add the potato and continue to blend, pausing to scrape the sides or stir as needed. With the blender still running, stream in the oil and allow it to incorporate.

Scrape the frosting into an airtight container and refrigerate for up to 3 days before using.

TO MAKE THE COMPOTE: Combine the vinegar and saffron in a small bowl for at least 30 minutes to allow the saffron to bloom.

Meanwhile, combine the carrot juice, apricots, grated carrot, honey, and salt in a small saucepan or skillet over medium heat. Cook, stirring occasionally, until the apricots are tender, 8 to 10 minutes. Add the vinegar and saffron threads and bring back to a simmer, allowing the liquid to reduce just a bit; it should still be pretty loose but will thicken as it cools.

Remove from the heat and allow to cool completely at room temperature or refrigerate in an airtight container for up to 3 days before using.

Apricot-Saffron Compote

Makes 1 cup [240 ml]

¼ cup [60 ml] brine from Vinegar-Pickled Red Carrots (page 189) or apple cider vinegar

8 saffron threads

½ cup [120 ml] carrot juice

½ cup [75 g] diced dried apricots

¼ cup [25 g] grated carrot

¼ cup [85 g] honey

½ tsp kosher salt

SWEET PEA AND OLIVE OIL CAKE WITH WHIPPED MINT YOGURT AND LEMON-JASMINE COOKIES

This cake is all about the natural sweetness of vegetables. Peas are little gems waiting to be popped from their protective shells. Since we praise peas for their natural sugars, why not fold them into a dessert? Here, sweet emerald peas get swirled into a yogurt and almond flour cake with dried mint and green tea. It's moist, which means it keeps well for a few days on the counter, but I especially enjoy the fudgy consistency when eaten straight from the refrigerator with a spoon. Once frosted, the cake should be consumed in 1 day, so if you want to keep it around, consider serving the whipped yogurt on the side.

Makes 8 servings

Whipped Mint Yogurt

Makes 2 cups [480 ml]

1 lb [455 g] Japanese sweet potato (about 2)

¾ cup [180 g] full-fat yogurt, strained

¾ cup [180 g] Fresh Ricotta (page 204), drained

1 Tbsp honey

¼ tsp kosher salt

Zest of 1 lemon

2 Tbsp extra-virgin olive oil

TO MAKE THE WHIPPED YOGURT: Preheat the oven to 350°F [180°C]. With a fork, prick the sweet potato all over so steam can escape and roast until mushy-tender, about 1 hour.

When the potato is cool enough to handle but still warm, peel away the skin and purée the flesh in a food processor until very smooth. Add the yogurt, ricotta, honey, salt, and lemon zest and blend until light and airy. Scrape down the sides of the bowl and continue processing as you stream in the oil. Refrigerate in an airtight container for at least 2 hours and up to 2 days.

CONTINUED

TO MAKE THE CAKE: Set a rack in the middle of the oven and preheat to 350°F [180°C]. Oil and flour the bottom and sides of a 9 in [23 cm] springform pan and line the bottom with parchment paper.

In a medium bowl, mix the almond flour, corn flour, rice flour, ground mint, green tea, baking powder, baking soda, and salt. Separately, in a blender, purée the peas with the oil and yogurt. Set both mixtures aside.

In a large bowl or in the bowl of a stand mixer fitted with the whisk attachment, whip the eggs on medium speed until foamy, about 1 minute. Add the honey, fresh mint, and lemon zest; increase the speed to high and whip until the mixture is fluffy and pale yellow, about 5 minutes.

Reduce the speed to medium and, with the mixer running, slowly pour in the pea mixture and mix to combine, about 1 minute. Add half of the flour mixture and continue mixing on low speed until fully incorporated, then repeat with the remaining flour, scraping down the bowl as needed.

Pour the batter into the prepared pan and bake until the cake is deeply browned on top and a tester inserted in the center comes out mostly clean with just a few crumbs, 40 to 45 minutes. Allow to cool completely and store, covered, in the refrigerator for up to 1 day before assembling.

To serve, use a serrated knife to cut the cake horizontally into 2 even layers. Gently transfer the bottom layer to a serving platter. With a butter knife or offset spatula, spread the whipped yogurt evenly over the top. Add the second cake layer, and frost the top and sides with more whipped yogurt. Serve each slice with frozen yogurt and lemon cookies on the side. This cake is best on the day it's frosted.

Cake

⅔ cup [160 ml] extra-virgin olive oil, plus more for the pan

¾ cup [90 g] almond flour

⅓ cup plus 1 Tbsp [50 g] corn flour

¼ cup [35 g] rice flour, plus more for the pan

2 Tbsp ground dried mint

2 tsp dry jasmine green tea leaves, finely ground

½ tsp baking powder

½ tsp baking soda

¼ tsp kosher salt

1⅓ cups [200 g] shelled fresh or thawed frozen peas

¼ cup [60 g] strained full-fat Greek yogurt

4 eggs, at room temperature

⅓ cup [115 g] honey

3 Tbsp finely chopped mint leaves

Zest of 2 lemons

Lemon–Jasmine Cookies

Makes 18 to 24 cookies

¼ cup plus 2 Tbsp [75 g] jasmine rice, toasted

1 tsp dry jasmine green tea leaves

⅔ cup [80 g] corn flour

¼ cup [30 g] almond flour

¼ cup [30 g] tapioca starch

2 Tbsp cornmeal

¾ tsp baking powder

¼ tsp kosher salt

½ cup [70 g] Maple Sugar (page 203)

Zest of 3 lemons

1 tsp lemon powder (see Drying section, page 196), plus more for garnish

1 egg

¼ cup [60 ml] grapeseed oil

Ground dried mint for garnish

TO MAKE THE COOKIES: Use a spice grinder to grind the rice until very fine. Add the tea and continue to grind until it's a uniform powder. In a medium bowl, combine the rice powder mixture with the corn flour, almond flour, tapioca, cornmeal, baking powder, and salt. Set aside.

Add the maple sugar, lemon zest, and lemon powder to the bowl of a stand mixer or to a large bowl. Rub the zest and powder into the sugar until it resembles wet sand. Add the egg and, using your stand mixer's paddle attachment or an electric mixer, beat until the mixture is completely smooth. With the mixer on low, slowly stream in the oil, then increase the speed and beat for another 1 to 2 minutes until thick.

Add half of the flour mixture, mix to combine, then incorporate the rest. The dough will be very thick and a bit sticky. Refrigerate in an airtight container until it firms up, then transfer the dough to a sheet of parchment paper and roll it into a log about 1½ in [4 cm] in diameter. Wrap tightly in plastic and refrigerate for at least 30 minutes and up to 5 days.

Preheat the oven to 350°F [180°C]. Line a baking sheet with parchment paper. Cut the cookies in roughly ½ in [12 mm] slices and space them 1 in [2.5 cm] apart. Dust the tops with ground mint and more lemon powder and bake for 14 to 16 minutes, rotating the tray halfway through; the cookies should be soft but not puffy, with a slight golden tinge around the edges. Allow to cool completely on the baking sheet and serve right away or store at room temperature in an airtight container for up to 2 days.

CONTINUED

Jasmine and Mint Frozen Yogurt

Makes 1 qt [960 g]

½ cup [100 g] jasmine rice, toasted

15 mint leaves

1 Tbsp dry jasmine green tea

¾ cup [180 g] heavy cream

⅔ cup [160 g] buttermilk

¼ cup [45 g] buttermilk powder

½ cup [80 g] maple sugar

¼ cup [85 g] honey

2 tsp kosher salt

2 Tbsp vodka

2⅓ cups [550 g] strained full-fat Greek yogurt

TO MAKE THE FROZEN YOGURT: Combine the rice, mint, and tea in a heat-proof bowl or container. In a small saucepan, bring the cream and buttermilk to a gentle simmer over medium-low heat, then immediately pour over the rice. Cover, refrigerate, and leave to infuse for at least 4 hours or overnight.

Use a fine-mesh sieve to strain the infused cream into a saucepan, pressing with a spatula to extract as much liquid as possible. Discard the solids.

In a small bowl, combine the buttermilk powder with about 6 Tbsp [90 ml] of the infused cream mixture to make a slurry. Whisk the slurry back into the cream mixture along with the sugar, honey, and salt; warm over medium heat just until the sugar and honey dissolve. Remove from the heat and add the vodka.

Allow the base to cool to room temperature or refrigerate in an airtight container overnight before whisking in the yogurt; if necessary, refrigerate again until completely cool. Freeze in your ice cream maker according to the manufacturer's directions; once frozen, it can be served right away, like soft serve, or frozen to firm up more. If frozen solid, place in the refrigerator for 20 minutes before serving to soften slightly.

CORN MOON PUDDING WITH BLUEBERRIES AND HONEY

I originally set out to make a savory boiled corn pudding, honoring a staple food of the Hoosic River Algonquin tribe, but once I got into the kitchen, my hands turned this dish sweet. I was told by an Algonquin elder, Grace, that they have names for each of the moon phases. She shared with me that the fifth moon is known as the Flower Moon, or the Corn Planting Moon. It is said that during this full moon, all plants display life-giving energy, ready to sprout, grow, and nourish us and the soil. The corn is tended until the ninth moon, called the Corn or Harvest Moon; at this time the corn's silk turns brown and wilts, telling us the corn has reached maturity. Within each husk are rows of seeds, some to be eaten, some to be saved for next year's planting, representing future generations for whom we must prepare. With this dish, I honor all ancestors and relatives of North Adams, Massachusetts.

Makes about 6 servings

Corn Moon Pudding

1 Japanese sweet potato
(6 to 7 oz [170 to 200 g])

1½ Tbsp cold unsalted butter, plus more for the pan and for frying

¼ cup [40 g] Maple Sugar (page 203)

2 Tbsp corn flour, plus more for the pan

2 Tbsp potato starch

¼ tsp kosher salt

8 ears sweet corn, husked

¼ cup [60 g] strained full-fat Greek-style yogurt

Zest of ½ lemon

1 egg

2 egg yolks

TO MAKE THE PUDDING: Preheat the oven to 375°F [190°C]. Use a fork to prick a few holes in the sweet potato, allowing the steam to escape. Roast until it feels tender and mashable, 60 to 90 minutes. Leave the oven on (you'll use it again to bake the custard) and allow the potato to cool to room temperature. Butter and flour a 2 cup [480 ml] loaf pan or small, deep baking dish; alternatively, for individual servings, butter and flour four ½ cup [120 ml] ramekins.

Combine the sugar, flour, potato starch, and salt in a small bowl and set aside.

Preheat a grill to high heat or set a metal grate directly over a gas burner on high. Char the ears of corn directly over the flame, rotating occasionally until they are blackened in places. Cut the kernels from the cob; you should have about 6 cups [840 g] of kernels.

Add 5 cups [700 g] of the charred corn kernels to a blender (save the rest, about 1 cup [140 g], for garnish) and purée until very smooth. Strain through a fine-mesh sieve to make the corn milk, pressing with a spatula to extract as much liquid as you can—you will need 2¼ cups [540 ml] total (you may have a bit extra, depending on the corn). Set aside 2 cups [480 ml] for use in the Corn Anglaise.

Cut into the sweet potato and scoop out its flesh; discard the skin. In a large bowl or in the bowl of a stand mixer fitted with the whisk attachment, combine the potato with ¼ cup [60 ml] of the corn milk, the yogurt, and lemon zest. Mix for a few minutes, until the mixture is very smooth and light. Add the egg and yolks, one at a time, mixing between additions, until completely incorporated. If you're using a stand mixer, switch to the paddle attachment. Mix in the flour mixture. Cut the butter into ½ in [12 mm] pieces and dot it over the batter; continue to mix on low speed until the butter is almost but not completely incorporated (the largest pieces should be smaller than peas).

CONTINUED

Pour the pudding into the prepared pan and set it in a larger pan. Pour very hot tap water into the larger pan so it comes about halfway up the prepared pan and bake until the pudding is completely set, 30 to 40 minutes. Allow to cool or refrigerate, covered, for up to 2 days before serving.

TO MAKE THE CONFITURE: In a blender combine ½ cup [70 g] of the blueberries with the lemon juice and purée until smooth.

In a medium saucepan, combine the puréed berries, the remaining 1½ cups [210 g] of fresh blueberries, the dried blueberries, lemon zest, honey, and salt. Bring to a simmer over medium heat, stirring frequently until the mixture is thick; when you scrape the bottom of the pan with your spoon, it should stay clean for a couple of seconds before the fruit starts to fill in.

Stir the pine needles into the warm confiture. Remove the pan from the heat and cool to room temperature. Use immediately or refrigerate in an airtight container for up to 1 month or more.

Blueberry and Pine Honey Confiture

2 cups [280 g] fresh or frozen blueberries

¼ cup [60 ml] fresh lemon juice

¼ cup [35 g] dried wild blueberries

Zest of 2 lemons

1½ Tbsp honey, preferably pine honey

½ tsp kosher salt

1½ tsp fresh pine needles, such as fir or spruce, finely minced or ground

TO MAKE THE ANGLAISE: While the custard bakes, whisk the egg yolks in a bowl and set aside. Combine the reserved corn milk with the honey and salt in a small saucepan. Warm the mixture over medium-low heat, stirring occasionally to prevent scalding, just until steam is rising off the surface. Whisk a ladleful of the warm milk into the yolks, then whisk the tempered yolks back into the saucepan and continue to cook until the mixture coats the back of a spoon, 8 to 12 minutes. Remove from the heat and allow to cool slightly before refrigerating in an airtight container.

When you are ready to serve, remove the pudding from the pan and cut it into ½ in [12 mm] slices. Set a skillet over medium heat and warm a big pat of butter until the foaming subsides. Working in batches, sear the pudding slices until they're crisp and golden brown, about 2 minutes per side.

To serve, swipe a big spoonful of the anglaise on individual serving plates and top with the pudding slices. Spoon some warm confiture over the top and garnish with the chopped pine cones and blueberries. Leftovers can be refrigerated in separate airtight containers; bring the pudding to room temperature before searing it.

Corn Anglaise

4 egg yolks

2 cups [480 ml] corn milk (from the pudding)

¼ cup [85 g] honey, preferably pine honey

1 tsp kosher salt

Honeyed Pine Cones (page 202), chopped, for garnish

Fresh blueberries for garnish

HAZELNUT AND ORANGE BLOSSOM CUSTARD WITH SALT-ROASTED PEARS

Perhaps it is the pure lusciousness of set egg custards that makes them so decadent. They require patience and a bit of grace. Cook them too quickly and the overcooked eggs will create little air bubbles that tickle your tongue. This version relies on toasted hazelnut milk instead of dairy for the base, which makes for a rich and nutty custard that marries beautifully with orange blossoms and coriander. The spice may seem like an unusual addition, but it lends a subtle citrus tone. Roasting the pears in an igloo of salt is, sure, a bit of playful culinary theatrics, but the briny cloak renders the fruit soft and juicy. Don't limit yourself to pears; try this technique with other fruits and vegetables as well. Anything will make a lovely surprise when you crack past the salt.

Makes 4 servings

Salt-Roasted Pears

3 egg whites

2½ cups [340 g] kosher salt

1 Tbsp orange blossom water

1 Tbsp coriander seeds, toasted and finely ground

2 firm, ripe pears

TO MAKE THE PEARS: Preheat the oven to 350°F [180°C]. Line a baking sheet or baking dish with parchment paper.

In a large bowl with an electric mixer or a whisk, whip the egg whites until foamy. Stir in the salt, orange blossom water, and coriander, mixing by hand until the mixture looks and feels like damp sand. Cut a thin slice from the bottom of each pear so they stand on their own.

Make two mounds with some of the salt mixture on your prepared baking sheet, about ¼ in [6 mm] thick and a little wider than the pears themselves. Top each mound with a pear and cover completely with the remaining salt mixture, pressing firmly to hermetically seal them. Only the stems will stick out.

Bake for 45 to 55 minutes, until the crust is rock-hard and golden brown. To check for doneness, punch a cake tester or toothpick through the crust; the pear should feel very soft. If it's not there yet, continue to bake in 10-minute increments before checking again. Allow the pears to cool slightly.

Shatter the salt crust, either delicately with a knife around the equator or more dramatically with a gentle crush. Remove the pears, brushing off any excess salt. Halve the pears lengthwise and use a paring knife to remove the tough core. Set aside to come to room temperature or cover and refrigerate overnight. Cut the pears into bite-size pieces before serving.

CONTINUED

Orange Blossom Custard

2¼ cups [305 g] toasted hazelnuts
or 2 cups [480 ml] store-bought
unsweetened hazelnut milk

¼ cup plus 3 Tbsp [140 g] honey

1 tsp dried orange blossoms or ¼ tsp
orange blossom water

1½ tsp kosher salt

Zest of 1 orange

¼ cup [60 ml] fresh orange juice

1½ Tbsp unsalted butter

1 egg

7 egg yolks

¼ cup [60 ml] extra-virgin olive oil

Freshly ground black pepper

TO MAKE THE CUSTARD: Soak 2 cups [270 g] of the hazelnuts, if using, in plenty of water for at least 4 hours or overnight.

Drain the hazelnuts and use a blender to purée them with 2¼ cups [540 ml] of fresh water until the mixture is completely smooth. Transfer to a nut milk bag or line a fine-mesh sieve with several layers of cheesecloth and use a spatula to gently extract as much excess liquid as possible. You should have 2 cups [480 ml] of hazelnut milk; if you don't, top it off with a bit more water.

In a medium saucepan, combine the hazelnut milk with ¼ cup [85 g] of the honey, the orange blossoms, and 1 tsp of the salt. Bring to a simmer over medium-low heat and cook, stirring occasionally, until it's as thick as cream. Remove from the heat, add half of the orange zest, and cool over an ice bath or refrigerate, uncovered, until completely cool. This mixture can be made up to 5 days in advance.

Preheat the oven to 250°F [120°C]. Meanwhile, make the caramel. Add the remaining 3 Tbsp [55 g] of the honey to a small saucepan and cook over medium heat, stirring occasionally, until it's the color of maple syrup. Add the orange juice and bring back up to an active simmer until the liquid has reduced to a thick sauce. Remove from the heat and swirl in the butter and the remaining ½ tsp of salt. Set aside.

In a medium bowl, whisk the egg and egg yolks until frothy, about 2 minutes. Strain the infused hazelnut milk into the eggs and stir to combine.

Divide the caramel evenly among four individual ½ cup [120 ml] custard cups or ramekins or pour it into one larger 2 cup [480 ml] baking dish. Gently pour the custard over the caramel and set the dish or dishes into a larger, deep baking pan. Pour very hot tap water into the pan so it comes about halfway up the sides of the dishes and bake until the custard is completely set but still soft, about 2 to 2½ hours. Remove from the water bath, chill completely, and cover. The custard can be made up to 3 days in advance.

To serve, chop the remaining ¼ cup [35 g] of toasted hazelnuts and toss them with the oil and the remaining orange zest; season with pepper. Gently loosen the sides of the custards with a butter knife and invert them onto serving plates, then spoon the hazelnut mixture over the top. Place the cut pears on the side and serve.

AETHER

IMAGINATION AND ALCHEMY

CHAPTER 6

Aether in the spiritual realm

Aether, also known as quintessence, is the place of limitlessness, representing the spirit element and the power of divine intelligence, potentiality, and alchemy. Aether is the great connector of all things, immaterial and invisible, the super-force behind the other elements, and present in all things. It does not exist apart from anything else, yet it balances, aligns, and contains within it all the earthly elements.

Here we dream, create, and imagine, transforming our everyday reality into something otherworldly. It's the alchemy of creation, rooted in the notion that everything around us contains a universal spirit. Alchemy began as a quest to know the world around us—its composition as well as our own—a science of the aether. And it continues to dazzle and affirm, to root us in the magic of the world.

Aether in the physical realm

To me, the spirit is the synergy of the divine. I need something to honor and thank for the magic that surrounds me, so I look to the aether and stand in gratitude for another day to experience it all. Every morning when we rise, my partner JP and I begin our day by lighting a sage bundle. In the cooler months, I do this directly from the crackling wood within the stove, letting the smoke swirl up to the rafters, blessing our home. We wave it over a cup of water; this water is a symbol of our fluidity in the world. While sipping it, we share our gratitude list for the day and ask the spirits to protect us and those we love as we move through the world as gracefully as possible. We ingest the daily blessing, setting our energetic intentions for the day. It's how we ground ourselves to each other, the natural world, the people in our lives, and all living beings everywhere.

This ritual has been adopted in our home through the teachings of my brother-in-law, Richard. As the one who wakes up first on most mornings, Richard blesses a cup of water. Sage and prayers fill the home and signal the dawn of a new day. As the rest of the home comes to life, each person is welcome to go to the altar and sip from the cup. In his home, it's called "morning water"; in ours, it's "magic water," playfully named by the little ones who think it has magical powers. We think they're right.

This chapter delves into the world of juices and tonics, switchels and shrubs, herbal distillates, infusions, and spirits (the alcohol distillate variety). It's centered around the ancient idea of drink as both celebratory and curative.

Barks, Roots, Leaves, Flowers, and Seeds for Tonics and Remedies

Herbal medicine is the oldest known remedy for anything that ails you. Ancient medical systems from Europe, India, China, and Africa all viewed illness as imbalance in the body and looked to plants to restore equilibrium. Prior to 500 B.C.E., plants were the only known medicines and carried great healing properties, both medically and spiritually.

As trade routes spread, herbs and spices migrated across the globe. By the nineteenth century, with the birth of modern medicine, herbalist concepts were largely dismissed as remnants of superstitious practices. However, modern-day Western herbal medicine still draws from a pharmacopoeia of European and North American herbs, mainly native plants, to treat or prevent a variety of illnesses and diseases.

Many studies suggest that spending time outside in a place rich with plants and wildlife can strengthen immune systems, decrease stress, increase focus, and reduce inflammation, among other less tangible benefits such as encouraging playfulness. The Japanese call it "forest bathing," and consider it a form of preventative health care.

For me, this is the absolute truth. I rely on the outside world to help me find clarity in difficult situations. I look to the forest to calm my nerves, clear my head, and ignite my creative fire. Another reason I keep coming back to nature is for its wild edible foods. I'm amazed that in spring, I can eat so many things as they begin to emerge from the ground: hosta shoots, ramps, fiddlehead ferns, morels, magnolia flowers, violets, and a myriad of barks. Later come pine buds, spruce tips, locust flowers, dandelions, garlic mustard, wild carrot seeds, cattail roots, wild berries, and autumn olives, not to mention the fruits. It's a virtual cornucopia of wild, healing, nourishing foods.

As a child, when asked what I wanted to be when I grew up, I would respond with "a doctor or a cook." My answer decades later would be much the same, but "doctor" would mean something different to me. I'm not a doctor, nor do I make prescriptive claims, but I do know from personal experience that food heals. I know that the miraculous plant world can be preserved with a myriad of techniques disguising their medicinal essense behind wondrous flavors and aromas; they become bold new flavors that nourish.

One of my favorite ways to use edible barks, flowers, herbs, and their roots, leaves, and seeds is to make them into tonics and health remedies by steeping them into infusions, shrubs, tinctures, and distillates, and by preserving them in honey, capturing their medicinal properties and collecting their aromas. The list that follows is by no means exhaustive; it includes just a few of my favorites. I am not a doctor; the information provided is what I've learned along the way and put into practice for myself. It is intended to pique your interest and serve as a jumping-off point. Please research what you're using, especially if you have a specific medical condition. Never use anything you're not 100 percent certain of, as some dangerous plants resemble edible plants.

Some common methods for producing edible herbal remedies:

Decoction: Decoction is an extraction method traditionally used for tougher parts of medicinal plants: the roots, stems, and bark. A water-based infusion is made and boiled down by one-half to one-third.

Dried: Drying plant material is a wonderful way to preserve medicinal properties for later use, and can be applied to all parts of the plant: flowers, pollens, leaves, barks, and roots.

Infused syrups: Made by steeping honey or maple syrup with medicinal plants.

Infused water: Made by immersing medicinal plants in hot or cold water (making a tisane) or other liquid or blend.

Oil infusion: Made by steeping medicinal plants in oil to harness aromas.

Pastilles: Pastilles are created by rolling powdered medicinal plants or syrups with honey into concentrated medicine balls or lozenges.

Shrub: The American version of a shrub has its origins in seventeenth-century England, where vinegar was used as an alternative to citrus juice in the preservation of medicinal plants, berries, and other fruits for tonics.

Steam-distilled: A type of extraction method used to separate the essential oil from the plant water, known as a hydrosol.

Tincture: Produced by soaking medicinal plants in alcohol.

Common Trees, Flowers, and Plants with Medicinal Qualities and Recipes

Anise

Throughout history, anise played a dual role, both medicinal and culinary. A flavorful digestive spice that may be soothing, stimulating, or carminative, its medicinal properties and fresh flavor make it popular in drinks. Many spirits from around the world, such as ouzo (Greece), Sambuca (Italy), absinthe (France), and arak (Palestine), use anise's sweet, licorice-like aroma. My version uses fennel fronds and aniseeds to bolster the already heady scent of fronds alone.

Medicinal qualities: It's an aromatic digestant, therefore preventing gas and bloating. Antiviral. Relieves congestion, great for tea blends for colds. An oil of leaves and flowers is good for arthritic joints.

Flowers: Use fresh in tisanes, as dessert garnishes, or in tinctures, herbal syrups, or pastilles.

Leaves: Dry and use in tisanes, tinctures, pastilles, or herbal syrups.

Anise Tincture

MAKES ABOUT 3 CUPS [720 ML]

3¼ cups [840 ml] organic vodka

2 cups [40 g] tightly packed bronze fennel, fennel flowers, fennel tops, and/or anise hyssop, or substitute ¼ cup [40 g] toasted fennel seeds

2 Tbsp toasted aniseeds

Combine the vodka, fennel, and aniseeds in a large jar or container. Seal and leave in a cool, dark place for 3 weeks to infuse. The tighter the seal, the better to keep all the essential oils. Strain and store in a sealed container indefinitely.

Anise Syrup

MAKES ABOUT 2 CUPS [480 ML]

1½ cups [510 g] honey

2 cups [40 g] tightly packed bronze fennel, fennel flowers, fennel tops, and/or anise hyssop, or substitue ¼ cup [40 g] toasted fennel seeds

2 Tbsp toasted aniseeds

Combine 1½ cups [360 ml] of water with the honey in a medium saucepan. Bring to a simmer and cook for 8 to 10 minutes, reducing the liquid slightly. Place the fennel and aniseeds in a heatproof jar or container, then pour the syrup so that they're completely submerged. Cool to room temperature, cover, and infuse for 3 days or longer depending on how strong you want the flavor. Strain and store, refrigerated, for months.

Anise Elixir

MAKES 1 DRINK

3 Tbsp Anise Tincture (recipe precedes)

2 Tbsp gin

2 Tbsp dry vermouth

1 Tbsp Anise Syrup (recipe precedes)

In a mixing glass filled with ice, combine the tincture, gin, dry vermouth, and syrup. Stir until well chilled, then strain into a chilled coupe glass.

Apple

Sweet apple blossoms have the faint aroma of their fruit, with a violet aroma as well.

Medicinal qualities: Bark for upset stomachs, heartburn, and inflammation; leaves for mouth disorders such as bleeding gums.

Bark: Make into a tincture, infusion, or herbal syrup.

Flowers: Make into a tincture, infusion, or herbal syrup.

Fruit: Juice to make syrups, shrubs, or alcohol. Apple peels make a lovely tisane.

Artichoke Leaves

When I was a child, my mother and I would have private artichoke feasts: just us, two steamed green beauties, and a vat of salty, melted butter. No one else in the house was interested in the elusive artichoke flower. After all our diligent plucking, we were rewarded with the meaty heart, its flavor a concentrated version of all those petals.

Fast-forward to one day as a young cook, when I was tasked with cleaning cases of baby artichokes. It was here that I discovered the bracingly bitter leaves of a raw artichoke. I took the leaves destined to be discarded and steeped them in vodka to create my own take on Cynar, a medicinal Italian after-dinner liqueur made from thirteen herbs and plants, including, most predominately, the artichoke thistle.

Artichoke Tincture

MAKES 3¼ CUPS [750 ML]

3 cups [420 g] packed artichoke leaves or a mixture of leaves and hearts

3¼ cups [750 ml] vodka

Pack the leaves into a large sealable jar or container. Add the vodka to cover. Seal and allow to sit at room temperature for at least 3 weeks, tasting regularly after this until the tincture achieves the flavor you desire. Strain and refrigerate indefinitely.

Artichoke Leaf Syrup

MAKES 6 CUPS [1.4 L]

1 large artichoke

3 cups [720 ml] honey

Pull the leaves from the raw artichoke and pack them into a large sealable jar or container. When you get to the heart, coarsely chop it and combine it with the leaves. Combine 3 cups [720 ml] water and the honey in a medium saucepan. Bring to a boil over high heat, then reduce the heat to medium and simmer for 8 to 10 minutes, reducing it slightly. Pour the syrup over the artichoke so it's completely submerged. Press a piece of parchment paper or plastic wrap over the entire surface of the syrup, top with a small weight to keep the artichoke submerged, and tightly cover. Set aside at cool room temperature for 3 to 5 days before testing. When the flavor is to your taste, strain out the artichokes and refrigerate the syrup indefinitely.

Basil

Medicinal qualities: Anti-inflammatory, contains vitamins K and A and calcium.

Leaves: Consume raw, use in tinctures, tisanes, pastilles, herbal syrups, or dry.

Birch

Birch, especially black sweet birch, has a wintergreen aroma.

Medicinal qualities: Leaves, buds, and bark have powerful anti-inflammatory properties. Birch tea soothes cramps, and is used to keep skin elastic and as a diuretic for cleansing the kidneys and treating urinary tract infections.

Bark: Make into an infusion, tincture, or oil.

Buds: Spring buds are edible; make into a tincture, or dry for tisane.

Leaves: Young leaves are edible; make into an infusion.

Sap: Can be tapped and consumed raw or cooked down into a syrup.

Calendula

Medicinal qualities: Antiseptic, anti-inflammatory, lymph cleansing.

Flowers: Use in tea blends, tinctures, infusions, syrups, shrubs, and honey infusions, or dry.

Cedar

Cedar has a bright, piney, peppery flavor.

Medicinal qualities: Cedar tea is used to treat fevers, rheumatism, the flu, and chest colds. The berries are high in ascorbic acid, or vitamin C, for immune support.

Bark: Make an infusion, tincture, or tea.

Berries: Make into an infusion, tincture, or syrup.

Needles: Use sparingly as they can be slightly toxic in large quantities; their aromatic properties are lovely blended into tinctures.

Chamomile

Medicinal qualities: Calmative and anti-inflammatory.

Flowers: Use in tea blends, tinctures, infusions, herbal syrups, pastilles, oil, shrubs, or dry.

Leaves: Eat raw, use in tinctures, or dry.

Coriander/Cilantro

Medicinal qualities: Antibacterial, has some properties known to kill Salmonella.

Flowers: Consume raw, or dry and use in tisanes, tinctures, pastilles, and herbal syrups.

Leaves: Consume raw or use in tinctures, tisanes, pastilles, and herbal syrups.

Seeds: Consume raw or use in tinctures, tisanes, pastilles, and herbal syrups.

Roots: Use in tinctures or decotions.

Red Currant and Green Coriander Shrub

When Nick and I traveled through Hungary and Slovakia in 2012, the summer markets overflowed with currants and gooseberries. I became obsessed with their tart-sweet flavor. When I moved east to Massachusetts, I found a few farmers growing red, white, and pink currants. I loaded up on them in the summer of 2017, enlisting a group of helpers with the fiddly task of destemming the berries. Once cleaned, some were made into jam, others were dried or turned into vinegar, and still others infused into vodka.

Currants are known as "superfruits," as they are naturally high in antioxidants due to the pigmented polyphenol cyanidin found in their skins. They are

CONTINUED

also a good source of vitamins C and K, manganese, and potassium.

MAKES 1 QT [1 L]

1 qt [960 ml] currant vinegar or white wine vinegar

¾ cup [255 g] honey (coriander honey if you can find it)

1 cup [50 g] fresh green coriander berries, still tender

2 lb [910 g] red currants pulled from the stems

¼ cup [3 g] cilantro flowers

Place the vinegar, honey, and green coriander berries in a food processor and pulse to break up the coriander. Add the currants and gently pulse to break up the fruit, but be careful not to open all the seeds, which can be bitter. Transfer to an airtight container, add in the flowers, and infuse overnight or for up to 1 month until the currant aroma and coriander aroma are both strong.

Strain through a fine-mesh sieve lined with a cheesecloth, getting as much of the juice as you can by squeezing down on the cheesecloth once the liquid has drained through. Save the pulp to start a new batch of currant vinegar.

Red Currant Tincture

MAKES 4½ CUPS [1 L]

1 lb [455 g] red currants

1 cup [140 g] dried currants (optional, but adds depth of flavor)

3¼ cups [750 ml] vodka

Remove the currants from their stems, gently crush the fruit but not so much that you smash the seeds, and place in a large jar or container with the dried currants if you are using them. Add the vodka, cover, and leave in a cool, dark place for 3 weeks

to infuse. Strain and store in a sealed container indefinitely.

Red Currant Shandy

MAKES 1 DRINK

2 oz [60 ml] Red Currant and Green Coriander Shrub (page 273)

10 oz [300 ml] lager

In a tall glass, combine the shrub and lager. Serve immediately.

Dandelion

Medicinal qualities: Blood purifier and good for the liver, overall body cleanser.

Flowers: Use in tea blends, tinctures, infusions, syrups, oils, shrubs, honey, pastilles, dry, or make wine.

Leaves: Consume raw.

Root: Use in decoctions, infusions, and syrups.

Dill

Medicinal qualities: Antibacterial properties similar to those associated with garlic. Helps protect against free radicals and carcinogens found in grill smoke. Diminishes hiccups and aids in bone health.

Flowers: Harvest the flowers when they're just starting to open, leaving a few flowers behind if you want to harvest seeds from them later. Use in tinctures, tisanes, pastilles, herbal syrups, or dry.

Leaves: Consume raw or use in tinctures, tisanes, pastilles, herbal syrups, or dry.

Seeds: Consume raw or use in tinctures, tisanes, pastilles, herbal syrups, or dry.

Roots: Use in tinctures and decoctions.

Elderflowers and Elderberries

Elderflowers have an intoxicating aroma, but their fragility reminds me to be gentle and focused during their fleeting season. Soon, the blossoms will turn to dark, almost black fruit. It's a dichotomous bush, ranging from light to dark, floral to fruity, and ethereal to unctuous.

The British are most familiar with the flavors of this hedge, which is touted as one of the best remedies for colds and flus, but it's most well known as starring in the French liqueur St. Germain. Since the stems and leaves of the plant are technically poisonous, you want to strip the tiny flowers and berries off by hand. The berries also need to be cooked before consuming. Place them in the freezer first, as the stems pop off easily when the fruit is icy.

Medicinal qualities: Bark tea can be used to treat headaches and congestion, and to lower fever by inducing perspiration.

Bark: Make into tea.

Flowers: Use in tinctures, infusions, syrup, pastilles, and dried for tea.

Fruit: Use in tinctures, syrup, or dried for tea.

Elderflower Syrup

The infused flowers can be puréed and eaten on yogurt or ice cream; the flavor will be diminished as a result of them giving off their aroma to the syrup, but they're worth enjoying anyway.

MAKES 3 CUPS [720 ML]

1 cup [340 g] honey

¼ cup [60 ml] freshly squeezed lemon juice, or more to taste

1 cup [12 g] packed fresh-picked elder-flowers, stems removed

Warm 2 cups [480 ml] of water and the honey in a medium saucepan over low heat to dissolve the honey before bringing to a simmer. Add the lemon juice. Pack the flowers into a jar, pour in the honey water, and cover. Refrigerate for 3 to 5 days, until the flowers start to brown and the syrup takes on a pale yellow hue. Strain through a fine-mesh sieve, squeezing out all the goodness from the flowers, and store the syrup in a bottle in the refrigerator for up to 1 year.

Elderflower Tincture

MAKES 3¼ CUPS [750 ML]

1 cup [24 g] packed elderflowers, stems removed

3¼ cups [750 ml] vodka

Combine the elderflowers and vodka in a large jar or container. Seal and leave in a cool, dark place for 3 weeks to infuse. Strain and store in a sealed container.

Elderflower Sparkling Cocktail

MAKES 1 DRINK

2 Tbsp Elderflower Tincture (recipe precedes)

1 Tbsp Burnt Lemon Tincture (page 283)

1 Tbsp Elderflower Syrup (page 274)

1 Tbsp Elderberry Shrub (recipe follows)

¼ cup [60 ml] dry sparkling wine

Fill a cocktail shaker with ice. Add the tinctures, syrup, and shrub. Shake for 10 seconds. Strain into a champagne flute and top with sparkling wine.

Elderberry Shrub

MAKES ABOUT 1¼ CUPS [300 ML]

1 qt [1 L] dark, ripe elderberries

½ cup [170 g] honey

¼ cup [60 ml] champagne vinegar

In a medium saucepan, combine the elderberries with ¼ cup [60 ml] of water. Bring the mixture to a simmer over medium-high heat. Simmer until the berries are soft, then use a slotted spoon to gently smash the berries against the sides and bottom of the pan. Strain the liquids into a bowl. You should have approximately 1 cup [240 ml] of juice; discard the solids. Return the juice to the pan and reduce by half. Pour into a measuring cup, note the volume, and add an equal amount of honey and half the volume of vinegar. Store, refrigerated, in an airtight container for up to 1 year.

Fennel bronze

Naturally sweet anise flavor.

Medicinal qualities: Anti-inflammatory, relieves gastric distress.

Leaves: Consume raw, in tinctures, tisanes, pastilles, herbal syrups, or dry.

Fig Leaves

Fig leaves taste of the tropics. They're pure coconut, vanilla, and green walnuts, and when paired with rum, the theme deepens.

Fig Leaf Cocktail

3 Tbsp Fig Leaf Tincture (recipe follows)

2 Tbsp fresh lime juice

1 Tbsp Fig Leaf Syrup (recipe follows)

Soda water

Combine the tincture, lime juice, syrup, and a splash of soda in a Collins glass filled with ice.

Fig Leaf Tincture

MAKES 3¼ CUPS [750 ML]

12 mature fig leaves

3¼ cups [750 ml] white rum

Combine the leaves and rum in a large jar or container. Seal and leave in a cool, dark place for 3 weeks to infuse. Strain and store in a sealed container indefinitely.

Fig Leaf Syrup

MAKES 2 CUPS [480 ML]

10 mature fig leaves

2 cups [480 ml] maple syrup

Clean the fig leaves of any dirt or debris. Gently tear them a bit to expose the cell walls for maximum flavor extraction. Place them in a large heatproof jar or container. In a large saucepan, simmer 2 cups [480 ml] of water and the maple syrup over medium-low heat for 10 minutes. Pour the syrup over the fig leaves. Cool, cover, and leave in a cool, dark place to infuse overnight. Taste the syrup. It should be sweet and taste faintly of coconut. Strain and store, refrigerated, for up to 1 month.

Fir and Spruce Tips

The forest has long been my secret wonderland. It's where I go to rebalance and quiet my mind. In California, I'd traipse through the canyon by our house almost daily, my antidote to city life. I'd forage for wild edibles and crinkle pine tips in my hands, releasing the resin to calm my nervous system. According to Connie Green, the forest whisperer

and goddess forager in Northern California, "Each Douglas fir tree has a slightly different flavor. One may taste like Meyer lemon peel or tangerine peel. Another might taste like peach skin, and then another may be a sharp, resiny green flavor. You can taste the wondrous genetic variation in these surprisingly delicious wild trees."

Like other evergreen conifers, Douglas fir needles and spruce needles are high in aromatic resins that fight infection and stimulate immunity.

Notes on foraging: Never pinch or cut off the tip on the top of the tree or harvest more than one-fifth of each tree's new tips. You can take far more of the mature needles if they're what you're after. Harvest just a branch and strip the needles off.

Spruce

Floral and fruity flavor, with a hint of pine.

Medicinal qualities: The inner bark is high in prebiotic fiber; the needles are high in vitamins A and C.

Bark: Use in decoctions, tinctures, and oils; dry and grind for flour. Bark is edible when cooked.

Buds: Spring buds are edible. Use in tinctures, preserve in salt, or infuse honey.

Needles: Use to make tea, tinctures, or herbal syrups or oils, or dry them.

Fir Tip Tincture

MAKES 3¼ CUPS [750 ML]

2 cups [120 g] packed fir or spruce tips
3¼ cups [750 ml] gin

Combine the fir tips and gin in a large jar or container. Seal and leave in a cool, dark place for 3 weeks to infuse. Strain and store in a sealed container.

Fir or Spruce Syrup

MAKES 2 CUPS [480 ML]

1 cup [60 g] packed fir or spruce needles or tips
1 cup [340 g] honey

Hand chop the fir or spruce needles or place in a food processor and pulse until very roughly chopped. Place the needles in a large jar or container. Simmer 1 cup [240 ml] of water and the honey in a small saucepan over medium-low heat for 10 minutes. Increase the heat to bring the mixture to a rapid boil and pour over the needles. Cover and leave to infuse overnight, or longer if you want a stronger syrup. Strain and store in a lidded container indefinitely.

Fir Tip Cocktail

MAKES 1 DRINK

¼ cup [60 ml] Fir Tip Tincture (recipe precedes)
1½ Tbsp Elderflower Syrup (page 274)
2 Tbsp fresh lemon or lime juice
1 egg white
2 Tbsp soda water

Add the tincture, syrup, lemon juice, and egg white to a shaker and shake vigorously for about 20 seconds. Add 4 to 6 ice cubes, shake for another 10 seconds until well chilled, strain into a glass, and top with soda water.

Ginger

Medicinal qualities: Antinausea, anti-inflammatory, calmative.

Leaves: Use in tinctures, tisanes, pastilles, herbal syrups, or dry.

Root: Consume raw or use in tinctures, infusions, and syrups.

Goldenrod

Medicinal qualities: Antifungal, diuretic, diaphoretic, anti-inflammatory, expectorant, antiseptic. Good for the kidneys, urinary tract, and bladder.

Flowers: Use in teas, tinctures, infusions, oils, shrubs, and honey infusions, or dry.

Holy Basil

Medicinal qualities: Adaptogenic.

Flowers: Consume raw or use in teas, tinctures, and infusions.

Leaves: Consume raw or use in teas, tinctures, and infusions.

Lemon Balm

Medicinal qualities: Antiviral, calmative.

Leaves: Consume raw or use in tinctures, tisanes, pastilles, herbal syrups, or dry.

Lilac

Medicinal qualities: Reduces fever, anti-parasitic.

Flowers: Use in tinctures, infusions, syrups, shrubs, and honey infusions, or dry.

Lilac and Rhubarb Elixir

Spring rose slowly my first year living in Massachusetts, but when it finally emerged, my new yard overflowed with lilac bushes and a towering rhubarb plant. The lilacs reminded me of growing up in Chicago, where a tall bush grew outside my bedroom window.

Since lilac and rhubarb are the first flavors I tasted from my New England garden, I like to think of this drink as an ode to new beginnings. Charring the rhubarb helps caramelize sugars and coax sweetness, while the tannins from the raw stalks lend a bitter undertone.

MAKES 1 DRINK

3 Tbsp Charred Rhubarb Elixir (page 280)

2 Tbsp gin or sparkling water

1 Tbsp Lilac Syrup (recipe follows)

For each drink, combine together 3 parts rhubarb elixir, 2 parts gin or sparkling water, and 1 part lilac syrup with ice in a cocktail shaker. Shake well, strain, and serve neat.

Lilac Syrup

MAKES 1¾ CUPS [420 ML]

1 cup [340 g] honey

1 cup [240 ml] lemon juice

4 cups [50 g] tightly packed lilac flowers

Mix the honey and lemon juice in a 1 qt [960 ml] container until the honey dissolves; then stir in the lilacs. Press a piece of parchment or plastic wrap over the entire surface to minimize exposure to the air, top with a small weight to keep the flowers submerged, and tightly cover. Allow the mixture to infuse at room temperature, tasting it every few days; it's ready when it tastes as floral as you'd like. Transfer to an airtight container and refrigerate for up to 2 weeks or store in the freezer for up to 1 year.

Maple

The flavor of maple is distinctively sweet and familiar.

Medicinal qualities: Bark is high in vitamins A and C and can act as an expectorant and decongestant.

Bark: Make into a decoction, tincture, or oil.

Buds: Spring buds are edible; use in a tincture or pastilles.

Leaves: Young leaves are edible; use in an infusion.

Seeds: Maple seeds can be peeled at the bulbous end and toasted, boiled, and seasoned in any way that suits you. I like them mixed into rice.

Sap: Maple water is lovely as a stand-alone drink; it's rich in bioactive nutrients, minerals, and phytonutrients. Reduce it to make syrup.

Marjoram

Medicinal qualities: Super-high antioxidant content.

Leaves: Use in tinctures, tisanes, pastilles, herbal syrups, or dry.

Mint

Medicinal qualities: Aids digestion and calms tense muscles. Provides manganese and vitamins A and C.

Leaves: Consume raw or use in tinctures, tisanes, herbal syrups, pastilles, or dry.

Nasturtium

Medicinal qualities: Antimicrobial properties make nasturtium an effective remedy against colds and flu. It is also useful in treating infections of the lungs, bladder, and reproductive organs.

Flowers: Consume raw; preserve in oil or salt; use in honey infusions, shrubs, or dry.

Leaves: Consume raw or preserve in oil or salt.

Parsley

Medicinal qualities: Good for bladder and kidney health, high in vitamins A, K, and C.

Leaves: Consume raw or use in tinctures, tisanes, pastilles, herbal syrups, or dry.

Peach

Leaves and flowers have a bitter-almond aroma, like the seed within the pit.

Medicinal qualities: Laxative and diuretic properties, kidney cleanser, treats worms, relieves edema.

Leaves: Use in tisanes, infusions, and herbal syrups.

Bark: Use in tinctures, infusions, and herbal syrups.

Flowers: Use in tinctures, infusions, and herbal syrups.

Fruit: Use the juice to make shrubs, syrups, and alcohol. Use dried in teas.

Peach Leaf Wine

It was many years ago when a farmer friend brought me peach leaves from a day of pruning, knowing all too well my passion for capturing interesting aromas. He gently tore the leaf and warmed it between his hands. A bitter almond aroma rose from it, and I immediately sank some leaves into a jar with hot water to see what a tisane would taste like. I was hooked. I began infusing the leaves into spirits and made an amaretto-like tincture to play with in cocktails. Serendipitously, the first summer I moved east, a friend told me of a neighbor with an overabundant peach tree that was open for picking. I grabbed a few buckets and my clippers, and went right away. I returned home with leaves, fruit, and branches, which were quickly dunked into vinegar or made into peach leaf tinctures, peach pit extract, and tisanes. It was a small moment, but one that seemed to condense time and space. At least emotionally, I had been here before.

MAKES 3½ CUPS [840 ML]

50 mature peach leaves, slightly torn

3¼ cups [750 ml] red wine (for a traditional recipe), white wine, rosé, or Lillet (use a 50:50 ratio of Lillet Blanc to Lillet Rouge and omit the sweetener)

¼ cup [90 g] Maple Sugar (page 203) or honey

2 Tbsp Peach Pit Extract (recipe follows) or brandy

Place the leaves, wine, maple sugar, and extract in a large jar, seal the lid, and shake to combine. Leave to infuse for 10 days in a cool, dark place, agitating the mixture daily. Taste it every couple of days to see if it's flavored to your liking. When it is, strain the liquid through a fine-mesh sieve. Peach leaf wine keeps for up to 1 year in the refrigerator or in a cool, dark place.

Peach or Apricot Pit Extract

Crack the pit of any stone fruit, from cherries to peaches to apricots, and you'll find an edible seed inside. Known as *noyaux*, they have an aroma of orange peel and bitter almond. Use them to flavor liqueurs, syrups, custards, or ice cream. I like to use them to mock up my own almond extract, which can be added to anything you want to add an extra boost of almond to. While collecting enough pits to make this infusion, you can squirrel the pits away in an airtight container in the freezer and crack them all at once when the time comes. Toasting them not only enhances their aroma but also can kill the teeny bit of cyanide the pits contain. Don't be

nervous; it would be impossible to eat so much you'd poison yourself.

MAKES 2 CUPS [480 ML]

20 peach or apricot pits

10 mature peach leaves (optional)

15 almond blossoms (optional)

2 cups [480 ml] vodka

Preheat the oven to 325°F [160°C]. Thaw the pits fully if frozen. Spread them in a single layer on a flat, sturdy surface and lay a towel over them to keep the shells from scattering. With a hammer or mallet, crack the pits, taking care not to smash the inner seeds. Pull the seeds out of the shells and spread them on a rimmed baking sheet. Toast until they are dry and have turned a very light golden brown, 10 to 15 minutes. Remove from the oven and let cool.

Place the seeds in a glass jar with the leaves (if using), blossoms (if using), and vodka. Keep the jar in a dry, cool spot for 2 to 3 months to get a truly nutty aroma; shake it as often as you remember to. To use, strain the extract through a cheesecloth or coffee filter, and keep in a cool, dry place indefinitely.

Peony

Medicinal qualities: Muscle relaxant for general pain and menstrual cramping.

Flowers: Use in tea blends, tinctures, and infusions, or dry.

Pine

Pine tastes like it smells, strong and green. In mountain areas, there is ponderosa pine, which has a really special bark with a butterscotch-y note to it.

Medicinal qualities: Needles are high in vitamins A and C.

Bark: The outer bark of the tree is not edible. Only the inner, soft, white bark can be consumed. Use in decoctions.

Buds: Spring buds are edible. Use in tinctures, preserve in salt, or make herbal syrups.

Needles: Use in tinctures, tisanes, pastilles, and oil, or dry.

Queen Anne's Lace

Medicinal qualities: Kidney support, digestive aid.

Leaves: Consume raw; use to infuse oil and salt.

Flowers: Consume raw; use in shrubs and honey.

Roots: Use in teas or tinctures.

Seeds: Use in teas and tinctures, or dry. Do not consume if pregnant.

Red Clover

Medicinal qualities: Blood cleanser and circulator, immune booster, relieves menstrual symptoms, and can lower cholesterol levels.

Flowers: Use in teas, tinctures, herbal syrups, pastilles, or dry.

Rhubarb

Charred Rhubarb Elixir

MAKES 2 CUPS [480 ML]

2 lb [910 g] red rhubarb

6 juniper berries

Set aside ½ lb [230 g] of the rhubarb. Char the remaining 1½ lb [680 g] by setting a metal rack directly over a gas burner with a medium-high flame, preparing a grill with medium heat, or setting an oven rack 3 to 4 in [7.5 to 10 cm] below the broiler. Char in batches if necessary, until the stalks are

CONTINUED

browned in places but still firm and crisp. Cool to room temperature.

Roughly chop the raw and charred rhubarb and run through a juicer, or purée in a blender and use a cheesecloth to strain the solids. Using a mortar and pestle or the wide side of your knife's blade, smash the juniper berries and add them to the juice. Transfer to an airtight container and refrigerate for up to 1 week or store in the freezer for up to 1 month.

Rose

Medicinal qualities: Rose hips are high in vitamin C and flavonoids that counteract stress and strengthen the immune system. Antioxidant properties support the heart and cardiovascular system.

Petals: Use for tinctures, shrubs, herbal syrups, infused oil, infused salt, and teas, or dry.

Hips: Use in tinctures, teas, shrubs, honey infusions, pastilles, or dry.

Sage

Medicinal qualities: Reduces inflammation, rich in vitamin K, good for bone health.

Leaves: Consume raw or use in tinctures, tisanes, pastilles, herbal syrups, or dry.

Sesame

Sesame Syrup

MAKES 3 CUPS [720 ML]

1½ cups [210 g] sesame seeds
1 cup [240 ml] maple syrup

In a medium skillet over medium-low heat, brown the seeds until they smell very nutty, about 5 minutes. Place the seeds in a large bowl and add 2 cups [480 ml] of warm water; allow the seeds to soak for 4 hours. Pulse the seeds and water in a blender before straining through a cheesecloth or coffee filter into a bowl. Discard the solids.

In a small saucepan, heat the sesame milk over medium heat and add the maple syrup. Stir until well incorporated. Store, covered and refrigerated, for up to 3 months.

Sumac

Tart and citrusy, with a woodsy resin aroma.

Medicinal qualities: Antimicrobial, antioxidant, antiviral, good medicine for mouth issues.

Berries: Use in tinctures, teas, syrups, and oils; dry, make pastilles. Dried, ground, and used as a spice, it adds acidity to dishes.

Sumac Tincture

MAKES 3¼ CUPS [750 ML]

2 cups [100 g] fresh or dried sumac berries or ¼ cup [30 g] sumac powder
3¼ cups [750 ml] vodka

Combine the sumac and vodka in a large jar or container. Seal and leave in a cool, dark place for 3 weeks to infuse. Strain and store in a sealed container indefinitely.

Sumac Switchel

MAKES 2½ CUPS [550 ML]

1 cup [50 g] sumac berries, removed from the cones, or 2 Tbsp sumac powder

2 cups [480 ml] champagne vinegar or apple cider vinegar
½ cup [120 ml] maple syrup

Mix the sumac and vinegar in a jar, seal the lid, and let infuse for 3 weeks at room temperature. Strain through a fine-mesh sieve lined with a cheesecloth or coffee filter to remove as much sediment as possible.

Add the maple syrup to the vinegar and mix well. Store in the refrigerator indefinitely.

Sumac and Sesame Elixir

MAKES 1 DRINK

Handful fresh mint leaves
¼ cup [60 ml] Sumac Tincture (recipe precedes)
1½ Tbsp Sumac Switchel (recipe precedes)
1 Tbsp Sesame Syrup (recipe precedes)
1 egg white

Muddle the mint in a cocktail shaker before adding the tincture, switchel, syrup, and egg white. Shake vigorously for about 20 seconds. Add 4 to 6 ice cubes, shake for another 10 seconds or so, strain into a glass, and serve immediately.

Sunflower

Medicinal qualities: Improves digestion, increases energy, strengthens bones, and is high in vitamin E.

Petals: Use to make teas, tinctures, oils, herbal infusions, and shrubs.

Buds and leaves: Consume steamed or raw, or use in tea.

Seeds: Consume raw or use in herbal infusions.

Tarragon

Medicinal qualities: Relieves pain related to osteoarthritis and lowers insulin levels; aids sleep.

Leaves: Consume raw or use in tinctures, tisanes, pastilles, herbal syrups, or dry.

Thyme

Medicinal qualities: Thymus booster, rich in antioxidants that protect cell membranes, antimicrobial. Also rich in iron, manganese, and vitamin K.

Flowers: Consume raw or use in tinctures, tisanes, pastilles, herbal syrups, or dry.

Leaves: Consume raw or use in pastilles, herbal syrups, or dry.

Turmeric

Medicinal qualities: Anti-inflammatory, antinausea.

Leaves: Use to make tinctures, tisanes, pastilles, herbal syrups, or dry.

Roots: Use to make pastilles, herbal syrups, or decoctions.

Violet

Medicinal qualities: Cleans the blood, stimulates the lymphatic system, treats pulmonary issues.

Petals: Use in tinctures, oils, or dry.

Other Concoctions

Rum Fruit Punch

Some of our favorite drinks are made with the less desirable parts of fruits, like the cores, stems, and peels. The Italians have limoncello and grappa and the Hungarians infuse all types of fruits in brandy. This is my template for creating zero-waste "fruit punch," making sure nothing is wasted.

MAKES 3 CUPS [720 ML]

1 cup [140 g] densely packed seasonal fruit, cut up, pitted, and peeled as necessary

¼ to ½ cup [40 to 80 g] Maple Sugar (page 203)

3 cups [720 ml] rum, vodka, or a floral infusion of your choice

Mix the fruit with the maple sugar in a large container, cover, and macerate for 1 hour. Pour in the rum to cover the fruit, cover, and let sit at room temperature for 1 week or up to 3 months. As you remove one fruit, replace it with more, topping off the container with the alcohol of your choice as you pour some out.

Shaken Rum Punch Elixir

MAKES 1 DRINK

½ cup [120 ml] Rum Fruit Punch (recipe precedes)

1½ Tbsp lemon or lime juice

1 Tbsp infused syrup, such as anise or orange

Shake the rum, lemon juice, and infused syrup with ice, strain, and serve in a chilled coupe.

Frozen Rum Punch Elixir

MAKES 1 DRINK

¼ cup [60 ml] Rum Fruit Punch (recipe precedes)

¼ cup [60 g] fruit from punch or fresh fruit of your choice

1½ Tbsp lemon or lime juice

1 Tbsp infused fruit syrup, such as anise (see page 272)

⅔ cup [160 g] crushed ice

Pre-freeze your rum punch, fruit, lemon juice, and syrup for at least 4 hours. In a blender, combine the ice, rum punch, fruit, lemon juice, and infused syrup and blend until smooth. Serve immediately.

Burnt Lemon Tincture

MAKES 3¼ CUPS [750 ML]

6 lemons

3¼ cups [750 ml] vodka

Quarter the lemons and remove the seeds. Over an open flame, char the lemons until the flesh is blackened; leave the skins as unburnt as possible to retain the essential oils. Combine with the vodka in a large jar or container. Seal and leave in a cool, dark place for 3 weeks to infuse. Strain and store in a sealed container.

Smoked Orange Tincture

MAKES 4½ CUPS [1 L]

4 oranges

4½ cups [1 L] vodka, tequila, mezcal, or gin

Peel the oranges with a flat-head peeler, leaving behind as much of the white pith as possible. Save the orange flesh for another use. Set up your smoker and smoke the orange peels at 175° to 250°F [80° to 120°C]

CONTINUED

for 2 hours. Add the smoked orange peels to a large jar or container and pour in the vodka. Infuse for 2 weeks at room temperature, or warm the mixture to 150°F [65°C] and allow to infuse at that temperature for 1 hour. If you use the fast method, let your peels cool in the liquid, and leave for a couple of days, tasting every day to make sure you are happy with the flavor and it's not getting too bitter (I like 5 days). When the infusion is ready, strain through a fine-mesh sieve. You can usually get a second round of infusion with the peels; the aroma will be less intense but still lovely. Sometimes I blend the two batches together. Store in a lidded jar at room temperature indefinitely.

Smoked Orange and Artichoke Cocktail

MAKES 1 DRINK

3 Tbsp [45 ml] Smoked Orange Tincture (see preceding)

2 Tbsp Artichoke Tincture (page 273)

1 Tbsp dark vermouth

1 Tbsp light vermouth

Splash of maple syrup

Orange wedge

Fill a cocktail glass with ice. Add the tinctures, both kinds of vermouth, and the maple syrup, and stir until well chilled. Strain, add a squeeze of orange juice, and serve in a chilled coupe.

Forest and Garden Kvass

Kvass doesn't get the respect it deserves. The classic is made with whey, bread, and sometimes beets, and oftentimes flour starts the fermentation. Some recipes are sweet, others saline and acidic, and many are flavored with herbs, fruit, or vegetables—just about anything will work. I like to look to the forest and the garden

for inspiration. This is a template, so feel free to experiment and use what you find on your walks or in your own garden.

MAKES 1 QT [1 L]

1 cup raw oats [100 g], groats [180 g], or steel-cut oats [160 g]

2 Tbsp Maple Sugar (page 203)

2 Tbsp raisins or 2 pitted dates, plus more for storing

¼ cup [35 g] sunflower or sesame seeds, toasted

2 Tbsp maple syrup

Preheat the oven to 350°F [180°C]. Toast ¼ cup [25 g] of the oats until nutty, about 10 minutes. The rest of the oats must remain raw, as the natural starches and yeast in the oats aid in the fermentation of the beverage.

Combine the toasted oats with the raw oats, maple sugar, 1 Tbsp of the raisins, and 6 cups [1.4 L] of water in a 2 qt [2 L] jar and cover tightly. Shake the jar and leave it out in a cool, dark space for 3 days. Shake occasionally.

After 3 days, strain the mixture through a fine-mesh sieve, reserving the solids and discarding the liquid (or use the liquid to make soup to simmer vegetables in).

Return the strained oats to the jar, add the sunflower seeds, maple syrup, and the remaining 1 Tbsp of raisins. Top with water, seal, and shake to combine.

Leave at room temperature for 3 to 5 days, or until the fermented oat kvass tastes delicious. Some foam may form on top of the beverage as it ferments. If this happens, open the jar and scoop it off with a spoon. Return the lid, shake the jar, and let it be. The finished oat kvass will be quite opaque and have some tang and a little fizz.

When the kvass is ready, transfer to airtight bottles, add 3 or 4 raisins, and store in the refrigerator for 2 weeks.

Kvass Variations

For the following variations, repeat the steps using the original starter grains up to 10 times. After that, discard half the starter grains, and add ½ to 1 cup [50 to 100 g] of oats, another 2 Tbsp of maple sugar, and another 1 Tbsp of raisins. Then add the aromatics and infuse as directed for 3 to 5 days. Refrigerate the finished kvass and serve chilled.

Forest flavors

- Winterberries
- Wild ginger root
- Creeping Charlie
- Wild berries
- Autumn olive flowers and berries
- Wild cherry bark
- Maple leaves
- Pine
- Spruce
- Spice bush
- Lilac

Garden flavors

- Anise hyssop flowers
- Lemon balm
- Lemon verbena
- Tomato leaf
- Cucumber blossoms
- Mint
- Chamomile
- Bee balm
- Rue
- Coriander root
- Fennel flowers
- Dill flowers
- Calendula

Cider, Cranberry, and Chaga Elixir

In North America, the Narragansett nation is said to have introduced cranberries to colonists in Massachusetts. These little, ruby antioxidant powerhouses are cultivated all over New England nowadays. I especially like how they provide a pleasant sharpness and rouge glow to these drinks and how their acidity tempers the muskiness of chaga, an acorn-like mushroom that grows on birch trees and contains enormous medicinal power. High amounts of antioxidants, zinc, copper, and iron promote digestion, aid circulation, and strengthen the immune system. Chaga has an earthy, woodsy, slightly nutty flavor that mixes well with maple's leafy sweetness. It looks like a strange black growth on the birch bark, but its honeycomb-like golden interior and spicy vanilla scent is what you're after.

MAKES 1 DRINK

¼ cup [60 ml] Tea Tincture (recipe follows)

2 Tbsp hard cider

1½ Tbsp "Cranberry Sauce" Shrub (recipe follows)

1 Tbsp Cider Syrup (recipe follows)

1 egg white

1 dry chaga mushroom for garnish

Fill a cocktail shaker with a bit of ice and add the tincture, cider, shrub, and syrup. Shake until your arm hurts, making the drink frothy. Strain into a glass and grate the chaga over the top.

Tea Tincture

MAKES 3¼ CUPS [780 ML]

6 Tbsp [50 g] lapsong souchung tea leaves

3¼ cup [750 ml] rum (white, amber, or a combination)

Combine the tea and the rum in a large jar or container. Seal and leave in a cool, dark place for 2 days to infuse. Strain and store in a sealed container indefinitely.

"Cranberry Sauce" Shrub

MAKES ABOUT 3 CUPS [720 ML]

2 cups [240 g] cranberries

½ cup [160 ml] maple syrup

2 Tbsp grated fresh ginger

1 cup [240 ml] apple cider vinegar

In a small saucepan, combine the cranberries, syrup, and ginger. Simmer just until warm, about 5 minutes (the fruit should still be raw). Use a blender to purée this mixture with the vinegar until smooth. Transfer to an airtight container, press a piece of parchment paper or plastic wrap against the surface, and leave to infuse at room temperature for 2 days. Strain and discard the solids. Refrigerate the shrub in an airtight container for up to 1 month.

Cider Syrup

MAKES ABOUT 1½ CUPS [360 ML]

2 cups [480 ml] apple cider

1 cup [320 ml] maple syrup

One 1 oz [30 g] chunk dry chaga mushroom

Combine the cider, syrup, and mushroom in a small saucepan and bring to a very gentle simmer. Cover and lower the heat to medium-low. Continue to simmer for 1 hour, which assists in extracting the chaga's amazing nutrients.

Strain the syrup, discarding the mushroom, and bring the syrup back to a simmer until reduced by half. Cool and transfer to an airtight container. Refrigerate for up to 2 months.

Opening the Circle

I end this book much like I began it: honoring the circle of protection used to hold the creative space sacred. In the first pages, I cast a circle, celebrating the sanctity of the kitchen and blessing it for the work about to be done. Here I open the circle, allowing the magic created within to flow openly out into the world.

People ask why I chose cooking, and my answer is always that it is what held my attention the longest. I'm a tactile doer, a creator of things. Like most doers, I have a garage filled with half-finished projects— ceramic pendant lamps waiting to be strung, oil paintings longing for another coat, fiber art wall pieces awaiting the next knot—but cooking, its ephemeral ability to connect me to land, history, and other cultures, has always kept me entranced. As a restaurant chef, I cooked for hundreds of diners, and their delight filled me up in countless ways. Now I cook and share meals with my family, which feels even more profound.

The energy created in the kitchen, beyond just the food, should be shared. So it's here, once the braises have simmered and the sauce has been spooned on the plate, that I open the circle. Food nourishes physically, but the act of cooking can nourish emotionally. Cook for others, cook with wonderment, cook with intention. Believe in your magic: Cooking is sorcery at its most elemental level.

Menus

Here are menus to gather with friends so you can cook a feast together, whether it's a cookbook club, a holiday, an exploration of the season, a full moon party, or just a simple get-together. Cook together, nourish each other, and play!

Brunch

- Spring: Coddled Eggs (page 113), Smashed Potatoes (page 48)
- Summer: Green Eggs (page 129), Mushroom Medley (page 95)
- Autumn: Red Eggs (page 127), Simplest Rice (page 294)
- Winter: Orange Eggs (page 125) and Aioli (page 204), Black Seeded Bread (page 242), Simplest Salad (page 294)

Dinner

- Spring: Sprouted Lentil Salad (page 75), Slow-Cooked Pork Steak (page 169), Simplest Rice (page 294)
- Summer: Late Harvest Gazpacho (page 29), Chicken Wings (page 152), Simplest Vegetables (page 294)
- Autumn: Charred Lettuces with Green Tahini (page 71), Brined Whole Chicken (page 155), Simplest Vinegar Potatoes (page 294)
- Winter: British-Berkshire Hot Pot (page 171) with pickled cabbage, Simplest Salad (page 294)

Festive Menus for Merriment

- Spring: Creamed Nettle-Spinach Soup (page 43), Vernal Equinox Salad (page 65), Root Vegetable Fritters (page 97), Whole Roasted Leg of Lamb (page 173)
- Summer: Summer Bean Soup (page 25), Summer Squash Salad (page 69), Silver Dollar Corn Cakes (page 235), Grilled Whole Fish with Herbs and Spices (page 141)

- Autumn: Autumn Chowder (page 47), Charred Lettuces with Green Tahini (page 71), Beef Short Rib Steaks (page 166), Harissa Vinaigrette (page 207), Aioli (page 204), and Smoky Chimichurri (page 205)
- Winter: Beet Salad (page 81), Whole Roasted Cauliflower (page 103), Mom's Pot Roast (page 163), Light as a Feather Brown Bread (page 241)

Picnic menus for 2 to 12

Here's a way to break down the recipes and pull out components to make a mezze-style picnic menu for eating indoors or to be consumed immersed in nature.

Dips, Sauces, and Spreads

- Green Tahini Sauce (page 72)
- Feta Mousse (page 64)
- Ramp Salsa Verde (page 205)
- Parsnip Skordalia (page 81)
- Pumpkin Seed and Cilantro Sauce (page 206)

Proteins

- Orange Eggs (page 125)
- Smoked Fish and Potato Hand Pies (page 145)
- Green Eggs (page 129)
- Brined Whole Chicken (page 155), served at room temperature, with Aioli (page 204)

Vehicles

- Seeded Herb Crackers (page 232)
- Feta Crisps (page 63)
- Black Seeded Bread (page 242)
- Silver Dollar Corn Cakes (page 235)

Veggies and Grains

- Ratatouille (page 85)
- Oil-Preserved Tomatoes (page 193)
- Oil-Preserved Eggplant (page 192)

- Sprouted Lentil Salad (page 75)
- Root Vegetable Fritters (page 97)
- Any brine pickle (page 180)
- Mushroom Medley (page 95)
- Woven Rainbow Tart (page 105)

Sweets

- Date and Preserved Lemon Balls (page 221)
- Pumpkin Seed and Buckwheat Cookies (page 212)
- Chocolate and Fir Tip Cookies (page 210)
- Maple Halva (page 218)

Snacks for a Crowd

- Herby Smashed Sardine Dip with Crudités (page 61)
- Smoked Fish and Potato Hand Pies (page 145)
- Pickled Scotch Eggs (page 119)
- Green Tahini Sauce (page 72) and crudités
- Green Eggs (page 129) with Feta Mousse (page 64)
- Silver Dollar Corn Cakes (page 235) with Lacto-Fermented Corn (page 184) or Ratatouille (page 85)
- Chicken Wings in Garlic Butter (page 152)
- Smashed potatoes (page 48) with Smoky Chimichurri (page 205)

Pantry Staples to Punch Up Flavor

Green Tahini Sauce (page 72)

- Dollop on whole roasted sweet potato with seeds.
- Thin it out with buttermilk and dress a salad, in lieu of green goddess dressing.

Fermented Squash (page 181)

- Mix with shredded cheese and broil on top of roasted pumpkin.
- Serve with tortilla chips in place of guacamole.
- Serve cold as a dip or with crackers and crudités. Garnish with pumpkin seed oil and toasted pumpkin seeds.
- Use warm as a sauce for roasted vegetables.
- Use as a condiment in a sandwich.

Harissa Vinaigrette (page 207)

- Mix 1:1 with Aioli (page 204) for a grilled vegetable and grilled meat platter.
- Add to a pot of cooked beans.

Kombu Dashi (page 207)

- Use this broth as a base for a quick simmered fish stew or all-vegetable hot pot with glass noodles and kimchi.
- Poach an egg and mushrooms in the dashi and scatter lots of torn herbs on top for a simple breakfast or lunch.

Spiced Seed Mix (page 197)

- Toss into a salad with hearty leaves such as chicories or romaine.
- Use over grilled vegetables.

Pumpkin Spice Mix (page 199)

- Mix with equal parts olive oil or infused oil of your liking and use as a sauce for raw or roasted vegetables or as a dip for River Stone Flatbread (page 238).
- Amp up your eggs . . . try it over fried eggs, add a spoonful to egg salad, or garnish your deviled eggs with it.

Lemon-Dill Vinaigrette (page 207)

- Use as your go-to day-to-day salad vinaigrette; it holds well refrigerated for 1 month.
- Spoon over steamed fish.

Smoky Chimichurri (page 205)

- Use in place of mayonnaise for a new twist on a cold or hot potato salad.
- Use as the oil for your next aioli or gribiche.

Pickles (page 180)

- Shave into salads for an extra lactic funk.
- Grate into tzatziki in lieu of cucumber.

Simplest Solutions for Rounding Out a Quick Meal

Simplest Salad

Mix different lettuces—crisp ones like romaine with soft, spicy watercress and chicories for a bitter note. Tear or snip lots of herbs, whatever is on hand, into the bowl. Add crunch: shaved radish, fennel, sprouted legumes, seeds, carrots. Top with a simple vinaigrette of 2 parts oil to 1 part acid (I go a bit heavier on the oil as I like its flavor) drizzled right into the bowl. A quick toss with your hands—your best tools to ensure none of the tender leaves bruise—and a sprinkling of coarse salt and fresh black pepper, sometimes followed by a squeeze of lemon to brighten everything up a touch more, and it's ready.

Simplest Rice

Cook the rice of your choice and add before fluffing it:

2 Tbsp butter

Lots of chopped herbs

Spiced Seed Mix (page 197)

Sprouted legumes

Toasted sesame seeds

Simplest Vinegar Potatoes

Cut potatoes in half or in chunks, depending on the size of the potatoes you start with. Preheat the oven to 400°F [200°C]. In a large skillet over medium heat, char the cut side of your potatoes with a bit of oil until browned. Flip and brown all sides of the potatoes, then season with salt and a splash of malt vinegar or another vinegar of your choice. Immediately transfer the pan to the oven to finish cooking. Once the potatoes are completely tender when pierced with the tip of a knife, remove the pan from the oven, add 2 Tbsp of butter, and swirl the pan to coat the potatoes. Add a bit more malt vinegar, freshly ground black pepper, and salt to taste.

Simplest Vegetables

My favorite, simplest way to cook vegetables is to steam or water-simmer them. For kale, I tear the leaves up, place them in the top of a steamer basket, and simmer the water below until the kale is silky but still bright green, about 5 minutes, before removing the kale from the pot and tossing with oil, salt, usually some spices, and toasted seeds. For vegetables like broccolini, I place the stalks with the leaves in a shallow pan with a lid, add about ¼ in [6 mm] of water, and place over medium-high heat for a few minutes until the greens are tender but still al dente and the water has all but evaporated. Add some oil or butter, spices, and/or herbs and seeds, and serve immediately.

GRATITUDE LIST

Creating this book has resulted in a woven tapestry, rich with magical humans to thank for showing up, being present, and teaching me countless lessons along the way.

Great Spirit/Creator/Grandma, thank you for my life today and for the lives of my family, chosen and blood. Thank you for the abundance you provide, the animals, the forests, the waterways, and the wind. Thank you for the lessons, the patience, and the grace you share with every soul on earth.

To Loom, thank you for being one of my life's greatest teachers and for showing me that home is within me. You've taught me that true nourishment is shared moments with the people I love, feeding them and honoring them, and that food is medicine and a direct window into the soul.

To my parents, Bob and Marcia, who always catch me when I trip or fall. You brush me off, and point out the rainbow path to me just in case I can't see it sparkling and beckoning to me in the distance. Thank you for choosing this incarnation with me.

To my sister, Shana, for your unconditional, unwavering, unfiltered love. You make me feel seen, shadows and all. You allow me the space to grow—you are so deeply radiant, and I can only hope to keep inching toward you and your direction to the sun. Thank you for finding me again in this lifetime; we have many more to go together for certain.

To my partner, JP, who shows me daily what and where home is. Thank you for fighting for us, and for saving me from a path far less illuminated than the one we are on. Thank you for sharing your boys with me; I promise to always nourish their hearts and souls the best I can. Thank you for never forgetting to make magic water, and for helping me to see what you see. Thank you for asking the universe to send me to you, and for letting me love you with every cell in my being.

To my brother, Richard, who has shown me how deeply the word *family* can run. Thank you for making sure I know that Creator holds us all in the safety of the fire and the air and the earth and the water.

To Nick, thank you for being a constant rock in my life for the last decade. We have laughed, cried, created, destroyed, and grown together. I wouldn't want to do this life without you; thank you for being an evolved soul and staying my creative partner forever and a day. Keep your north node forever in sight.

To Jackie, humans like you don't come around very often; I stand in gratitude for the twenty-plus years of honesty, laughter, and growth we've shared. Thank you for naming me

Lucia's goddess mamma. She's everything that is right with the world. Love you too, Dev—your gentle, fun-loving spirit is forever contagious.

To Jaden, Hunter, Javier, and JJ, thank you for letting me share in your lives. You enhance my life, and the world around you is better with you in it. Most of all, thank you for sharing your dad with me.

To Kitty Cowles, my literary agent, friend, mentor, and confidant, thank you for seeing sides of me I don't see and pushing me to honor them. Thank you also for being my biggest advocate and always pointing me to the clearest path forward.

To Sarah Billingsley, my editor, thank you for believing in me and this book, and helping me make it into something greater than the sum of its parts. You are a magician.

To Vanessa Dina, my designer, thank you for listening and creating something deeply heartfelt and beautiful. Thank you also to the rest of the Chronicle production team: Magnolia Molcan, Cecilia Santini, Steve Kim, and Tera Killip.

To Heami and Rebecca, sometimes people find one another and get to create magic together. I believe we did this. Thank you for making something you truly embodied and for allowing the creative process to swirl around us infinitely.

To Remy, my recipe goddess, you moved miles away from your home to cartwheel into a chaotic kitchen and make sense of it and me. Thank you for introducing me to Josie, for the sotol moments, for being my voice from concept to plate, and for being a true friend. I appreciate you to the depth of my soul.

Hannah, my lyrical maven. You take my words and weave them into something much more delicate. Thank you for hearing me, seeing me, and truly helping me. I'd be so much less without you.

To Lauren and Susan, thank you for the years of friendship and trust. You always show up, you're always solid, and watching how you both do life inspires me daily. I aim to be more like you both in spirit and grace. Thank you for the love and support.

To the opening Tourist kitchen team: Erin, Corey, Alan, Shannon, Erica, Ellie, and Shih-yu. Thank you for sharing time and space with me and each other. Thank you for smudging the pastries and believing in what we were creating together; nothing would have been possible without you.